ABOUT THIS PUBLICATION

FOR SERVICE ASSISTANCE

Please call Customer Service Department At:
1.704.921.9271

North Carolina General Statues is published by The Muliti-Media Group of Greater Charlotte in Charlotte, North Carolina. Copyright 2015 by the Multi-Media Group of Greater Charlotte. This book or parts thereof may not be reproduced in any form, stored in a retrieval system, or transmitted in any form by any means—electronic, mechanical, photocopy, recording or otherwise—without prior written permission of the publisher, except as provided by United States of America copyright law. All persons in Pen-Pal Magazine are over the age of 18.

The records required by U.S. Code 2257(a) through (c) and the pertinent regulations 28 C.F.R. Cli. 1, Part 75 with respect to this publication and all materials associated with such records are maintained by The Multi-Media Group of Greater Charlotte, Publisher and available for review by Attorney General.

www.visionbooks.org

Copyright © 2015 by MMGGC
All rights reserved!

TID: 4988975
ISBN (10) digit: 1502301776
ISBN (13) digit: 978-1502301772

123-4-56789-01236-Paperback
123-4-56789-01236-Hardback

First Edition

090520140547

Printed in the United States of America

2015 EDITION

North Carolina Criminal Law And Procedure-Pamphlet # 3

Printed In conjunction with the Administration of the Courts

North Carolina Criminal Law and Procedure
Pamphlet Reference Guide

Chapters	Pamphlet
Chapter 1 Civil Procedure	1
Chapter 1 Civil Procedure (Continue)	2
Chapter 1A Rules of Civil Procedure	2
Chapter 1B Contribution.	2
Chapter 1C Enforcement of Judgments.	2
Chapter 1D Punitive Damages.	2
Chapter 1E Eastern Band of Cherokee Indians.	2
Chapter 1F North Carolina Uniform Interstate Depositions and Discovery Act.	2
Chapter 2 - Clerk of Superior Court [Repealed and Transferred.]	3
Chapter 3 - Commissioners of Affidavits and Deeds [Repealed.]	3
Chapter 4 - Common Law	3
Chapter 5 - Contempt [Repealed.]	3
Chapter 5A - Contempt	3
Chapter 6 - Liability for Court Costs	3
Chapter 7 - Courts [Repealed and Transferred.]	3
Chapter 7A – Judicial Department	3
Chapter 7A – Continuation (7A) Judicial Department	4
Chapter 7A – Continuation (7A) Judicial Department	5
Chapter 7B - Juvenile Code	5
Chapter 8 - Evidence	6
Chapter 8A - Interpreters for Deaf Persons [Recodified.]	6
Chapter 8B - Interpreters for Deaf Persons	6
Chapter 8C - Evidence Code	6
Chapter 9 - Jurors	6
Chapter 10 - Notaries [Repealed.]	6
Chapter 10A - Notaries [Recodified.]	6
Chapter 10B - Notaries	6
Chapter 11 - Oaths	6
Chapter 12 - Statutory Construction	6
Chapter 13 - Citizenship Restored	6
Chapter 14 - Criminal Law	7
Chapter 14 –Criminal Law (Continuation)	8
Chapter 15 - Criminal Procedure	9
Chapter 15A - Criminal Procedure Act (Continuation)	10
Chapter 15A - Criminal Procedure Act (Continuation)	11
Chapter 15B - Victims Compensation	11
Chapter 15C - Address Confidentiality Program	11
Chapter 16 - Gaming Contracts and Futures	11
Chapter 17 - Habeas Corpus	11

Chapter 17A - Law-Enforcement Officers [Recodified.]	11
Chapter 17B - North Carolina Criminal Justice Education and Training System [Recodified.] Chapter 17C - North Carolina Criminal Justice Education and Training Standards Commission	11
	11
Chapter 17D - North Carolina Justice Academy	11
Chapter 17E - North Carolina Sheriffs' Education and Training Standards Commission	11
Chapter 18 - Regulation of Intoxicating Liquors [Repealed.]	12
Chapter 18A - Regulation of Intoxicating Liquors [Repealed.]	12
Chapter 18B - Regulation of Alcoholic Beverages	12
Chapter 18C - North Carolina State Lottery	12
Chapter 19 - Offenses against Public Morals	12
Chapter 19A - Protection of Animals	12
Chapter 20 - Motor Vehicles	13
Chapter 20 - Motor Vehicles (Continuation)	14
Chapter 20 - Motor Vehicles (Continuation)	15
Chapter 20 - Motor Vehicles (Continuation)	16
Chapter 21 - Bills of Lading	17
Chapter 22 - Contracts Requiring Writing	17
Chapter 22A - Signatures	17
Chapter 22B - Contracts Against Public Policy	17
Chapter 22C - Payments to Subcontractors	17
Chapter 23 - Debtor and Creditor	17
Chapter 24 – Interest	17
Chapter 25 – Uniform Commercial Code	18
Chapter 25 – Uniform Commercial Code (Continuation)	19
Chapter 25A – Retail Installment Sales Act	20
Chapter 25B - Credit	20
Chapter 25C - Sales of Artwork	20
Chapter 26 - Suretyship	20
Chapter 27 - Warehouse Receipts [Repealed.]	20
Chapter 28 - Administration [Repealed.]	20
Chapter 28A - Administration of Decedents' Estates	20
Chapter 28B - Estates of Absentees in Military Service	20
Chapter 28C - Estates of Missing Persons	20
Chapter 29 - Intestate Succession	21
Chapter 30 - Surviving Spouses	21
Chapter 31 - Wills	21
Chapter 31A - Acts Barring Property Rights	21
Chapter 31B - Renunciation of Property and Renunciation of Fiduciary Powers Act	21
Chapter 31C - Uniform Disposition of Community Property Rights at Death Act	21
Chapter 32 - Fiduciaries	21
Chapter 32A - Powers of Attorney	21
Chapter 33 - Guardian and Ward [Repealed and Recodified.]	21

Chapter 33A - North Carolina Uniform Transfers to Minors Act	21
Chapter 33B - North Carolina Uniform Custodial Trust Act	21
Chapter 34 - Veterans' Guardianship Act	22
Chapter 35 - Sterilization Procedures	22
Chapter 35A - Incompetency and Guardianship	22
Chapter 36 - Trusts and Trustees [Repealed.]	22
Chapter 36A - Trusts and Trustees	22
Chapter 36B - Uniform Management of Institutional Funds Act [Repealed.]	22
Chapter 36C - North Carolina Uniform Trust Code	22
Chapter 36D - North Carolina Community Third Party Trusts, Pooled Trusts	23
Chapter 36E - Uniform Prudent Management of Institutional Funds Act	23
Chapter 37 - Allocation of Principal and Income [Repealed.]	23
Chapter 37A - Uniform Principal and Income Act	23
Chapter 38 - Boundaries	23
Chapter 38A - Landowner Liability	23
Chapter 39 - Conveyances	23
Chapter 39A - Transfer Fee Covenants Prohibited	23
Chapter 40 - Eminent Domain [Repealed.]	23
Chapter 40A - Eminent Domain	23
Chapter 41 - Estates	23
Chapter 41A - State Fair Housing Act	23
Chapter 42 - Landlord and Tenant	23
Chapter 42A - Vacation Rental Act	23
Chapter 43 - Land Registration	23
Chapter 44 - Liens	24
Chapter 44A - Statutory Liens and Charges	24
Chapter 45 - Mortgages and Deeds of Trust	24
Chapter 45A - Good Funds Settlement Act	24
Chapter 46 - Partition	24
Chapter 47 - Probate and Registration	25
Chapter 47A - Unit Ownership	25
Chapter 47B - Real Property Marketable Title Act	25
Chapter 47C - North Carolina Condominium Act	25
Chapter 47D - Notice of Settlement Act [Expired.]	25
Chapter 47E - Residential Property Disclosure Act	25
Chapter 47F - North Carolina Planned Community Act	25
Chapter 47G - Option to Purchase Contracts	25
Chapter 47H - Contracts for Deed	25
Chapter 48 - Adoptions	26
Chapter 48A - Minors	26
Chapter 49 - Bastardy	26
Chapter 49A - Rights of Children	26
Chapter 50 - Divorce and Alimony	26
Chapter 50A - Uniform Child-Custody Jurisdiction and	

Enforcement Act	26
Chapter 50B - Domestic Violence	26
Chapter 50C - Civil No-Contact Orders	26
Chapter 51 - Marriage	26
Chapter 52 - Powers and Liabilities of Married Persons	27
Chapter 52A - Uniform Reciprocal Enforcement of Support Act [Repealed.]	27
Chapter 52B - Uniform Premarital Agreement Act	27
Chapter 52C - Uniform Interstate Family Support Act	27
Chapter 53 - Banks	27
Chapter 53A - Business Development Corporations and North Carolina Capital Resource Corporations	28
Chapter 53B - Financial Privacy Act	28
Chapter 54 - Cooperative Organizations	28
Chapter 54A - Capital Stock Savings and Loan Associations [Repealed.]	28
Chapter 54B - Savings and Loan Associations	29
Chapter 54C - Savings Banks	29
Chapter 55 - North Carolina Business Corporation Act	30
Chapter 55A - North Carolina Nonprofit Corporation Act	31
Chapter 55B - Professional Corporation Act	31
Chapter 55C - Foreign Trade Zones	31
Chapter 55D - Filings, Names, and Registered Agents for Corporations, Nonprofit Corporations, and Partnerships	31
Chapter 56 - Electric, Telegraph and Power Companies [Repealed.]	31
Chapter 57 - Hospital, Medical and Dental Service Corporations [Recodified.]	31
Chapter 57A - Health Maintenance Organization Act [Recodified.]	31
Chapter 57B - Health Maintenance Organization Act [Recodified.]	31
Chapter 57C - North Carolina Limited Liability Company Act.	31
Chapter 58 - Insurance.	32
Chapter 58 - Insurance (Continuation)	33
Chapter 58 - Insurance (Continuation)	34
Chapter 58 - Insurance (Continuation)	35
Chapter 58 - Insurance (Continuation)	36
Chapter 58 - Insurance (Continuation)	37
Chapter 58 - Insurance (Continuation)	38
Chapter 58A - North Carolina Health Insurance Trust Commission [Recodified.]	38
Chapter 59 - Partnership.	39
Chapter 59B - Uniform Unincorporated Nonprofit Association Act.	39
Chapter 60 - Railroads and Other Carriers [Repealed and Transferred.]	39
Chapter 61 - Religious Societies	39
Chapter 62 - Public Utilities	39

Chapter 62 - Public Utilities (Continuation)	40
Chapter 62A - Public Safety Telephone Service And Wireless Telephone Service	40
Chapter 63 - Aeronautics	40
Chapter 63A - North Carolina Global TransPark Authority	40
Chapter 64 - Aliens	40
Chapter 65 – Cemeteries	40
Chapter 66 - Commerce and Business	41
Chapter 67 - Dogs	41
Chapter 68 - Fences and Stock Law	41
Chapter 69 - Fire Protection	41
Chapter 70 - Indian Antiquities, Archaeological Resources and Unmarked Human Skeletal Remains Protection	42
Chapter 71 - Indians [Repealed.]	42
Chapter 71A - Indians	42
Chapter 72 - Inns, Hotels and Restaurants	42
Chapter 73 - Mills	42
Chapter 74 - Mines and Quarries	42
Chapter 74A - Company Police [Repealed.]	42
Chapter 74B - Private Protective Services Act [Repealed.]	42
Chapter 74C - Private Protective Services	42
Chapter 74D - Alarm Systems	42
Chapter 74E - Company Police Act	42
Chapter 74F - Locksmith Licensing Act	42
Chapter 74G - Campus Police Act	42
Chapter 75 - Monopolies, Trusts and Consumer Protection	42
Chapter 75A - Boating and Water Safety	43
Chapter 75B - Discrimination in Business	43
Chapter 75C - Motion Picture Fair Competition Act	43
Chapter 75D - Racketeer Influenced and Corrupt Organizations	43
Chapter 75E - Unlawful Activities in Connection With Certain Corporate Transactions	43
Chapter 76 - Navigation	43
Chapter 76A - Navigation and Pilotage Commissions	43
Chapter 77 - Rivers, Creeks, and Coastal Waters	43
Chapter 78 - Securities Law [Repealed.]	43
Chapter 78A - North Carolina Securities Act	43
Chapter 78B - Tender Offer Disclosure Act [Repealed.]	43
Chapter 78C - Investment Advisers	43
Chapter 78D - Commodities Act	43
Chapter 79 - Strays [Repealed.]	43
Chapter 80 - Trademarks, Brands, etc.	44
Chapter 81 - Weights and Measures [Recodified.]	44
Chapter 81A - Weights and Measures Act of 1975.	44
Chapter 82 - Wrecks [Repealed.]	44
Chapter 83 - Architects [Recodified.]	44

Chapter 83A - Architects	44
Chapter 84 - Attorneys-at-Law	44
Chapter 84A - Foreign Legal Consultants	44
Chapter 85 - Auctions and Auctioneers [Repealed.]	44
Chapter 85A - Bail Bondsmen and Runners [Recodified.]	44
Chapter 85B - Auctions and Auctioneers	44
Chapter 85C - Bail Bondsmen and Runners [Recodified.]	44
Chapter 86 - Barbers [Recodified.]	44
Chapter 86A - Barbers	44
Chapter 87 - Contractors	44
Chapter 88 - Cosmetic Art [Repealed.]	44
Chapter 88A - Electrolysis Practice Act	44
Chapter 88B - Cosmetic Art	45
Chapter 89 - Engineering and Land Surveying [Recodified.]	45
Chapter 89A - Landscape Architects	45
Chapter 89B - Foresters	45
Chapter 89C - Engineering and Land Surveying	45
Chapter 89D - Landscape Contractors	45
Chapter 89E - Geologists Licensing Act	45
Chapter 89F - North Carolina Soil Scientist Licensing Act	45
Chapter 89G - Irrigation Contractors	45
Chapter 90 - Medicine and Allied Occupations	45
Chapter 90 - Medicine and Allied Occupations (Continuation)	46
Chapter 90 - Medicine and Allied Occupations (Continuation)	47
Chapter 90 - Medicine and Allied Occupations (Continuation)	48
Chapter 90A - Sanitarians and Water and Wastewater Treatment Facility Operators	48
Chapter 90B - Social Worker Certification and Licensure Act	48
Chapter 90C - North Carolina Recreational Therapy Licensure Act	48
Chapter 90D - Interpreters and Transliterators	48
Chapter 91 - Pawnbrokers [Repealed.]	48
Chapter 91A - Pawnbrokers Modernization Act of 1989	48
Chapter 92 - Photographers [Deleted.]	48
Chapter 93 - Certified Public Accountants	48
Chapter 93A - Real Estate License Law	49
Chapter 93B - Occupational Licensing Boards	49
Chapter 93C - Watchmakers [Repealed.]	49
Chapter 93D - North Carolina State Hearing Aid Dealers and Fitters Board.	49
Chapter 93E - North Carolina Appraisers Act	49
Chapter 94 - Apprenticeship	49
Chapter 95 - Department of Labor and Labor Regulations	49
Chapter 95 - Department of Labor and Labor Regulations (Continuation)	50
Chapter 96 - Employment Security	50
Chapter 97 - Workers' Compensation Act	50
Chapter 97 - Workers' Compensation Act (Continuation)	51

Chapter 98 - Burnt and Lost Records	51
Chapter 99 - Libel and Slander	51
Chapter 99A - Civil Remedies for Criminal Actions	51
Chapter 99B - Products Liability	51
Chapter 99C - Actions Relating to Winter Sports Safety and Accidents	51
Chapter 99D - Civil Rights	51
Chapter 99E - Special Liability Provisions	51
Chapter 100 - Monuments, Memorials and Parks	51
Chapter 101 - Names of Persons	51
Chapter 102 - Official Survey Base	51
Chapter 103 - Sundays, Holidays and Special Days	51
Chapter 104 - United States Lands	51
Chapter 104A - Degrees of Kinship	51
Chapter 104B - Hurricanes or Other Acts of Nature	51
Chapter 104C - Atomic Energy, Radioactivity and Ionizing Radiation [Repealed and Recodified.]	51
Chapter 104D - Southern States Energy Compact	51
Chapter 104E - North Carolina Radiation Protection Act	51
Chapter 104F - Southeast Interstate Low-Level Radioactive Waste Management Compact [Repealed]	51
Chapter 104G - North Carolina Low-Level Radioactive Waste Management Authority Act of 1987 [Repealed]	51
Chapter 105 - Taxation	51
Chapter 105 - Taxation (Continuation)	52
Chapter 105 - Taxation (Continuation)	53
Chapter 105 - Taxation (Continuation)	54
Chapter 105A - Setoff Debt Collection Act	55
Chapter 105B - Defaulted Student Loan Recovery Act	55
Chapter 106 - Agriculture	55
Chapter 106 - Agriculture (Continue)	56
Chapter 106 - Agriculture (Continue)	57
Chapter 107 - Agricultural Development Districts [Repealed.]	57
Chapter 108 - Social Services [Repealed and Recodified.]	57
Chapter 108A - Social Services	57
Chapter 108B - Community Action Programs	58
Chapter 108C Medicaid and Health Choice Provider Requirements.	58
Chapter 108D Medicaid Managed Care for Behavioral Health Services.	58
Chapter 109 - Bonds [Recodified.]	58
Chapter 110 - Child Welfare	58
Chapter 111 - Aid to the Blind	58
Chapter 112 - Confederate Homes and Pensions [Repealed.]	58
Chapter 113 - Conservation and Development	58
Chapter 113 - Conservation and Development (Continuation)	59

Chapter 113A - Pollution Control and Environment	59
Chapter 113A - Pollution Control and Environment (Continuation)	60
Chapter 113B - North Carolina Energy Policy Act of 1975	60
Chapter 114 - Department of Justice	60
Chapter 115 - Elementary and Secondary Education [Repealed.]	60
Chapter 115A - Community Colleges, Technical Institutes, and Industrial Education Centers [Repealed.]	60
Chapter 115B - Tuition and Fee Waivers	60
Chapter 115C - Elementary and Secondary Education	60
Chapter 115C - Elementary and Secondary Education (Continuation)	61
Chapter 115C - Elementary and Secondary Education (Continuation)	62
Chapter 115C - Elementary and Secondary Education (Continuation)	63
Chapter 115D - Community Colleges	63
Chapter 115E - Private Educational Facilities Finance Act [Recodified]	63
Chapter 116 - Higher Education	63
Chapter 116 - Higher Education (Continuation)	63
Chapter 116A - Escheats and Abandoned Property [Repealed.]	64
Chapter 116B - Escheats and Abandoned Property	64
Chapter 116C - Continuum of Education Programs	64
Chapter 116D - Higher Education Bonds	64
Chapter 116E -Education Longitudinal Data System	64
Chapter 117 - Electrification	64
Chapter 118 - Firemen's and Rescue Squad Workers' Relief and Pension Funds [Recodified.]	64
Chapter 118A - Firemen's Death Benefit Act [Repealed.]	64
Chapter 118B - Members of a Rescue Squad Death Benefit Act [Repealed.]	64
Chapter 119 - Gasoline and Oil Inspection and Regulation	64
Chapter 120 - General Assembly	65
Chapter 120 - General Assembly (Continuation)	66
Chapter 120 - General Assembly (Continuation)	67
Chapter 120C - Lobbying	67
Chapter 121 - Archives and History	67
Chapter 122 - Hospitals for the Mentally Disordered [Repealed.]	67
Chapter 122A - North Carolina Housing Finance Agency	67
Chapter 122B - North Carolina Agricultural Facilities Finance Act [Repealed.]	67
Chapter 122C - Mental Health, Developmental Disabilities, and Substance Abuse Act of 1985	67
Chapter 122C - Mental Health, Developmental Disabilities, and Substance Abuse Act of 1985 (Continuation)	68

Chapter 122D - North Carolina Agricultural Finance Act	68
Chapter 122E - North Carolina Housing Trust and Oil Overcharge Act	68
Chapter 123 - Impeachment	69
Chapter 123A - Industrial Development [Repealed.]	69
Chapter 124 - Internal Improvements	69
Chapter 125 - Libraries	69
Chapter 126 - State Personnel System	69
Chapter 127 - Militia [Repealed.]	69
Chapter 127A - Militia	69
Chapter 127B - Military Affairs	69
Chapter 127C - Advisory Commission on Military Affairs	69
Chapter 128 - Offices and Public Officers	69
Chapter 128 - Offices and Public Officers (Continuation)	70
Chapter 129 - Public Buildings and Grounds	70
Chapter 130 - Public Health [Repealed.]	70
Chapter 130A - Public Health	70
Chapter 130A - Public Health (Continuation)	71
Chapter 130A - Public Health (Continuation)	72
Chapter 130B - Hazardous Waste Management Commission [Repealed.]	72
Chapter 131 - Public Hospitals [Repealed.]	72
Chapter 131A - Health Care Facilities Finance Act	72
Chapter 131B - Licensing of Ambulatory Surgical Facilities [Repealed.]	72
Chapter 131C - Charitable Solicitation Licensure Act [Repealed.]	72
Chapter 131D - Inspection and Licensing of Facilities	72
Chapter 131E - Health Care Facilities and Services	72
Chapter 131E - Health Care Facilities and Services (Continuation)	73
Chapter 131F - Solicitation of Contributions	73
Chapter 132 - Public Records	73
Chapter 133 - Public Works	74
Chapter 134 - Youth Development [Recodified.]	74
Chapter 134A - Youth Services [Repealed.]	74
Chapter 135 - Retirement System for Teachers and State Employees; Social Security; Health Insurance Program for Children	74
Chapter 135 - Retirement System for Teachers and State Employees; Social Security; Health Insurance Program for Children	75
Chapter 136 - Transportation	75
Chapter 136 - Transportation (Continuation)	76
Chapter 137 - Rural Rehabilitation [Repealed.]	76
Chapter 138 - Salaries, Fees and Allowances	76
Chapter 138A - State Government Ethics Act	76

Chapter 139 - Soil and Water Conservation Districts	76
Chapter 140 - State Art Museum; Symphony and Art Societies	76
Chapter 140A - State Awards System	76
Chapter 141 - State Boundaries	76
Chapter 142 - State Debt	76
Chapter 143 - State Departments, Institutions, and Commissions	77
Chapter 143 - State Departments, Institutions, and Commissions (Continuation)	78
Chapter 143 - State Departments, Institutions, and Commissions (Continuation)	79
Chapter 143 - State Departments, Institutions, and Commissions (Continuation)	80
Chapter 143A - State Government Reorganization	80
Chapter 143B - Executive Organization Act of 1973	80
Chapter 143B - Executive Organization Act of 1973 (Continuation)	81
Chapter 143B - Executive Organization Act of 1973 (Continuation)	82
Chapter 143C - State Budget Act	83
Chapter 143D - The State Governmental Accountability and Internal Control Act	83
Chapter 144 - State Flag, Official Governmental Flags, Motto, and Colors	83
Chapter 145 - State Symbols and Other Official Adoptions.	83
Chapter 146 - State Lands	83
Chapter 147 - State Officers	83
Chapter 148 - State Prison System	84
Chapter 149 - State Song and Toast	84
Chapter 150 - Uniform Revocation of Licenses [Repealed.]	84
Chapter 150A - Administrative Procedure Act [Recodified.]	84
Chapter 150B - Administrative Procedure Act	84
Chapter 151 - Constables [Repealed.]	84
Chapter 152 - Coroners	84
Chapter 152A - County Medical Examiner [Repealed.]	84
Chapter 152A - County Medical Examiner [Repealed.] (Continuation)	85
Chapter 153 - Counties and County Commissioners [Repealed.]	85
Chapter 153A - Counties	85
Chapter 153B - Mountain Resources Planning Act	85
Chapter 153C - Uwharrie Regional Resources Act	85
Chapter 154 - County Surveyor [Repealed.]	85
Chapter 155 - County Treasurer [Repealed.]	85
Chapter 156 - Drainage	85

Chapter 156 – Drainage (Continuation)	86
Chapter 157 - Housing Authorities and Projects	86
Chapter 157A - Historic Properties Commissions [Transferred.]	86
Chapter 158 - Local Development	86
Chapter 159 - Local Government Finance	86
Chapter 159 - Local Government Finance (Continuation)	87
Chapter 159A - Pollution Abatement and Industrial Facilities Financing Act [Unconstitutional.]	87
Chapter 159B - Joint Municipal Electric Power and Energy Act	87
Chapter 159C - Industrial and Pollution Control Facilities Financing Act	87
Chapter 159D - The North Carolina Capital Facilities Financing Act	87
Chapter 159E - Registered Public Obligations Act	87
Chapter 159F - North Carolina Energy Development Authority [Repealed.]	87
Chapter 159G - Water Infrastructure	87
Chapter 159H - [Reserved.]	87
Chapter 159I - Solid Waste Management Loan Program and Local Government Special Obligation Bonds	87
Chapter 160 - Municipal Corporations [Repealed And Transferred.]	87
Chapter 160A - Cities and Towns	88
Chapter 160A - Cities and Towns (Continuation)	89
Chapter 160B - Consolidated City-County Act	89
Chapter 160C - Baseball Park Districts [Repealed.]	90
Chapter 161 - Register of Deeds	90
Chapter 162 - Sheriff	90
Chapter 162A - Water and Sewer Systems	90
Chapter 162B Continuity of Local Government in Emergency.	90
Chapter 163 Elections and Election Laws.	90
Chapter 163 Elections and Election Laws. (Continuation)	91
Chapter 164 Concerning the General Statutes of North Carolina.	92
Chapter 165 Veterans.	92
Chapter 166 Civil Preparedness Agencies [Repealed.]	92
Chapter 166A North Carolina Emergency Management Act.	92
Chapter 167 State Civil Air Patrol [Repealed.]	92
Chapter 168 Persons with Disabilities.	92
Chapter 168A Persons With Disabilities Protection Act.	92

Chapter 2

Clerk of Superior Court.

§§ 2-1 through 2-60. Repealed and transferred by Session Laws 1971, c. 363.

Chapter 3

Commissioners of Affidavits and Deeds.

§§ 3-1 through 3-8. Repealed by Session Laws 1971, c. 202.

Chapter 4

Common Law.

§ 4-1. Common law declared to be in force.

All such parts of the common law as were heretofore in force and use within this State, or so much of the common law as is not destructive of, or repugnant to, or inconsistent with, the freedom and independence of this State and the form of government therein established, and which has not been otherwise provided for in whole or in part, not abrogated, repealed, or become obsolete, are hereby declared to be in full force within this State. (1715, c. 5, ss. 2, 3, P.R.; 1778, c. 133, P.R.; R.C., c. 22; Code, s. 641; Rev., s. 932; C.S., s. 970.)

Chapter 5

Contempt.

§§ 5-1 through 5-9: Repealed by Session Laws 1977, c. 711, s. 33.

Chapter 5A.

Contempt.
Article 1.

Criminal Contempt.

§ 5A-1. Reserved for future codification purposes.

§ 5A-2. Reserved for future codification purposes.

§ 5A-3. Reserved for future codification purposes.

§ 5A-4. Reserved for future codification purposes.

§ 5A-5. Reserved for future codification purposes.

§ 5A-6. Reserved for future codification purposes.

§ 5A-7. Reserved for future codification purposes.

§ 5A-8. Reserved for future codification purposes.

§ 5A-9. Reserved for future codification purposes.

§ 5A-10. Reserved for future codification purposes.

Chapter 5A.

Contempt.

Article 1

Criminal Contempt.

§§ 5A-1 through 5A-10. Reserved for future codification purposes.

§ 5A-11. Criminal contempt.

(a) Except as provided in subsection (b), each of the following is criminal contempt:

(1) Willful behavior committed during the sitting of a court and directly tending to interrupt its proceedings.

(2) Willful behavior committed during the sitting of a court in its immediate view and presence and directly tending to impair the respect due its authority.
(3) Willful disobedience of, resistance to, or interference with a court's lawful process, order, directive, or instruction or its execution.

(4) Willful refusal to be sworn or affirmed as a witness, or, when so sworn or affirmed, willful refusal to answer any legal and proper question when the refusal is not legally justified.

(5) Willful publication of a report of the proceedings in a court that is grossly inaccurate and presents a clear and present danger of imminent and serious threat to the administration of justice, made with knowledge that it was false or with reckless disregard of whether it was false. No person, however, may be punished for publishing a truthful report of proceedings in a court.

(6) Willful or grossly negligent failure by an officer of the court to perform his duties in an official transaction.

(7) Willful or grossly negligent failure to comply with schedules and practices of the court resulting in substantial interference with the business of the court.

(8) Willful refusal to testify or produce other information upon the order of a judge acting pursuant to Article 61 of Chapter 15A, Granting of Immunity to Witnesses.

(9) Willful communication with a juror in an improper attempt to influence his deliberations.

(9a) Willful refusal by a defendant to comply with a condition of probation.

(9b) Willful refusal to accept post-release supervision or to comply with the terms of post-release supervision by a prisoner whose offense requiring post-release supervision is a reportable conviction subject to the registration requirement of Article 27A of Chapter 14 of the General Statutes. For purposes of this subdivision, "willful refusal to accept post-release supervision or to comply with the terms of post-release supervision" includes, but is not limited to, knowingly violating the terms of post-release supervision in order to be returned to prison to serve out the remainder of the supervisee's sentence.

(10)   Any other act or omission specified elsewhere in the General Statutes of North Carolina as grounds for criminal contempt.

The grounds for criminal contempt specified here are exclusive, regardless of any other grounds for criminal contempt which existed at common law.

(b)   No person may be held in contempt under this section on the basis of the content of any broadcast, publication, or other communication unless it presents a clear and present danger of an imminent and serious threat to the administration of criminal justice.

(c)   This section is subject to the provisions of G.S. 7A-276.1, Court orders prohibiting publication or broadcast of reports of open court proceedings or reports of public records banned. (1977, c. 711, s. 3; 1994, Ex. Sess., c. 19, s. 1; 2011-307, s. 6.)

§ 5A-12. Punishment; circumstances for fine or imprisonment; reduction of punishment; other measures.

(a)   A person who commits criminal contempt, whether direct or indirect, is subject to censure, imprisonment up to 30 days, fine not to exceed five hundred dollars ($500.00), or any combination of the three, except that:
(1)   A person who commits a contempt described in G.S. 5A-11(8) is subject to censure, imprisonment not to exceed 6 months, fine not to exceed five hundred dollars ($500.00), or any combination of the three;

(2)   A person who has not been arrested who fails to comply with a nontestimonial identification order, issued pursuant to Article 14 of Chapter 15A of the General Statutes is subject to censure, imprisonment not to exceed 90 days, fine not to exceed five hundred dollars ($500.00), or any combination of the three; and

(3)   A person who commits criminal contempt by failing to comply with an order to pay child support is subject to censure, imprisonment up to 30 days, fine not to exceed five hundred dollars ($500.00), or any combination of the three. However, a sentence of imprisonment up to 120 days may be imposed for a single act of criminal contempt resulting from the failure to pay child support, provided the sentence is suspended upon conditions reasonably related to the contemnor's payment of child support.

(b) Except for contempt under G.S. 5A-11(5) or 5A-11(9), fine or imprisonment may not be imposed for criminal contempt, whether direct or indirect, unless:

(1) The act or omission was willfully contemptuous; or

(2) The act or omission was preceded by a clear warning by the court that the conduct is improper.

(c) The judicial official who finds a person in contempt may at any time withdraw a censure, terminate or reduce a sentence of imprisonment, or remit or reduce a fine imposed as punishment for contempt if warranted by the conduct of the contemnor and the ends of justice.

(d) A person held in criminal contempt under this Article shall not, for the same conduct, be found in civil contempt under Article 2 of this Chapter, Civil Contempt.

(e) A person held in criminal contempt under G.S. 5A-11(9) may nevertheless, for the same conduct, be found guilty of a violation of G.S. 14-225.1, but he must be given credit for any imprisonment resulting from the contempt. (1977, c. 711, s. 3; 1985 (Reg. Sess., 1986), c. 843, s. 1; 1987 (Reg. Sess., 1988), c. 1040, ss. 2, 4; 1989 (Reg. Sess., 1990), c. 1039, s. 4; 1991, c. 686, s. 3; 1999-361, s. 3; 2009-335, s. 1.)

§ 5A-13. Direct and indirect criminal contempt; proceedings required.

(a) Criminal contempt is direct criminal contempt when the act:

(1) Is committed within the sight or hearing of a presiding judicial official; and

(2) Is committed in, or in immediate proximity to, the room where proceedings are being held before the court; and

(3) Is likely to interrupt or interfere with matters then before the court.

The presiding judicial official may punish summarily for direct criminal contempt according to the requirements of G.S. 5A-14 or may defer adjudication and sentencing as provided in G.S. 5A-15. If proceedings for direct criminal contempt are deferred, the judicial official must, immediately following the conduct, inform the person of his intention to institute contempt proceedings.

(b) Any criminal contempt other than direct criminal contempt is indirect criminal contempt and is punishable only after proceedings in accordance with the procedure required by G.S. 5A-15. (1977, c. 711, s. 3.)

§ 5A-14. Summary proceedings for contempt.

(a) The presiding judicial official may summarily impose measures in response to direct criminal contempt when necessary to restore order or maintain the dignity and authority of the court and when the measures are imposed substantially contemporaneously with the contempt.

(b) Before imposing measures under this section, the judicial official must give the person charged with contempt summary notice of the charges and a summary opportunity to respond and must find facts supporting the summary imposition of measures in response to contempt. The facts must be established beyond a reasonable doubt. (1977, c. 711, s. 3.)

§ 5A-15. Plenary proceedings for contempt.

(a) When a judicial official chooses not to proceed summarily against a person charged with direct criminal contempt or when he may not proceed summarily, he may proceed by an order directing the person to appear before a judge at a reasonable time specified in the order and show cause why he should not be held in contempt of court. A copy of the order must be furnished to the person charged. If the criminal contempt is based upon acts before a judge which so involve him that his objectivity may reasonably be questioned, the order must be returned before a different judge.

(b) Proceedings under this section are before a district court judge unless a court superior to the district court issued the order, in which case the proceedings are before that court. Venue lies throughout the district court district as defined in G.S. 7A-133 or superior court district or set of districts as defined in G.S. 7A-41.1, as the case may be, where the order was issued.

(c) The person ordered to show cause may move to dismiss the order.

(d) The judge is the trier of facts at the show cause hearing.

(e)   The person charged with contempt may not be compelled to be a witness against himself in the hearing.

(f)   At the conclusion of the hearing, the judge must enter a finding of guilty or not guilty. If the person is found to be in contempt, the judge must make findings of fact and enter judgment. The facts must be established beyond a reasonable doubt.

(g)   The judge presiding over the hearing may appoint a prosecutor or, in the event of an apparent conflict of interest, some other member of the bar to represent the court in hearings for criminal contempt. (1977, c. 711, s. 3; 1987 (Reg. Sess., 1988), c. 1037, s. 44.)

§ 5A-16. Custody of person charged with criminal contempt.

(a)   A judicial official may orally order that a person he is charging with direct criminal contempt be taken into custody and restrained to the extent necessary to assure his presence for summary proceedings or notice of plenary proceedings.

(b)   If a judicial official who initiates plenary proceedings for contempt under G.S. 5A-15 finds, based on sworn statement or affidavit, probable cause to believe the person ordered to appear will not appear in response to the order, he may issue an order for arrest of the person, pursuant to G.S. 15A-305. A person arrested under this subsection is entitled to release under the provisions of Article 26, Bail, of Chapter 15A of the General Statutes. (1977, c. 711, s. 3.)

§ 5A-17. Appeals; bail proceedings.

(a)   A person found in criminal contempt may appeal in the manner provided for appeals in criminal actions, except appeal from a finding of contempt by a judicial official inferior to a superior court judge is by hearing de novo before a superior court judge.

(b)   Upon appeal in a case where the judicial official imposes confinement, a bail hearing shall be held within a reasonable time period after imposition of the confinement. The judicial official holding the bail hearing shall be:

(1)   A district court judge if the confinement is imposed by a clerk or magistrate.

(2)   A superior court judge if the confinement is imposed by a district court judge.

(3)   A superior court judge other than the superior court judge that imposed the confinement.

(c)   A person found in contempt and who has given notice of appeal may be retained in custody not more than 24 hours from the time of imposition of confinement without a bail determination being made by a judicial official as designated under subdivisions (1) through (3) of subsection (b) of this section. If a designated judicial official has not acted within 24 hours of the imposition of confinement, any judicial official shall act under the provisions of subsection (b) of this section and hold the bail hearing. (1977, c. 711, s. 3; 2013-303, s. 1.)

§ 5A-18. Reserved for future codification purposes.

§ 5A-19. Reserved for future codification purposes.
§ 5A-20. Reserved for future codification purposes.

Article 2

Civil Contempt.

§ 5A-21. Civil contempt; imprisonment to compel compliance.

(a)   Failure to comply with an order of a court is a continuing civil contempt as long as:

(1)   The order remains in force;

(2)   The purpose of the order may still be served by compliance with the order;

(2a)   The noncompliance by the person to whom the order is directed is willful; and

(3) The person to whom the order is directed is able to comply with the order or is able to take reasonable measures that would enable the person to comply with the order.

(b) A person who is found in civil contempt may be imprisoned as long as the civil contempt continues, subject to the limitations provided in subsections (b1) and (b2) of this section. Notwithstanding subsection (b2) of this section, if a person is found in civil contempt for failure to pay child support or failure to comply with a court order to perform an act that does not require the payment of a monetary judgment, the person may be imprisoned as long as the civil contempt continues without further hearing.

(b1) A person who is found in civil contempt, but was not arrested, for failure to comply with a nontestimonial identification order issued pursuant to Article 14, Nontestimonial Identification Order, of Chapter 15A of the General Statutes may not be imprisoned more than 90 days unless the person is arrested on probable cause.

(b2) The period of imprisonment for a person found in civil contempt shall not exceed 90 days for the same act of disobedience or refusal to comply with an order of the court. A person who has not purged himself or herself of the contempt within the period of imprisonment imposed by the court under this subsection may be recommitted for one or more successive periods of imprisonment, each not to exceed 90 days. However, the total period of imprisonment for the same act of disobedience or refusal to comply with the order of the court shall not exceed 12 months, including both the initial period of imprisonment imposed under this section and any additional period of imprisonment imposed under this subsection. Before the court may recommit a person to any additional period of imprisonment under this subsection, the court shall conduct a hearing de novo. The court must enter a finding for or against the alleged contemnor on each of the elements of G.S. 5A-21(a), and must find that all of elements of G.S. 5A-21(a) continue to exist before the person can be recommitted. For purposes of this subsection, a person's failure or refusal to purge himself or herself of contempt shall not be deemed a separate or additional act of disobedience, failure, or refusal to comply with an order of the court.

(c) A person who is found in civil contempt under this Article shall not, for the same conduct, be found in criminal contempt under Article 1 of this Chapter. (1977, c. 711, s. 3; 1979, 2nd Sess., c. 1080, s. 1; 1999-361, s. 1.)

§ 5A-22. Release when civil contempt no longer continues.

(a)   A person imprisoned for civil contempt must be released when his civil contempt no longer continues. The order of the court holding a person in civil contempt must specify how the person may purge himself of the contempt. Upon finding compliance with the specifications, the sheriff or other officer having custody may release the person without a further order from the court.

(b)   On motion of the contemnor, the court must determine if he is subject to release and, on an affirmative determination, order his release. The motion must be directed to the judge who found civil contempt unless he is not available. Then the motion must be made to a judge of the same division in the same district court district as defined in G.S. 7A-133 or superior court district or set of districts as defined in G.S. 7A-41.1, as the case may be. The contemnor may also seek his release under other procedures available under the law of this State. (1977, c. 711, s. 3; 1987 (Reg. Sess., 1988), c. 1037, s. 45.)

§ 5A-23. Proceedings for civil contempt.

(a)   Proceedings for civil contempt are by motion pursuant to G.S. 5A-23(a1), by the order of a judicial official directing the alleged contemnor to appear at a specified reasonable time and show cause why he should not be held in civil contempt, or by the notice of a judicial official that the alleged contemnor will be held in contempt unless he appears at a specified reasonable time and shows cause why he should not be held in contempt. The order or notice must be given at least five days in advance of the hearing unless good cause is shown. The order or notice may be issued on the motion and sworn statement or affidavit of one with an interest in enforcing the order, including a judge, and a finding by the judicial official of probable cause to believe there is civil contempt.

(a1)   Proceedings for civil contempt may be initiated by motion of an aggrieved party giving notice to the alleged contemnor to appear before the court for a hearing on whether the alleged contemnor should be held in civil contempt. A copy of the motion and notice must be served on the alleged contemnor at least five days in advance of the hearing unless good cause is shown. The motion must include a sworn statement or affidavit by the aggrieved party setting forth the reasons why the alleged contemnor should be held in civil contempt. The burden of proof in a hearing pursuant to this subsection shall be on the aggrieved party.

(b)   Except when the General Statutes specifically provide for the exercise of contempt power by the clerk of superior court, proceedings under this section are before a district court judge, unless a court superior to the district court issued the order in which case the proceedings are before that court. When the proceedings are before a superior court, venue is in the superior court district or set of districts as defined in G.S. 7A-41.1 of the court which issued the order. Otherwise, venue is in the county where the order was issued.

(c)   The person ordered to show cause may move to dismiss the order.

(d)   The judicial official is the trier of facts at the show cause hearing.
(e)   At the conclusion of the hearing, the judicial official must enter a finding for or against the alleged contemnor on each of the elements set out in G.S. 5A-21(a). If civil contempt is found, the judicial official must enter an order finding the facts constituting contempt and specifying the action which the contemnor must take to purge himself or herself of the contempt.

(f)   A person with an interest in enforcing the order may present the case for a finding of civil contempt for failure to comply with an order.
(g)   A person who is found in civil contempt under this Article shall not, for the same conduct, be found in criminal contempt under Article 1 of this Chapter. (1977, c. 711, s. 3; 1979, 2nd Sess., c. 1080, ss. 2-4; 1987 (Reg. Sess., 1988), c. 1037, s. 46; 1999-361, ss. 2, 4, 5; 2000-140, s. 35.)

§ 5A-24. Appeals.

A person found in civil contempt may appeal in the manner provided for appeals in civil actions. (1977, c. 711, s. 3.)

§ 5A-25. Proceedings as for contempt and civil contempt.

Whenever the laws of North Carolina call for proceedings as for contempt, the proceedings are those for civil contempt set out in this Article. (1977, c. 711, s. 3.)

§ 5A-26. Reserved for future codification purposes.

§ 5A-27. Reserved for future codification purposes.

§ 5A-28. Reserved for future codification purposes.

§ 5A-29. Reserved for future codification purposes.

§ 5A-30. Reserved for future codification purposes.

Article 3

Contempt by Juveniles.

§ 5A-31. Contempt by a juvenile.

(a) Each of the following, when done by an unemancipated minor who (i) is at least six years of age, (ii) is not yet 16 years of age, and (iii) has not been convicted of any crime in superior court, is contempt by a juvenile:
(1) Willful behavior committed during the sitting of a court and directly tending to interrupt its proceedings.

(2) Willful behavior committed during the sitting of a court in its immediate view and presence and directly tending to impair the respect due its authority.

(3) Willful disobedience of, resistance to, or interference with a court's lawful process, order, directive, or instruction or its execution.

(4) Willful refusal to be sworn or affirmed as a witness, or, when so sworn or affirmed, willful refusal to answer any legal and proper question when the refusal is not legally justified.

(5) Willful or grossly negligent failure to comply with schedules and practices of the court resulting in substantial interference with the business of the court.

(6)   Willful refusal to testify or produce other information upon the order of a judge acting pursuant to Article 61 of Chapter 15A of the General Statutes, Granting of Immunity to Witnesses.

(7)   Willful communication with a juror in an improper attempt to influence the juror's deliberations.

(8)   Any other act or omission specified in another Chapter of the General Statutes as grounds for criminal contempt.

(b)   Contempt by a juvenile is direct contempt by a juvenile when each of the following conditions is met:

(1)   The act is committed within the sight or hearing of a presiding judicial official.

(2)   The act is committed in, or in the immediate proximity to, the room where proceedings are being held before the court.

(3)   The act is likely to interrupt or interfere with matters then before the court.

(c)   Contempt by a juvenile that is not direct contempt by a juvenile is indirect contempt by a juvenile. (2007-168, s. 1.)
§ 5A-32. Direct contempt by a juvenile.

(a)   A presiding judicial official may summarily impose measures in response to direct contempt by a juvenile when necessary to restore order or maintain the dignity and authority of the court and when the measures are imposed substantially contemporaneously with the contempt. Before imposing measures summarily, the judicial official shall do all of the following:

(1)   Give the juvenile summary notice of the contempt allegation and a summary opportunity to respond.

(2)   Appoint an attorney to represent the juvenile and allow time for the juvenile and attorney to confer.

(3)   Find facts supporting the summary imposition of measures in response to contempt by a juvenile. The facts shall be established beyond a reasonable doubt.

(b)   When a judicial official chooses not to proceed summarily, the official may enter an order appointing counsel for the juvenile and directing the juvenile to appear before a judge in a juvenile proceeding at a reasonable time specified in the order and show cause why the juvenile should not be held in contempt. A copy of the order shall be furnished to the juvenile and to the juvenile's attorney. If the direct contempt by a juvenile is based on acts before a judge that so involve the judge that the judge's objectivity may reasonably be questioned, the order shall be returned before a different judge presiding in juvenile court.

(c)   After a determination is made pursuant to subsection (a) or (b) of this section that a juvenile has committed direct contempt, the court may order any or all of the following:

(1)   That the juvenile be detained in a juvenile detention facility for up to five days.

(2)   That the juvenile perform up to 30 hours of supervised community service as arranged by a juvenile court counselor.

(3)   That the juvenile be required to undergo any evaluation necessary for the court to determine the needs of the juvenile.

The court shall not impose any of these sanctions without finding first that the juvenile's act or omission was willfully contemptuous or that the act or omission was preceded by a clear warning by the court that the conduct is improper.

(d)   A judicial official who finds a juvenile in direct contempt may at any time terminate or reduce a sanction of detention or eliminate or reduce the number of hours of community service ordered if warranted by the juvenile's conduct and the ends of justice.

(e)   A judicial official may orally order that a juvenile the official is charging with direct contempt be taken into custody and restrained to the extent necessary to assure the juvenile's presence for summary proceedings or notice of plenary proceedings.

(f)   The clerk shall place a copy of any order or other paper issued pursuant to this section in the juvenile's juvenile file, if one exists, or in a new juvenile file.

(g) Appeal from an order finding a juvenile in direct contempt is to the Court of Appeals. (2007-168, s. 1.)

§ 5A-33. Indirect contempt by a juvenile.

Indirect contempt by a juvenile may be adjudged and sanctioned only pursuant to the procedures in Subchapter II of Chapter 7B of the General Statutes. (2007-168, s. 1.)

§ 5A-34. When minor can be in contempt.

(a) No act or omission by a minor younger than six years of age constitutes contempt.

(b) The provisions of Article 1 and Article 2 of this Chapter apply to acts or omissions by a minor who:

(1) Is 16 years of age or older;

(2) Is married or otherwise emancipated; or

(3) Before the act or omission, was convicted in superior court of any criminal offense. (2007-168, s. 1.)

Chapter 6.

Liability for Court Costs.

Article 1.

Generally.

§ 6-1. Items allowed as costs.

To the party for whom judgment is given, costs shall be allowed as provided in Chapter 7A and this Chapter. (Code, s. 528; Rev., s. 1249; C.S., s. 1225; 1955, c. 922; 1971, c. 269, s. 1.)

§ 6-2. Repealed by Session Laws 1971, c. 269, s. 15.

§ 6-3. Sureties on prosecution bonds liable for costs.

When an action is brought in any court in which security is given for the prosecution thereof, or when any case is brought up to a court by an appeal or otherwise, in which security for the prosecution of the suit has been given, and judgment is rendered against the plaintiff for the costs of the defendant, the appellate court shall also give judgment against the surety for said costs, and execution may issue jointly against the plaintiff and his surety. (1831, c. 46; R.S., c. 31, s. 133; R.C., c. 31, s. 126; Code, s. 543; Rev., s. 1251; 1913, c. 189, s. 1; C.S., s. 1227.)

§ 6-4. Execution for unpaid costs; bill of costs to be attached.

When costs are not paid by the party from whom they are due, the clerk of superior court shall issue an execution for the costs, and attach a bill of costs to each execution. The sheriff shall levy the execution as in other cases. (R.C., c. 102, s. 24; Code, s. 3762; Rev., s. 1252; C.S., s. 1228; 1969, c. 44, s. 17; 1971, c. 269, s. 2.)

§§ 6-5 through 6-6. Repealed by Session Laws 1971, c. 269, s. 15.

§ 6-7. Clerk to enter costs in case file.

The clerk of superior court shall enter in the case file, after judgment, the costs allowed by law. (Code, s. 532; Rev., s. 1255; C.S., s. 1231; 1971, c. 269, s. 3.)

§§ 6-8 through 6-12. Repealed by Session Laws 1971, c. 269, s. 15.

Article 2.

When State Liable for Costs.

§ 6-13. Civil actions by the State; joinder of private party.

In all civil actions prosecuted in the name of the State, by an officer duly authorized for that purpose, the State shall be liable for costs in the same cases and to the same extent as private parties. If a private person be joined with the State as plaintiff, he shall be liable in the first instance for the defendant's costs, which shall not be recovered of the State till after execution is issued therefor against such private party and returned unsatisfied. (Code, s. 536; Rev., s. 1259; C.S., s. 1236.)

§ 6-14. Civil action by and against State officers.

In all civil actions depending, or which may be instituted, by any of the officers of the State, or which have been or shall be instituted against them, when any such action is brought or defended pursuant to the advice of the Attorney General, and the same is decided against such officers, the cost thereof shall be paid by the State Treasurer upon properly drawn warrants. (1874-75, c. 154; Code, s. 3373; Rev., s. 1260; C.S., s. 1237; 1971, c. 269, s. 4.)

§ 6-15. Actions by State for private persons, etc.

In an action prosecuted in the name of the State for the recovery of money or property, or to establish a right or claim for the benefit of any county, city, town, village, corporation or person, costs awarded against the plaintiff shall be a charge against the party for whose benefit the action was prosecuted, and not against the State. (Code, s. 537; Rev., s. 1261; C.S., s. 1238.)

§ 6-16. Repealed by Session Laws 1971, c. 269, s. 15.

§ 6-17. Costs of State on appeals to federal courts.

In all cases, whether civil or criminal, to which the State of North Carolina is a party, and which are carried from the courts of this State, or from the district court of the United States, by appeal or writ of error, to the United States circuit court of appeals, or to the Supreme Court of the United States, and the State is adjudged to pay the costs, it is the duty of the Attorney General to certify the amount of such costs to the Treasurer, who shall pay them upon properly drawn warrants. (1871-2, c. 26; Code, s. 538; Rev., s. 1263; C.S., s. 1240; 1971, c. 269, s. 5.)

§ 6-17.1. Costs and expenses of State in connection with federal litigation arising out of State cases.

In all cases of litigation in any court of the United States arising out of or by reason of any cases pending or tried in any court of the State of North Carolina, or in any action originally instituted in any court of the United States, the expenses for State court costs, securing of court records and transcripts, and other necessary expenses in representing the State of North Carolina or any of its departments, officials or agencies shall be allocated from and paid out of the State Contingency and Emergency Fund. (1963, c. 844.)

Article 3.

Civil Actions and Proceedings.

§ 6-18. When costs allowed as of course to plaintiff.

Costs shall be allowed of course to the plaintiff, upon a recovery, in the following cases:

(1) In an action for the recovery of real property, or when a claim of title to real property arises on the pleadings, or is certified by the court to have come in question at the trial.

(2) In an action to recover the possession of personal property.

(3) In an action for assault, battery, false imprisonment, libel, slander, malicious prosecution, criminal conversation or seduction, if the plaintiff recovers less than fifty dollars ($50.00) damages, he shall recover no more costs than damages.

(4) When several actions are brought on one bond, recognizance, promissory note, bill of exchange or instrument in writing, or in any other case, for the same cause of action against several parties who might have been joined as defendants in the same action, no costs other than disbursements

shall be allowed to the plaintiff in more than one of such actions, which shall be at his election, provided the party or parties proceeded against in such other action or actions were within the State and not secreted at the commencement of the previous action or actions.

(5)   In an action brought under Article 1 of Chapter 19A. (R.C., c. 31, s. 78; 1874-5, c. 119; Code, s. 525; Rev., s. 1264; C.S., s. 1241; 1971, c. 269, s. 6; 1979, c. 808, s. 5.)

§ 6-19. When costs allowed as of course to defendant.

Costs shall be allowed as of course to the defendant, in the actions mentioned in G.S. 6-18 unless the plaintiff be entitled to costs therein. In all actions where there are several defendants not united in interest, and making separate defenses by separate answers, and the plaintiff fails to recover judgment against all, the court may award costs to such of the defendants as have judgment in their favor or any of them. (C.C.P., s. 277; Code, ss. 526, 527; Rev., s. 1266; C.S., s. 1242; 2007-212, s. 1.)

§ 6-19.1. Attorney's fees to parties appealing or defending against agency decision.

(a)   In any civil action, other than an adjudication for the purpose of establishing or fixing a rate, or a disciplinary action by a licensing board, brought by the State or brought by a party who is contesting State action pursuant to G.S. 150B-43 or any other appropriate provisions of law, unless the prevailing party is the State, the court may, in its discretion, allow the prevailing party to recover reasonable attorney's fees, including attorney's fees applicable to the administrative review portion of the case, in contested cases arising under Article 3 of Chapter 150B, to be taxed as court costs against the appropriate agency if:

(1)   The court finds that the agency acted without substantial justification in pressing its claim against the party; and

(2)   The court finds that there are no special circumstances that would make the award of attorney's fees unjust. The party shall petition for the attorney's

fees within 30 days following final disposition of the case. The petition shall be supported by an affidavit setting forth the basis for the request.

Nothing in this section shall be deemed to authorize the assessment of attorney's fees for the administrative review portion of the case in contested cases arising under Article 9 of Chapter 131E of the General Statutes.

Nothing in this section grants permission to bring an action against an agency otherwise immune from suit or gives a right to bring an action to a party who otherwise lacks standing to bring the action.

Any attorney's fees assessed against an agency under this section shall be charged against the operating expenses of the agency and shall not be reimbursed from any other source.

(b)   Expired. (1983, c. 918, s. 1; 1987, c. 827, s. 1; 2000-190, s. 1; 2009-475, s. 8.)

§ 6-19.2: Repealed by Session Laws 1995, c. 388, s. 6.

§ 6-20. Costs allowed or not, in discretion of court.

In actions where allowance of costs is not otherwise provided by the General Statutes, costs may be allowed in the discretion of the court. Costs awarded by the court are subject to the limitations on assessable or recoverable costs set forth in G.S. 7A-305(d), unless specifically provided for otherwise in the General Statutes. (Code, s. 527; Rev., s. 1267; C.S., s. 1243; 2007-212, s. 2.)

§ 6-21. Costs allowed either party or apportioned in discretion of court.

Costs in the following matters shall be taxed against either party, or apportioned among the parties, in the discretion of the court:

(1)   Application for years' support, for surviving spouse or children.

(2)   Caveats to wills and any action or proceeding which may require the construction of any will or trust agreement, or fix the rights and duties of parties thereunder; provided, that in any caveat proceeding under this subdivision, the

court shall allow attorneys' fees for the attorneys of the caveators only if it finds that the proceeding has substantial merit.

(3)   Habeas corpus; and the court shall direct what officer shall tax the costs thereof.

(4)   In actions for divorce or alimony; and the court may both before and after judgment make such order respecting the payment of such costs as may be incurred by either spouse from the sole and separate estate of either spouse, as may be just.

(5)   Application for the establishment, alteration or discontinuance of a public road, cartway or ferry. The board of county commissioners may order the costs incurred before them paid in their discretion.

(6)   The compensation of referees and commissioners to take depositions.

(7)   All costs and expenses incurred in special proceedings for the division or sale of either real estate or personal property under the Chapter entitled Partition.

(8)   In all proceedings under the Chapter entitled Drainage, except as therein otherwise provided.

(9)   In proceedings for reallotment of homestead for increase in value, as provided in the Chapter, Civil Procedure.

(10)   In proceedings under Article 3 of Chapter 49 of the General Statutes regarding children born out of wedlock.

(11)   In custody proceedings under Chapter 50A of the General Statutes.

(12)   In actions brought for misappropriation of a trade secret under Article 24 of Chapter 66 of the General Statutes.

The word "costs" as the same appears and is used in this section shall be construed to include reasonable attorneys' fees in such amounts as the court shall in its discretion determine and allow: provided that attorneys' fees in actions for alimony shall not be included in the costs as provided herein, but shall be determined and provided for in accordance with G.S. 50-16.4. (Code, ss. 533, 1294, 1323, 1422, 1660, 2039, 2056, 2134, 2161; 1889, c. 37; 1893, c.

149, s. 6; Rev., s. 1268; C.S., s. 1244; 1937, c. 143; 1955, c. 1364; 1965, c. 633; 1967, c. 993, s. 2; c. 1152, s. 5; 1977, c. 576; 1979, c. 110, s. 3; 1981, c. 809, s. 1; c. 890, s. 2; 2013-198, s. 1.)

§ 6-21.1. Allowance of counsel fees as part of costs in certain cases.

(a)   In any personal injury or property damage suit, or suit against an insurance company under a policy issued by the defendant insurance company in which the insured or beneficiary is the plaintiff, instituted in a court of record, upon findings by the court (i) that there was an unwarranted refusal by the defendant to negotiate or pay the claim which constitutes the basis of such suit, (ii) that the amount of damages recovered is twenty-five thousand dollars ($25,000) or less, and (iii) that the amount of damages recovered exceeded the highest offer made by the defendant no later than 90 days before the commencement of trial, the presiding judge may, in the judge's discretion, allow a reasonable attorneys' fees to the duly licensed attorneys representing the litigant obtaining a judgment for damages in said suit, said attorneys' fees to be taxed as a part of the court costs. The attorneys' fees so awarded shall not exceed ten thousand dollars ($10,000).

(b)   When the presiding judge determines that an award of attorneys' fees is to be made under this statute, the judge shall issue a written order including findings of fact detailing the factual basis for the finding of an unwarranted refusal to negotiate or pay the claim, and setting forth the amount of the highest offer made 90 days or more before the commencement of trial, and the amount of damages recovered, as well as the factual basis and amount of any such attorneys' fees to be awarded. (1959, c. 688; 1963, c. 1193; 1967, c. 927; 1969, c. 786; 1979, c. 401; 1985 (Reg. Sess., 1986), c. 976; 2011-283, s. 3.1; 2011-317, s. 1.1; 2013-159, s. 5.)

§ 6-21.2. Attorneys' fees in notes, etc., in addition to interest.

Obligations to pay attorneys' fees upon any note, conditional sale contract or other evidence of indebtedness, in addition to the legal rate of interest or finance charges specified therein, shall be valid and enforceable, and collectible as part of such debt, if such note, contract or other evidence of indebtedness be collected by or through an attorney at law after maturity, subject to the following provisions:

(1) If such note, conditional sale contract or other evidence of indebtedness provides for attorneys' fees in some specific percentage of the "outstanding balance" as herein defined, such provision and obligation shall be valid and enforceable up to but not in excess of fifteen percent (15%) of said "outstanding balance" owing on said note, contract or other evidence of indebtedness.

(2) If such note, conditional sale contract or other evidence of indebtedness provides for the payment of reasonable attorneys' fees by the debtor, without specifying any specific percentage, such provision shall be construed to mean fifteen percent (15%) of the "outstanding balance" owing on said note, contract or other evidence of indebtedness.

(3) As to notes and other writing(s) evidencing an indebtedness arising out of a loan of money to the debtor, the "outstanding balance" shall mean the principal and interest owing at the time suit is instituted to enforce any security agreement securing payment of the debt and/or to collect said debt.

(4) As to conditional sale contracts and other such security agreements which evidence both a monetary obligation and a security interest in or a lease of specific goods, the "outstanding balance" shall mean the "time price balance" owing as of the time suit is instituted by the secured party to enforce the said security agreement and/or to collect said debt.

(5) The holder of an unsecured note or other writing(s) evidencing an unsecured debt, and/or the holder of a note and chattel mortgage or other security agreement and/or the holder of a conditional sale contract or any other such security agreement which evidences both a monetary obligation and a security interest in or a lease of specific goods, or his attorney at law, shall, after maturity of the obligation by default or otherwise, notify the maker, debtor, account debtor, endorser or party sought to be held on said obligation that the provisions relative to payment of attorneys' fees in addition to the "outstanding balance" shall be enforced and that such maker, debtor, account debtor, endorser or party sought to be held on said obligation has five days from the mailing of such notice to pay the "outstanding balance" without the attorneys' fees. If such party shall pay the "outstanding balance" in full before the expiration of such time, then the obligation to pay the attorneys' fees shall be void, and no court shall enforce such provisions.

(6) If the attorneys' fees are for services rendered to an assignee or a debt buyer, as defined in G.S. 58-70-15, all of the following materials setting forth a

party's obligation to pay attorneys' fees shall be provided to the court before a court may enforce those provisions:

a. A copy of the contract or other writing evidencing the original debt, which must contain a signature of the defendant. If a claim is based on credit card debt and no such signed writing evidencing the original debt ever existed, then copies of documents generated when the credit card was actually used must be attached.

b. A copy of the assignment or other writing establishing that the plaintiff is the owner of the debt. If the debt has been assigned more than once, then each assignment or other writing evidencing transfer of ownership must be attached to establish an unbroken chain of ownership. Each assignment or other writing evidencing transfer of ownership must contain the original account number of the debt purchased and must clearly show the debtor's name associated with that account number.

Notwithstanding the foregoing, however, if debtor has defaulted or violated the terms of the security agreement and has refused, on demand, to surrender possession of the collateral to the secured party as authorized by G.S. 25-9-609, with the result that said secured party is required to institute an ancillary claim and delivery proceeding to secure possession of said collateral; no such written notice shall be required before enforcement of the provisions relative to payment of attorneys' fees in addition to the outstanding balance. (1967, c. 562, s. 4; 2000-169, s. 27; 2009-573, s. 7.)

§ 6-21.3. Remedies for returned check.

(a) Notwithstanding any criminal sanctions that may apply, a person, firm, or corporation who knowingly draws, makes, utters, or issues and delivers to another any check or draft drawn on any bank or depository that refuses to honor the same because the maker or drawer does not have sufficient funds on deposit in or credit with the bank or depository with which to pay the check or draft upon presentation or because the check has previously been presented and honored for the payment of money or its equivalent, and who fails to pay the same amount, any service charges imposed on the payee by a bank or depository for processing the dishonored check, and any processing fees imposed by the payee pursuant to G.S. 25-3-506 in cash to the payee within 30 days following written demand therefor, shall be liable to the payee (i) for the amount owing on the check, the service charges, and processing fees and (ii) for additional damages of three times the amount owing on the check, not to exceed five hundred dollars ($500.00) or to be less than one hundred dollars ($100.00). If the amount claimed in the first demand letter is not paid, the claim for the amount of the check, the service charges and processing fees, and the treble damages provided for in this subsection may be made by a subsequent letter of demand prior to filing an action. In an action under this section the court or jury may, however, waive all or part of the additional damages upon a finding that the defendant's failure to satisfy the dishonored check or draft was due to economic hardship.

The initial written demand for the amount of the check, the service charges, and processing fees shall be mailed by certified mail to the defendant at the defendant's last known address and shall be in the form set out in subsection (a1) of this section. The subsequent demand letter demanding the amount of the check, the service charges, the processing fees, and treble damages shall be mailed by certified mail to the defendant at the defendant's last known address and shall be in the form set out in subsection (a2) of this section. If the payee chooses to send the demand letter set out in subsection (a2) of this section, then the payee may not file an action to collect the amount of the check, the service charges, the processing fees, or treble damages until 30 days following the written demand set out in subsection (a2) of this section.

(a1) The first notification letter shall be substantially in the following form:

This letter is written pursuant to G.S. 6-21.3 to inform you that on _____, you made and delivered to the business listed above a check payable to this business containing your name and address in the sum of $_____, drawn upon _____ (bank or institution), account #_____. [If the check was received in a face-to-face transaction insert this sentence: This check contained a drivers license identification number from a card with your photograph and mailing address, which was used to identify you at the time the check was accepted.] [If the check was delivered by mail insert this sentence: We have compared your name, address, and signature on the check with the name, address, and signature on file in the account previously established by you or on your behalf, and the signature on the check appears to be genuine.] Also, we have received no information that this was a stolen check, if that is the circumstance.

The check has been dishonored by the bank for the following reasons:

As acceptor of the check, we give you notice to rectify any bank error or other error in connection with the transaction, and to pay the face value of the check, plus the fees as authorized under G.S. 25-3-506 and G.S. 6-21.3(a) as follows:

Face value of the check #
$_____

Processing fee authorized

under G.S. 25-3-506
$_____

Bank service fees authorized

under G.S. 6-21.3
$_____

Total amount due:
$_____

If the total amount due listed above is not paid within 30 days of the mailing of this letter, thereafter we may file a civil action to seek civil damages of three times the amount of the check (with a minimum damage of one hundred dollars ($100.00) and a maximum damage of five hundred dollars ($500.00)) for allegedly giving a worthless check in violation of law (G.S. 6-21.3), in addition to the amount of the check and the fees specified above.

Appropriate relief will then be sought before a court of proper jurisdiction for full payment of the check plus all costs, treble damages, and witness fees.

If you do not believe you are liable for these amounts, you will have a right to present your defense in court. To pay the check or obtain information, contact the undersigned at the above business location. Cash or a bank official check will be the only acceptable means of redeeming the dishonored check.

If you do not believe that you owe the amount claimed in this letter or if you believe you have received this letter in error, please notify the undersigned at the above business location as soon as possible.

(a2)   If the total amount due in subsection (a1) has not been paid within 30 days after the mailing of the notification letter, a subsequent demand letter may be sent and shall be substantially in the following form:

On _____, we informed you that we received a check payable to this business containing your name and address in the sum of $_____, drawn upon _____ (bank or institution), account #_____. This check contained identification information which was used to identify you as the maker of the check. Also, we have received no information that this was a stolen check, if that is the circumstance.

The check has been dishonored by the bank for the following reasons:

_____

We notified you that you were responsible for the face value of the check ($_____) plus the fees authorized under G.S. 25-3-506 ($_____) and G.S. 6-21.3(a) ($_____) for a total amount due of $_____. Thirty days have passed since the mailing of that notification letter, and you have not made payment to us for that total amount due.

Under G.S. 6-21.3, we claim you are now liable for the face value of the check, the fees, and treble damages. The damages we claim are three times the amount of the check or one hundred dollars ($100.00), whichever is greater, but cannot exceed five hundred dollars ($500.00). The total amount we claim now due is:

Face value of the check
$_____

Processing fee authorized

under G.S. 25-3-506
$_____

Bank service fees authorized

under G.S. 6-21.3
$_____

Three times the face value of the

check, with a minimum of $100.00

and a maximum of $500.00
$_____

Total amount due:
$_____

Payment of the total amount claimed above within 30 days of the mailing of this letter shall satisfy this civil remedy for the returned check.

If payment has not been received within this 30-day period, we will seek appropriate relief before a court of proper jurisdiction for full payment of the check plus all costs, treble damages, and witness fees.

If you do not believe you are liable for these amounts, you will have a right to present your defense in court. To pay the check or obtain information, contact the undersigned at the above business location. Cash or a bank official check will be the only acceptable means of redeeming the dishonored check.

If you do not believe that you owe the amount claimed in this letter or if you believe you have received this letter in error, please notify the undersigned at the above business location as soon as possible.

(b) In an action under subsection (a) of this section, the presiding judge or magistrate may award the prevailing party, as part of the court costs payable, a reasonable attorney's fee to the duly licensed attorney representing the prevailing party in such suit.

(c) It shall be an affirmative defense, in addition to other defenses, to an action under this section if it is found that: (i) full satisfaction of the amount of the check or draft was made prior to the commencement of the action, or (ii) that the bank or depository erred in dishonoring the check or draft, or (iii) that the acceptor of the check knew at the time of acceptance that there were insufficient funds on deposit in the bank or depository with which to cause the check to be honored.

(d) The remedy provided for herein shall apply only if the check was drawn, made, uttered or issued with knowledge there were insufficient funds in the account, that no credit existed with the bank or depository with which to pay the check or draft upon presentation, or that the check was presented with the knowledge that the check had previously been presented and honored for the payment of money or its equivalent.

(e) A check or draft refused by a bank or depository, or the image of that check or draft, may be submitted as evidence for the remedy provided by this section if the bank or depository has returned it in the regular course of business stamped, marked, or with an attachment indicating the reason for the dishonor with terms that include, but are not limited to, the following: "insufficient funds," "no account," "account closed," "NSF," "uncollected," "unable to locate," "stale dated," "postdated," "endorsement irregular," "signature irregular," "nonnegotiable," "altered," "unable to process," "refer to maker," "duplicate presentment," "forgery," "noncompliant," or "UCD noncompliant." (1975, c. 129, s. 1; 1981, c. 781, s. 2; 1985, c. 643; 1993, c. 374, s. 1; 1995, c. 356, s. 1; 1995 (Reg. Sess., 1996), c. 742, s. 5; 2013-244, ss. 1-3.)

§ 6-21.4. Allowance of counsel fees and costs in certain cases involving principals or teachers.

In any civil action brought against a public school principal or teacher as defined in G.S. 115C-390 arising or resulting from the use of corporal punishment, upon a determination that the principal or teacher has prevailed and that the plaintiff's action was frivolous or without substantial merit, the presiding judge may, in his discretion, allow a reasonable attorney fee to the duly licensed attorney representing the principal or teacher. The attorney's fee shall be taxed as part of the court costs. (1981, c. 381, s. 1; c. 682, s. 22.)

§ 6-21.5. Attorney's fees in nonjusticiable cases.

In any civil action, special proceeding, or estate or trust proceeding, the court, upon motion of the prevailing party, may award a reasonable attorney's fee to the prevailing party if the court finds that there was a complete absence of a justiciable issue of either law or fact raised by the losing party in any pleading. The filing of a general denial or the granting of any preliminary motion, such as a motion for judgment on the pleadings pursuant to G.S. 1A-1, Rule 12, a motion to dismiss pursuant to G.S. 1A-1, Rule 12(b)(6), a motion for a directed verdict pursuant to G.S. 1A-1, Rule 50, or a motion for summary judgment pursuant to G.S. 1A-1, Rule 56, is not in itself a sufficient reason for the court to award attorney's fees, but may be evidence to support the court's decision to make such an award. A party who advances a claim or defense supported by a good faith argument for an extension, modification, or reversal of law may not be required under this section to pay attorney's fees. The court shall make findings of fact and conclusions of law to support its award of attorney's fees under this section. (1983 (Reg. Sess., 1984), c. 1039, s. 1; 2006-259, s. 13(I).)

§ 6-21.6. Reciprocal attorneys' fees provisions in business contracts.

(a)   As used in this section, the following definitions apply:

(1)   Business contract. - A contract entered into primarily for business or commercial purposes. The term does not include a consumer contract, an employment contract, or a contract to which a government or a governmental agency of this State is a party.

(2)   Consumer contract. - A contract entered into by one or more individuals primarily for personal, family, or household purposes.

(3)   Employment contract. - A contract between an individual and another party to provide personal services by that individual to the other party, whether the relationship is in the nature of employee-employer or principal-independent contractor.

(4)   Reciprocal attorneys' fees provisions. - Provisions in any written business contract by which each party to the contract agrees, in the manner set out in subsection (b) of this section, upon the terms and subject to the conditions set forth in the contract that are made applicable to all parties, to pay or reimburse the other parties for attorneys' fees and expenses incurred by reason of any suit, action, proceeding, or arbitration involving the business contract.

(b)   Reciprocal attorneys' fees provisions in business contracts are valid and enforceable for the recovery of reasonable attorneys' fees and expenses only if all of the parties to the business contract sign by hand the business contract. In any suit, action, proceeding, or arbitration primarily for the recovery of monetary damages, the award of reasonable attorneys' fees may not exceed the monetary damages awarded.

(c)   If a business contract governed by the laws of this State contains a reciprocal attorneys' fees provision, the court or arbitrator in any suit, action, proceeding, or arbitration involving the business contract may award reasonable attorneys' fees in accordance with the terms of the business contract. In determining reasonable attorneys' fees and expenses under this section, the court or arbitrator may consider all relevant facts and circumstances, including, but not limited to, the following:

(1)   The amount in controversy and the results obtained.
(2)   The reasonableness of the time and labor expended, and the billing rates charged, by the attorneys.

(3)   The novelty and difficulty of the questions raised in the action.

(4)   The skill required to perform properly the legal services rendered.

(5)   The relative economic circumstances of the parties.

(6)   Settlement offers made prior to the institution of the action.

(7)   Offers of judgment pursuant to Rule 68 of the North Carolina Rules of Civil Procedure and whether judgment finally obtained was more favorable than such offers.

(8)   Whether a party unjustly exercised superior economic bargaining power in the conduct of the action.

(9)   The timing of settlement offers.

(10)   The amounts of settlement offers as compared to the verdict.

(11)   The extent to which the party seeking attorneys' fees prevailed in the action.

(12)   The amount of attorneys' fees awarded in similar cases.

(13)   The terms of the business contract.

(d)   Reasonable attorneys' fees and expenses shall not be governed by (i) any statutory presumption or provision in the business contract providing for a stated percentage of the amount of such attorneys' fees or (ii) the amount recovered in other cases in which the business contract contains reciprocal attorneys' fees provisions.

(e) Nothing in this section shall in any way make valid or invalid attorneys' fees provisions in consumer contracts or in any note, conditional sale contract, or other evidence of indebtedness that is otherwise governed by G.S. 6-21.2. If the business contract is also a note, conditional sale contract, or other evidence of indebtedness that is otherwise governed by G.S. 6-21.2, then the parties that are entitled to recover attorneys' fees and expenses may elect to recover attorneys' fees and expenses either under this section or G.S. 6-21.2 but may recover only once for the same attorneys' fees and expenses.

(f) In any suit, action, proceeding, or arbitration primarily for the recovery of monetary damages, the award of reasonable attorneys' fees may not exceed the amount in controversy.

(g) Nothing in this section shall in any way make valid or invalid attorneys' fees provisions in a contract of insurance governed by Chapter 58 of the General Statutes. (2011-341, s. 2.)

§ 6-21.7. Attorneys' fees; cities or counties acting outside the scope of their authority.

In any action in which a city or county is a party, upon a finding by the court that the city or county acted outside the scope of its legal authority, the court may award reasonable attorneys' fees and costs to the party who successfully challenged the city's or county's action, provided that if the court also finds that the city's or county's action was an abuse of its discretion, the court shall award attorneys' fees and costs. (2011-299, s. 1.)

§ 6-22. Petitioner to pay costs in certain cases.

The petitioner shall pay the costs in the following proceedings:

(1) In petitions for draining or damming lowlands where the petitioner alone is benefited.

(2) In petitions for condemnation of water millsites when the petitioner is allowed to erect the mill; but when he is not allowed to erect the mill, the costs shall be paid by the person who is allowed to do so.

(3) In petitions for condemnation of land for railroads, street railways, telegraph, telephone or electric power or light companies, or for water supplies for public institutions, or for the use of other quasi-public or municipal corporations; unless in the opinion of the superior court the defendant improperly refused the privilege, use or easement demanded, in which case the costs must be adjudged as to the court may appear equitable and just.
(4) When the petition is refused. (Code, ss. 1299, 1855, 2013; 1893, c. 63; 1903, c. 562; Rev., s. 1269; C.S., s. 1245; 1945, c. 635.)

§ 6-23. Defendant unreasonably defending after notice of no personal claim to pay costs.

In case of a defendant, against whom no personal claim is made, the plaintiff may deliver to such defendant with the summons, a notice subscribed by the plaintiff or his attorney, setting forth the general object of the action, a brief description of the property affected by it, if it affects real or personal property, and that no personal claim is made against such defendant. If a defendant on whom such notice is served unreasonably defends the action, he shall pay costs to the plaintiff. (Code, s. 216; Rev., s. 1270; C.S., s. 1246.)

§ 6-24. Suits by an indigent; payment of costs by an indigent.

A person who sues as an indigent is not required to advance the required court costs and no officer shall require any fee of the person. If a court enters a judgment in favor of a person suing as an indigent and does not require another party to the suit to pay the costs of the suit, the court may require the indigent person to pay any costs of the suit that were not required to be paid because the person was indigent. (1868-9, c. 96, s. 3; Code, s. 212; 1895, c. 149; Rev., s. 1265; C.S., s. 1247; 1993, c. 435, s. 5.)

§ 6-25. Party seeking recovery on usurious contracts; no costs.

No costs shall be recovered by any party, whether plaintiff or defendant, who may endeavor to recover upon any usurious contract. (1895, c. 69; Rev., s. 1271; C.S., s. 1248.)

§ 6-26. Costs in special proceedings.

The costs in special proceedings shall be as allowed in civil actions, unless otherwise specially provided. (Code, s. 541; Rev., s. 1272; C.S., s. 1249.)

§ 6-27. Repealed by Session Laws 1971, c. 269, s. 15.

§ 6-28. Costs of laying off homestead and exemption.

The costs and expenses of appraising and laying off the homestead or personal property exemptions, when the same is made under execution, shall be charged and included in the officer's bill of fees upon such execution or other final process; and when made upon the petition of the owner, they shall be paid by such owner, and the latter costs shall be a lien on said homestead. (Code, s. 510; Rev., s. 1274; C.S., s. 1251.)

§ 6-29. Costs of reassessment of homestead.

If the superior court at term shall confirm the appraisal or assessment, or shall increase the exemption allowed the debtor or claimant, the levy shall stand only upon the excess remaining, and the creditor shall pay all the costs of the proceeding in court. If the amount allowed the debtor or claimant is reduced, the costs of the proceeding in court shall be paid by the debtor or claimant, and the levy shall cover the excess then remaining. (Code, s. 521; Rev., s. 1275; C.S., s. 1252.)

§ 6-30. Costs against infant plaintiff; guardian responsible.

When costs are adjudged against an infant plaintiff, the guardian by whom he appeared in the action shall be responsible therefor. (Code, s. 534; Rev., s. 1276; C.S., s. 1253.)

§ 6-31. Costs where executor, administrator, trustee of express trust, or person authorized by statute a party.

In an action prosecuted or defended by an executor, administrator, trustee of an express trust, or a person expressly authorized by statute, costs shall be recovered as in an action by and against a person prosecuting or defending in his own right; but such costs shall be chargeable only upon or collected out of the estate, fund or party represented, unless the court directs the same to be paid by the plaintiff or defendant, personally, for mismanagement or bad faith in such action or defense. And when any claim against a deceased person is referred, the prevailing party shall be entitled to recover the fees of referees and witnesses, and other necessary disbursements, to be taxed according to law. (Code, s. 535; Rev., s. 1277; C.S., s. 1254.)

§ 6-32. Costs against assignee after action brought.

In actions in which the cause of action becomes by assignment after the commencement of the action, or in any other manner, the property of a person not a party to the action, such person shall be liable for the costs in the same manner as if he were a party. (Code, s. 539; Rev., s. 1278; C.S., s. 1255.)

Article 4.

Costs on Appeal.

§ 6-33. Costs on appeal generally.

On appeal from a magistrate or any court of the General Court of Justice, if the appellant recovers judgment, he shall recover the costs of the appeal and also those costs he ought to have recovered below had the judgment of that court been correct. If in any court of appeal there is judgment for a new trial, or for a new jury, or if the judgment appealed from is not wholly reversed, but partly affirmed and partly disaffirmed, the costs shall be in the discretion of the appellate court. (Code, s. 540; Rev., s. 1279; C.S., s. 1256; 1969, c. 44, s. 19; 1971, c. 269, s. 7.)

§§ 6-34 through 6-35. Repealed by Session Laws 1971, c. 269, s. 15.

Article 5.

Liability of Counties in Criminal Actions.

§§ 6-36 through 6-39. Repealed by Session Laws 1971, c. 269, s. 15.

Article 5.

Liability of Counties in Criminal Actions.

§ 6-40. Liability of counties, where trial removed from one county to another.

When a prisoner is sent from one county to another to be held for trial, or for any other cause or purpose, the county from which he is sent shall pay his jail expenses, unless they are collected from the prisoner. (1889, c. 354; 1901, c. 718; Rev., s. 1285; C.S., s. 1263; 1971, c. 269, s. 8.)

§§ 6-41 through 6-44. Repealed by Session Laws 1971, c. 269, s. 15.

Article 6.

Liability of Defendant in Criminal Actions.

§§ 6-45 through 6-46. Repealed by Session Laws 1971, c. 269, s. 15.

Article 6.

Liability of Defendant in Criminal Actions.

§ 6-47. Judgment confessed; bond given to secure fine and costs.

In cases where a court permits a defendant convicted of any criminal offense to give bond or confess judgment, with sureties to secure the fine and costs which may be imposed, the acceptance of such security shall be upon the condition that it shall not operate as a discharge of the original judgment against the defendant nor as a discharge of his person from the custody of the law until the fine and costs are paid. (1879, c. 264; Code, s. 749; 1885, c. 364; Rev., s. 1293; C.S., s. 1269; 1971, c. 269, s. 9.)

§ 6-48. Arrest for nonpayment of fine and costs.

In default of payment of such fine and costs, it is the duty of the court at any subsequent term thereof, on motion of the solicitor of the State, to order a capias to issue to the end that such defendant may be again arrested and held for the fine and costs until discharged according to law. (1879, c. 264; Code, s. 750; 1885, c. 364; Rev., s. 1294; C.S., s. 1270; 1971, c. 269, s. 10.)
Article 7.

Liability of Prosecuting Witness for Costs.

§ 6-49. Prosecuting witness liable for costs in certain cases; court determines prosecuting witness.

In all criminal actions in any court, if the defendant is acquitted, nolle prosequi entered, or judgment against him is arrested, or if the defendant is discharged from arrest for want of probable cause, the costs, including the fees of all witnesses whom the judge before whom the trial took place shall certify to have been proper for the defense and prosecution, shall be paid by the prosecuting witness, whether marked on the bill or warrant or not, whenever the judge is of the opinion that there was not reasonable ground for the prosecution, or that it was not required by the public interest. If a greater number of witnesses have been summoned than were, in the opinion of the court, necessary to support the charge, the court may, even though it is of the opinion that there was reasonable ground for the prosecution, order the prosecuting witness to pay the attendance fees of such witnesses, if it appear that they were summoned at the prosecuting witness's special request.

Every judge is authorized to determine who the prosecuting witness is at any stage of a criminal proceeding, whether before or after the bill of indictment has been found, or the defendant acquitted: Provided, that no person shall be made a prosecuting witness after the finding of the bill, unless he shall have been notified to show cause why he should not be made the prosecuting witness of record. (1799, c. 4, s. 19, P.R.; 1880, c. 558, P.R.; R.C., c. 35, s. 37; 1868-9, c. 277; 1874-5, c. 151; 1879, c. 49; Code, s. 737; 1889, c. 34; Rev., s. 1295; C.S., s. 1271; 1947, c. 781; 1953, c. 675, s. 1; 1971, c. 269, s. 11.)

§ 6-50. Imprisonment of prosecuting witness for willful nonpayment of costs if prosecution frivolous.

Every such prosecuting witness may be adjudged not only to pay the costs, but he shall also be imprisoned for the willful nonpayment thereof, when the judge before whom the case was tried shall adjudge that the prosecution was frivolous or malicious. (1800, c. 558; R.C., c. 35, s. 37; 1879, c. 49; 1881, c. 176; Code, s. 738; Rev., s. 1297; C.S., s. 1272; 1971, c. 269, s. 11.1.)

Article 8.

Fees of Witnesses.

§ 6-51. Not entitled to fees in advance.

Witnesses are not entitled to receive their fees in advance; but no witness in a civil action or special proceeding, unless summoned on behalf of the State or a municipal corporation, shall be compelled to attend more than one day, if the party by or for whom he was summoned shall, after one day's attendance, on request and presentation of a certificate, fail or refuse to pay what then may be due for traveling to the place of examination and for the number of days of attendance. (1868-9, c. 279, subch. 11, s. 3; Code, s. 1368; Rev., s. 1298; C.S., s. 1273.)

§ 6-52. Repealed by Session Laws 1971, c. 269, s. 15.

§ 6-53. Witness to prove attendance; action for fees.

Every person summoned, who shall attend as a witness in any suit, shall, before the clerk of the court, or before the referee or officer taking the testimony, ascertain by his own oath or affirmation the sum due for traveling to and from court, attendance and ferriage, which shall be certified by the clerk; and on failure of the party, at whose instance such witness was summoned (witnesses for the State and municipal corporations excepted), to pay the same previous to the departure of the witness from court, such witness may at any time sue for and recover the same from the party summoning him; and the certificate of the clerk shall be sufficient evidence of the debt. (1777, c. 115, s. 46, P.R.; 1796, c. 458, P.R.; R.C., c. 31, s. 73; 1868-9, c. 279, subch. 11, ss. 2, 4; Code, s. 1369; Rev., s. 1299; C.S., s. 1274; 1971, c. 269, s. 12.)

§§ 6-54 through 6-56. Repealed by Session Laws 1971, c. 269, s. 15.

§ 6-57. Repealed by Session Laws 1947, c. 781.

§§ 6-58 through 6-59. Repealed by Session Laws 1971, c. 269, s. 15.

§ 6-60. No more than two witnesses may be subpoenaed to prove single material fact; liability for fees of such witnesses; one fee for day's attendance.

No district attorney shall direct that more than two witnesses be subpoenaed for the State to prove a single material fact, nor shall the State or defendant in any such prosecution be liable for the fees of more than two witnesses to prove a single material fact, unless the court, upon satisfactory reasons appearing, otherwise directs. And no witness subpoenaed in a criminal action shall be paid by the State for attendance in more than one case for any one day. (1871-2, c. 186; 1879, c. 264; Code, s. 744; Rev., s. 1303; C.S., s. 1284; 1971, c. 269, s. 13; 1973, c. 47, s. 2.)

§ 6-61. Repealed by Session Laws 1971, c. 269, s. 15.

§ 6-62. District attorney to announce discharge of State's witnesses.

It is the duty of all district attorneys prosecuting in the several courts, as each criminal prosecution is disposed of by trial, removal, continuance or otherwise, to call, in open court, and announce the discharge of witnesses for the State, either finally or otherwise as the disposition of the case may require. (1879, c. 264; 1881, c. 312; Code, s. 746; Rev., s. 1305; C.S., s. 1286; 1935, c. 26; 1971, c. 269, s. 14; 1973, c. 47, s. 2.)

§ 6-63. Repealed by Session Laws 1971, c. 269, s. 15.

Article 9.

Criminal Costs before Justices, Mayors, County or Recorders' Courts.

§§ 6-64 through 6-65. Repealed by Session Laws 1971, c. 269, s. 15.

Chapter 7.

Courts.

§§ 7-1 through 7-456. Repealed and transferred.
Chapter 7A.

Judicial Department.

Subchapter I. GeneRal Court of Justice.

Article 1.

Judicial Power and Organization.

§ 7A-1. Short title.

This Chapter shall be known and may be cited as the "Judicial Department Act of 1965." (1965, c. 310, s. 1.)

§ 7A-2. Purpose of Chapter.

This Chapter is intended to implement Article IV of the Constitution of North Carolina and promote the just and prompt disposition of litigation by:

(1)   Providing a new chapter in the General Statutes into which, at a time not later than January 1, 1971, when the General Court of Justice is fully operational in all counties of the State, all statutes concerning the organization, jurisdiction and administration of each division of the General Court of Justice may be placed;

(2)   Amending certain laws with respect to the superior court division to conform them to the laws set forth in this Chapter, to the end that each trial division may be a harmonious part of the General Court of Justice;

(3)   Creating the district court division of the General Court of Justice, and the Administrative Office of the Courts;

(4) Establishing in accordance with a fixed schedule the various district courts of the district court division;

(5) Providing for the organization, jurisdiction and procedures necessary for the operation of the district court division;

(6) Providing for the financial support of the judicial department, and for uniform costs and fees in the trial divisions of the General Court of Justice;

(7) Providing for an orderly transition from the present system of courts to a uniform system completely operational in all counties of the State not later than January 1, 1971;

(8) Repealing certain laws inconsistent with the foregoing purposes; and

(9) Effectuating other purposes incidental and supplemental to the foregoing enumerated purposes. (1965, c. 310, s. 1.)

§ 7A-3. Judicial power; transition provisions.

Except for the judicial power vested in the court for the trial of impeachments, and except for such judicial power as may from time to time be vested by the General Assembly in administrative agencies, the judicial power of the State is vested exclusively in the General Court of Justice. Provided, that all existing courts of the State inferior to the superior courts, including justice of the peace courts and mayor's courts, shall continue to exist and to exercise the judicial powers vested in them by law until specifically abolished by law, or until the establishment within the county of their situs of a district court, or until January 1, 1971, whichever event shall first occur. Judgments of inferior courts which cease to exist under the provisions of this section continue in force and effect as though the issuing court continued to exist, and the General Court of Justice is hereby vested with jurisdiction to enforce such judgments. (1965, c. 310, s. 1.)

§ 7A-4. Composition and organization.

The General Court of Justice constitutes a unified judicial system for purposes of jurisdiction, operation and administration, and consists of an appellate division, a superior court division, and a district court division. (1965, c. 310, s. 1.)

Article 1A.

§§ 7A-4.1 through 7A-4.19. Reserved for future codification purposes.

Article 1B.

Age Limits for Service as Justice or Judge.

§ 7A-4.20. Age limit for service as justice or judge: exception.

No justice or judge of the General Court of Justice may continue in office beyond the last day of the month in which he attains his seventy-second birthday, but justices and judges so retired may be recalled for periods of temporary service as provided in Subchapters II and III of this chapter. (1971, c. 508, s. 1; c. 1194; 1973, c. 248; 1977, c. 736, s. 5; 1981, c. 455, s. 1; 1991 (Reg. Sess., 1992), c. 873, s. 1.)

§ 7A-4.21. Validation of official actions of district court judges of twenty-fifth judicial district performed after mandatory retirement age.

No official action performed by any judge of the twenty-fifth judicial district of the district court division of the General Court of Justice shall be declared to be invalid by reason of the fact that the judge was beyond the mandatory retirement age set out in G.S. 7A-4.20 at the time of his performing any such act; provided this section shall only apply to those official actions performed prior to May 1, 1977. (1977, c. 389.)

SUBCHAPTER II. APPELLATE DIVISION OF THE GENERAL COURT OF JUSTICE.

Article 2.

Appellate Division Organization.

§ 7A-5. Organization.

The appellate division of the General Court of Justice consists of the Supreme Court and the Court of Appeals. (1965, c. 310, s. 1; 1967, c. 108, s. 1.)

§ 7A-6. Appellate division reporters; reports.

(a) The Supreme Court shall appoint one or more reporters for the appellate division, to serve at its pleasure. It shall be the duty of the reporters to prepare for publication the opinions of the Supreme Court and the Court of Appeals. The salary of the reporters shall be fixed by the Administrative Officer of the Courts, subject to the approval of the Supreme Court.

(b) The Administrative Officer of the Courts shall contract for the printing of the reports of the Supreme Court and the Court of Appeals, and for the advance sheets of each court. He shall select a printer for the reports and prescribe such contract terms as will insure issuance of the reports as soon as practicable after a sufficient number of opinions are filed. He shall make such contract after consultation with the Department of Administration and comparison of prices for similar work in other states to such an extent as may be practicable. He shall also sell the reports and advance sheets of the appellate division, to the general public, at a price not less than cost nor more than cost plus ten percent (10%), to be fixed by him in his discretion. Proceeds of such sales shall be remitted to the State treasury.

(b1) In addition to and as an alternative to the provisions for the publication and sale of the appellate division reports of subsection (a) and subsection (b) of this section, the Supreme Court may designate a commercial law publisher's reports and advance sheets of the opinions of the Supreme Court and the Court of Appeals as the Official Reports of the Appellate Division, or the Administrative Officer of the Courts, with the approval of the Supreme Court, may contract with a commercial law publisher or publishers to act as printer and vendor of the reports and advance sheets of the Supreme Court and the Court of Appeals upon such terms as the Supreme Court deems advisable after consultation with the Department of Administration.

(c) The Administrative Officer of the Courts shall furnish, without charge, one copy of the advance sheets of the appellate division to each justice and judge of the General Court of Justice, to each superior court district attorney, to each superior court clerk, to each district court prosecutor, to each special counsel at regional psychiatric facilities, and, in such numbers as may be reasonably necessary, to the Supreme Court library. (1967, c. 108, s. 1; c. 691, s. 57; 1969, c. 1190, s. 1; 1971, c. 377, s. 2; 1975, c. 879, s. 46; 1977, c. 721, s. 1; 1987, c. 404.)

§ 7A-7. Law clerks; secretaries and stenographers.

(a) Each justice and judge of the appellate division is entitled to the services of not more than two research assistants, who must be graduates of an accredited law school. The salaries of research assistants shall be set by the Administrative Officer of the Courts, subject to the approval of the Supreme Court.

(b) The Administrative Officer of the Courts shall determine the number and salaries of all secretaries and stenographers in the appellate division. (1967, c. 108, s. 1; 1985, c. 698, s. 8(a).)

§ 7A-8. Reserved for future codification purposes.

§ 7A-9. Reserved for future codification purposes.

Article 3.

The Supreme Court.

§ 7A-10. Organization; compensation of justices.

(a) The Supreme Court shall consist of a Chief Justice and six associate justices, elected by the qualified voters of the State for terms of eight years. Before entering upon the duties of his office, each justice shall take an oath of office. Four justices shall constitute a quorum for the transaction of the business of the court. Except as otherwise provided in this subsection, sessions of the court shall be held in the city of Raleigh, and scheduled by rule of court so as to discharge expeditiously the court's business. The court may by rule hold sessions not more than twice annually in the Old Chowan County Courthouse (1767) in the Town of Edenton, which is a State-owned court facility that is designated as a National Historic Landmark by the United States Department of the Interior.

(b) The Chief Justice and each of the associate justices shall receive the annual salary provided in Current Operations Appropriations Act. Each justice is entitled to reimbursement for travel and subsistence expenses at the rate allowed State employees generally.
(b1) In addition to the reimbursement for travel and subsistence expenses authorized by subsection (b) of this section, and notwithstanding G.S. 138-6, each justice whose permanent residence is at least 50 miles from the City of Raleigh shall also be reimbursed for the mileage the justice travels each week to the City of Raleigh from the justice's home for business of the court. The reimbursement authorized by this subsection shall be calculated for each justice by multiplying the actual round-trip mileage from that justice's home to the City of Raleigh by a rate-per-mile established by the Director of the Administrative Office of the Courts, but not to exceed the business standard mileage rate set by the Internal Revenue Service.

(c) In lieu of merit and other increment raises paid to regular State employees, the Chief Justice and each of the Associate Justices shall receive as longevity pay an annual amount equal to four and eight-tenths percent (4.8%) of the annual salary set forth in the Current Operations Appropriations Act payable monthly after five years of service, nine and six-tenths percent (9.6%) after 10 years of service, fourteen and four-tenths percent (14.4%) after 15 years of service, nineteen and two-tenths percent (19.2%) after 20 years of service, and twenty-four percent (24%) after 25 years of service. "Service" means service as a justice or judge of the General Court of Justice or as a member of the Utilities Commission. Service shall also mean service as a district attorney or as a clerk of superior court. (1967, c. 108, s. 1; 1983, c. 761, s. 242; 1983 (Reg. Sess., 1984), c. 1034, s. 165; c. 1109, ss. 11, 13.1; 1985, c. 698, s. 10(a); 1997-56, s. 1; 2007-323, ss. 14.21(a), 28.18A(a).)

§ 7A-10.1. Authority to prescribe standards of judicial conduct.

The Supreme Court is authorized, by rule, to prescribe standards of judicial conduct for the guidance of all justices and judges of the General Court of Justice. (1973, c. 89.)

§ 7A-11. Clerk of the Supreme Court; salary; bond; fees; oath.

The clerk of the Supreme Court shall be appointed by the Supreme Court to serve at its pleasure. The annual salary of the clerk shall be fixed by the Administrative Officer of the Courts, subject to the approval of the Supreme Court. The clerk may appoint assistants in the number and at the salaries fixed by the Administrative Officer of the Courts. The clerk shall perform such duties as the Supreme Court may assign, and shall be bonded to the State, for faithful performance of duty, in the same manner as the clerk of the superior court, and in such amount as the Administrative Officer of the Courts shall determine. He shall adopt a seal of office, to be approved by the Supreme Court. A fee bill for services rendered by the clerk shall be fixed by rules of the Supreme Court, and all such fees shall be remitted to the State treasury. Charges to litigants for the reproduction of appellate records and briefs shall be fixed by rule of the Supreme Court and remitted to the Appellate Courts Printing and Computer Operations Fund established in G.S. 7A-343.3. The operations of the Clerk of the Supreme Court shall be subject to the oversight of the State Auditor pursuant to Article 5A of Chapter 147 of the General Statutes. Before entering upon the duties of his office, the clerk shall take the oath of office prescribed by law. (1967, c. 108, s. 1; 1969, c. 1190, s. 2; 1973, c. 750; 1983, c. 913, s. 3; 2002-126, s. 2.2(j).)

§ 7A-12. Supreme Court marshal.

The Supreme Court may appoint a marshal to serve at its pleasure, and to perform such duties as it may assign. The marshal shall have the criminal and civil powers of a sheriff, and any additional powers necessary to execute the orders of the appellate division in any county of the State. His salary shall be fixed by the Administrative Officer, subject to the approval of the Supreme Court. The marshal may appoint such assistants, and at such salaries, as may be authorized by the Administrative Officer of the Courts. The Supreme Court, in its discretion, may appoint the Supreme Court librarian, or some other suitable employee of the court, to serve in the additional capacity of marshal. (1967, c. 108, s. 1.)

§ 7A-13. Supreme Court library; functions; librarian; library committee; seal of office.

(a) The Supreme Court shall appoint a librarian of the Supreme Court library, to serve at the pleasure of the court. The annual salary of the librarian shall be fixed by the Administrative Officer of the Courts, subject to the approval of the Supreme Court. The librarian may appoint assistants in numbers and at salaries to be fixed by the Administrative Officer of the Courts.

(b)   The primary function of the Supreme Court library is to serve the appellate division of the General Court of Justice, but it may render service to the trial divisions of the General Court of Justice, to State agencies, and to the general public, under such regulations as the librarian, subject to the approval of the library committee, may promulgate.

(c)   The library shall be maintained in the city of Raleigh, except that if the Court of Appeals sits regularly in locations other than the city of Raleigh, branch libraries may be established at such locations for the use of the Court of Appeals.

(d)   The librarian shall promulgate rules and regulations for the use of the library, subject to the approval of a library committee, to be composed of two justices of the Supreme Court appointed by the Chief Justice, and one judge of the Court of Appeals appointed by the Chief Judge.

(e)   The librarian may adopt a seal of office.

(f)   The librarian may operate a copying service by means of which he may furnish certified or uncertified copies of all or portions of any document, paper, book, or other writing in the library that legally may be copied. When a certificate is made under his hand and attested by his official seal, it shall be received as prima facie evidence of the correctness of the matter therein contained, and as such shall receive full faith and credit. The fees for copies shall be approved by the library committee, and the fees so collected shall be administered in the same manner as the charges to litigants for the reproduction of appellate records and briefs. (1967, c. 108, s. 1.)

§ 7A-14. Reprints of Supreme Court Reports.

The Supreme Court is authorized to have such of the Reports of the Supreme Court of the State of North Carolina as are not on hand for sale, republished and numbered consecutively, retaining the present numbers and names of the reporters and by means of star pages in the margin retaining the original numbering of the pages. The Supreme Court is authorized to have such Reports reprinted without any alteration from the original edition thereof, except as may be directed by the Supreme Court. The contract for such reprinting and republishing shall be made by the Administrative Office of the Courts in the manner prescribed in G.S. 7A-6. Such republication shall thus continue until the State shall have for sale all of such Reports; and hereafter when the editions of any number or volume of the Supreme Court Reports shall be exhausted, it shall be the duty of the Supreme Court to have the same reprinted under the provisions of this section and G.S. 7A-6. In reprinting the Reports that have already been annotated, the annotations and the additional indexes therein shall be retained. (Code, s. 3634; 1885, c. 309; 1889, c. 473, ss. 1-4, 6; Rev., s. 5361; 1907, c. 503; 1917, cc. 201, 292; C.S., s. 7671; 1923, c. 176; 1929, c. 39, s. 2; 1975, c. 328.)

§ 7A-15. Reserved for future codification purposes.

Article 4.

Court of Appeals.

§ 7A-16. Creation and organization.

The Court of Appeals is created effective January 1, 1967. It shall consist initially of six judges, elected by the qualified voters of the State for terms of eight years. The Chief Justice of the Supreme Court shall designate one of the judges as Chief Judge, to serve in such capacity at the pleasure of the Chief Justice. Before entering upon the duties of his office, a judge of the Court of Appeals shall take the oath of office prescribed for a judge of the General Court of Justice.

The Governor on or after July 1, 1967, shall make temporary appointments to the six initial judgeships. The appointees shall serve until January 1, 1969. Their successors shall be elected at the general election for members of the General Assembly in November, 1968, and shall take office on January 1, 1969, to serve for the remainder of the unexpired term which began on January 1, 1967.

Upon the appointment of at least five judges, and the designation of a Chief Judge, the court is authorized to convene, organize, and promulgate, subject to the approval of the Supreme Court, such supplementary rules as it deems necessary and appropriate for the discharge of the judicial business lawfully assigned to it.

Effective January 1, 1969, the number of judges is increased to nine, and the Governor, on or after March 1, 1969, shall make temporary appointments to the additional judgeships thus created. The appointees shall serve until January 1, 1971. Their successors shall be elected at the general election for members of the General Assembly in November, 1970, and shall take office on January 1, 1971, to serve for the remainder of the unexpired term which began on January 1, 1969.

Effective January 1, 1977, the number of judges is increased to 12; and the Governor, on or after July 1, 1977, shall make temporary appointments to the additional judgeships thus created. The appointees shall serve until January 1, 1979. Their successors shall be elected at the general election for members of the General Assembly in November, 1978, and shall take office on January 1, 1979, to serve the remainder of the unexpired term which began on January 1, 1977.

On or after December 15, 2000, the Governor shall appoint three additional judges to increase the number of judges to 15.

The Court of Appeals shall sit in panels of three judges each. The Chief Judge insofar as practicable shall assign the members to panels in such fashion that each member sits a substantially equal number of times with each other member. He shall preside over the panel of which he is a member, and shall designate the presiding judge of the other panel or panels.

Three judges shall constitute a quorum for the transaction of the business of the court, except as may be provided in G.S. 7A-32.

In the event the Chief Judge is unable, on account of absence or temporary incapacity, to perform the duties placed upon him as Chief Judge, the Chief Justice shall appoint an acting Chief Judge from the other judges of the Court, to temporarily discharge the duties of Chief Judge. (1967, c. 108, s. 1; 1969, c. 1190, s. 3; 1973, c. 301; 1977, c. 1047; 2000-67, s. 15.5(a); 2004-203, s. 16.)

§ 7A-17: Repealed by Session Laws 1969, c. 1190, s. 57.

§ 7A-18. Compensation of judges.

(a) The Chief Judge and each associate judge of the Court of Appeals shall receive the annual salary provided in the Current Operations Appropriations Act. Each judge is entitled to reimbursement for travel and subsistence expenses at the rate allowed State employees generally.

(a1) In addition to the reimbursement for travel and subsistence expenses authorized by subsection (a) of this section, and notwithstanding G.S. 138-6, each judge whose permanent residence is at least 50 miles from the City of Raleigh shall also be reimbursed for the mileage the judge travels each week to the City of Raleigh from the judge's home for business of the court. The reimbursement authorized by this subsection shall be calculated for each judge by multiplying the actual round-trip mileage from that judge's home to the City of Raleigh by a rate-per-mile established by the Director of the Administrative Office of the Courts, but not to exceed the business standard mileage rate set by the Internal Revenue Service.

(b) In lieu of merit and other increment raises paid to regular State employees, a judge of the Court of Appeals shall receive as longevity pay an annual amount equal to four and eight-tenths percent (4.8%) of the annual salary set forth in the Current Operations Appropriations Act payable monthly after five years of service, nine and six-tenths percent (9.6%) after 10 years of service, fourteen and four-tenths percent (14.4%) after 15 years of service, nineteen and two-tenths percent (19.2%) after 20 years of service, and twenty-four percent (24%) after 25 years of service. "Service" means service as a justice or judge of the General Court of Justice or as a member of the Utilities Commission. Service shall also mean service as a district attorney or as a clerk of superior court. (1967, c. 108, s. 1; 1983, c. 761, s. 243; 1983 (Reg. Sess., 1984), c. 1034, s. 165; c. 1109, ss. 11, 13.1; 1985, c. 698, s. 10(a); 2007-323, ss. 14.21(b), 28.18A(b).)

§ 7A-19. Seats and sessions of court.

(a) The Court of Appeals shall sit in Raleigh, and at such other locations within the State as the Supreme Court may designate.

(b) The Department of Administration shall provide adequate quarters for the Court of Appeals.

(c) The Chief Judge shall schedule sessions of the court as required to discharge expeditiously the court's business. (1967, c. 108, s. 1.)

§ 7A-20. Clerk; oath; bond; salary; assistants; fees.

(a) The Court of Appeals shall appoint a clerk to serve at its pleasure. Before entering upon his duties, the clerk shall take the oath of office prescribed for the clerk of the Supreme Court, conformed to the office of clerk of the Court of Appeals, and shall be bonded, in the same manner as the clerk of superior court, in an amount prescribed by the Administrative Officer of the Courts, payable to the State, for the faithful performance of his duties. The salary of the clerk shall be fixed by the Administrative Officer of the Courts, subject to the approval of the Court of Appeals. The number and salaries of his assistants, and their bonds, if required, shall be fixed by the Administrative Officer of the Courts. The clerk shall adopt a seal of office, to be approved by the Court of Appeals.

(b) Subject to approval of the Supreme Court, the Court of Appeals shall promulgate from time to time a fee bill for services rendered by the clerk, and such fees shall be remitted to the State Treasurer. Charges to litigants for the reproduction of appellate records and briefs shall be fixed by rule of the Supreme Court and remitted to the Appellate Courts Printing and Computer Operations Fund established in G.S. 7A-343.3. The operations of the Court of Appeals shall be subject to the oversight of the State Auditor pursuant to Article 5A of Chapter 147 of the General Statutes. (1967, c. 108, s. 1; 1983, c. 913, s. 4; 2002-126, s. 2.2(k).)

§ 7A-21. Marshal; powers; salary.

The Court of Appeals may appoint a marshal to serve at its pleasure and to perform such duties as it may assign. The marshal shall have the criminal and civil powers of a sheriff and any additional powers necessary to execute the orders of the appellate division in any county of the State. His salary shall be fixed by the Administrative Officer, subject to the approval of the Court of Appeals. (1981, c. 485.)

§ 7A-22. Reserved for future codification purposes.

§ 7A-23. Reserved for future codification purposes.

§ 7A-24. Reserved for future codification purposes.

Article 5.

Jurisdiction.

§ 7A-25. Original jurisdiction of the Supreme Court.

The Supreme Court has original jurisdiction to hear claims against the State, but its decisions shall be merely recommendatory; no process in the nature of execution shall issue thereon; the decisions shall be reported to the next session of the General Assembly for its action. The court shall by rule prescribe the procedures to be followed in the proper exercise of the jurisdiction conferred by this section. (1967, c. 108, s. 1.)

§ 7A-26. Appellate jurisdiction of the Supreme Court and the Court of Appeals.

The Supreme Court and the Court of Appeals respectively have jurisdiction to review upon appeal decisions of the several courts of the General Court of Justice and of administrative agencies, upon matters of law or legal inference, in accordance with the system of appeals provided in this Article. (1967, c. 108, s. 1.)

§ 7A-27. Appeals of right from the courts of the trial divisions.

(a) Appeal lies of right directly to the Supreme Court in all cases in which the defendant is convicted of murder in the first degree and the judgment of the superior court includes a sentence of death.

(b) Appeal lies of right directly to the Court of Appeals in any of the following cases:

(1) From any final judgment of a superior court, other than the one described in subsection (a) of this section, or one based on a plea of guilty or nolo contendere, including any final judgment entered upon review of a decision of an administrative agency, except for a final judgment entered upon review of a court martial under G.S. 127A-62.

(2) From any final judgment of a district court in a civil action.

(3) From any interlocutory order or judgment of a superior court or district court in a civil action or proceeding which does any of the following:

a. Affects a substantial right.

b. In effect determines the action and prevents a judgment from which an appeal might be taken.

c. Discontinues the action.

d. Grants or refuses a new trial.

e. Determines a claim prosecuted under G.S. 50-19.1.

(4) From any other order or judgment of the superior court from which an appeal is authorized by statute.

(c) through (e) Repealed by Session Laws 2013-411, s. 1, effective August 23, 2013. (1967, c. 108, s. 1; 1971, c. 377, s. 3; 1973, c. 704; 1977, c. 711, s. 4; 1987, c. 679; 1995, c. 204, s. 1; 2010-193, s. 17; 2013-411, s. 1.)

§ 7A-28. Decisions of Court of Appeals on post-trial motions for appropriate relief, valuation of exempt property, or courts-martial are final.

(a) Decisions of the Court of Appeals upon review of motions for appropriate relief listed in G.S. 15A-1415(b) are final and not subject to further review in the Supreme Court by appeal, motion, certification, writ, or otherwise.

(b) Decisions of the Court of Appeals upon review of valuation of exempt property under G.S. 1C are final and not subject to further review in the Supreme Court by appeal, motion, certification, writ, or otherwise.

(c) Decisions of the Court of Appeals upon review of courts-martial under G.S. 127A-62 are final and not subject to further review in the Supreme Court by appeal, motion, certification, writ, or otherwise. (1981, c. 470, s. 1; 1981 (Reg. Sess., 1982), c. 1224, s. 16.; 2010-193, s. 18.)

§ 7A-29. Appeals of right from certain administrative agencies.

(a) From any final order or decision of the North Carolina Utilities Commission not governed by subsection (b) of this section, the Department of Health and Human Services under G.S. 131E-188(b), the North Carolina Industrial Commission, the North Carolina State Bar under G.S. 84-28, the Property Tax Commission under G.S. 105-290 and G.S. 105-342, the Commissioner of Insurance under G.S. 58-2-80, the State Board of Elections under G.S. 163-127.6, the Office of Administrative Hearings under G.S. 126-34.02, or the Secretary of Environment and Natural Resources under G.S. 104E-6.2 or G.S. 130A-293, appeal as of right lies directly to the Court of Appeals.

(b) From any final order or decision of the Utilities Commission in a general rate case, appeal as of right lies directly to the Supreme Court. (1967, c. 108, s. 1; 1971, c. 703, s. 5; 1975, c. 582, s. 12; 1979, c. 584, s. 1; 1981, c. 704, s. 28; 1983, c. 526, s. 1; c. 761, s. 188; 1983 (Reg. Sess., 1984), c. 1000, s. 2; c. 1087, s. 2; c. 1113, s. 2; 1985, c. 462, s. 3; 1987, c. 850, s. 2; 1991, c. 546, s. 2; c. 679, s. 2; 1993, c. 501, s. 2; 1995, c. 115, s. 1; c. 504, s. 2; c. 509, s. 2; 1997-443, ss. 11A.118(a), 11A.119(a); 2003-63, s. 1; 2006-155, s. 1.1; 2013-382, s. 6.4.)

§ 7A-30. Appeals of right from certain decisions of the Court of Appeals.

Except as provided in G.S. 7A-28, an appeal lies of right to the Supreme Court from any decision of the Court of Appeals rendered in a case:

(1) Which directly involves a substantial question arising under the Constitution of the United States or of this State, or

(2) In which there is a dissent. (1967, c. 108, s. 1; 1983, c. 526, s. 2.)

§ 7A-31. Discretionary review by the Supreme Court.

(a) In any cause in which appeal is taken to the Court of Appeals, except a cause appealed from the North Carolina Industrial Commission, the North Carolina State Bar pursuant to G.S. 84-28, the Property Tax Commission pursuant to G.S. 105-345, the Board of State Contract Appeals pursuant to G.S.

143-135.9, the Commissioner of Insurance pursuant to G.S. 58-2-80, a court-martial pursuant to G.S. 127A-62, a motion for appropriate relief, or valuation of exempt property pursuant to G.S. 7A-28, the Supreme Court may, in its discretion, on motion of any party to the cause or on its own motion, certify the cause for review by the Supreme Court, either before or after it has been determined by the Court of Appeals. A cause appealed to the Court of Appeals from any of the administrative bodies listed in the preceding sentence may be certified in similar fashion, but only after determination of the cause in the Court of Appeals. The effect of such certification is to transfer the cause from the Court of Appeals to the Supreme Court for review by the Supreme Court. If the cause is certified for transfer to the Supreme Court before its determination in the Court of Appeals, review is not had in the Court of Appeals but the cause is forthwith transferred for review in the first instance by the Supreme Court. If the cause is certified for transfer to the Supreme Court after its determination by the Court of Appeals, the Supreme Court reviews the decision of the Court of Appeals.

Except in courts-martial and motions within the purview of G.S. 7A-28, the State may move for certification for review of any criminal cause, but only after determination of the cause by the Court of Appeals.

(b) In causes subject to certification under subsection (a) of this section, certification may be made by the Supreme Court before determination of the cause by the Court of Appeals when in the opinion of the Supreme Court:

(1) The subject matter of the appeal has significant public interest, or

(2) The cause involves legal principles of major significance to the jurisprudence of the State, or

(3) Delay in final adjudication is likely to result from failure to certify and thereby cause substantial harm, or

(4) The work load of the courts of the appellate division is such that the expeditious administration of justice requires certification.

(c) In causes subject to certification under subsection (a) of this section, certification may be made by the Supreme Court after determination of the cause by the Court of Appeals when in the opinion of the Supreme Court:

(1) The subject matter of the appeal has significant public interest, or

(2)   The cause involves legal principles of major significance to the jurisprudence of the State, or

(3)   The decision of the Court of Appeals appears likely to be in conflict with a decision of the Supreme Court.

Interlocutory determinations by the Court of Appeals, including orders remanding the cause for a new trial or for other proceedings, shall be certified for review by the Supreme Court only upon a determination by the Supreme Court that failure to certify would cause a delay in final adjudication which would probably result in substantial harm.

(d)   The procedure for certification by the Supreme Court on its own motion, or upon petition of a party, shall be prescribed by rule of the Supreme Court. (1967, c. 108, s. 1; 1969, c. 1044; 1975, c. 555; 1977, c. 711, s. 5; 1981, c. 470, s. 2; 1981 (Reg. Sess., 1982), c. 1224, s. 17; c. 1253, s. 1; 1983, c. 526, s. 3; c. 761, s. 189; 2010-193, s. 19.)

§ 7A-31.1. Discretionary Review by the Court of Appeals.

(a)   In the case of a court-martial in which appeal is taken to the Wake County Superior Court under G.S. 127A-62, the Court of Appeals may, in its discretion, on motion of any party to the cause or on its own motion, certify the cause for review by the Court of Appeals after it has been reviewed by the Wake County Superior Court. The effect of such certification is to transfer the cause from the Wake County Superior Court to the Court of Appeals, and the Court of Appeals reviews the decision by the Wake County Superior Court.

(b)   In causes subject to certification under subsection (a) of this section, certification may be made by the Court of Appeals after determination of the cause by the Wake County Superior Court when in the opinion of the Court of Appeals:

(1)   The subject matter of the appeal has significant public interest, or

(2)   The cause involves legal principles of major significance to the jurisprudence of the State, or

(3) The decision of the Wake County Superior Court appears likely to be in conflict with a decision of the United States Court of Appeals for the Armed Forces.

Interlocutory determinations by the Wake County Superior Court, including orders remanding the cause for a new trial or for other proceedings, shall be certified for review by the Court of Appeals only upon a determination by the Court of Appeals that failure to certify would cause a delay in final adjudication which would probably result in substantial harm.

(c) Any rules for practice and procedure for review of courts-martial that may be required shall be prescribed pursuant to G.S. 7A-33. (2010-193, s. 20.)

§ 7A-32. Power of Supreme Court and Court of Appeals to issue remedial writs.

(a) The Supreme Court and the Court of Appeals have jurisdiction, exercisable by any one of the justices or judges of the respective courts, to issue the writ of habeas corpus upon the application of any person described in G.S. 17-3, according to the practice and procedure provided therefor in chapter 17 of the General Statutes, and to rule of the Supreme Court.

(b) The Supreme Court has jurisdiction, exercisable by one justice or by such number of justices as the court may by rule provide, to issue the prerogative writs, including mandamus, prohibition, certiorari, and supersedeas, in aid of its own jurisdiction or in exercise of its general power to supervise and control the proceedings of any of the other courts of the General Court of Justice. The practice and procedure shall be as provided by statute or rule of the Supreme Court, or, in the absence of statute or rule, according to the practice and procedure of the common law.

(c) The Court of Appeals has jurisdiction, exercisable by one judge or by such number of judges as the Supreme Court may by rule provide, to issue the prerogative writs, including mandamus, prohibition, certiorari, and supersedeas, in aid of its own jurisdiction, or to supervise and control the proceedings of any of the trial courts of the General Court of Justice, and of the Utilities Commission and the Industrial Commission. The practice and procedure shall be as provided by statute or rule of the Supreme Court, or, in the absence of statute or rule, according to the practice and procedure of the common law. (1967, c. 108, s. 1.)

§ 7A-33. Supreme Court to prescribe appellate division rules of practice and procedure.

The Supreme Court shall prescribe rules of practice and procedure designed to procure the expeditious and inexpensive disposition of all litigation in the appellate division. (1967, c. 108, s. 1.)

§ 7A-34. Rules of practice and procedure in trial courts.

The Supreme Court is hereby authorized to prescribe rules of practice and procedure for the superior and district courts supplementary to, and not inconsistent with, acts of the General Assembly. (1967, c. 108, s. 1.)

§ 7A-34.1: Repealed by Session Laws 2011-145, s. 31.23(f), effective July 1, 2011.

§ 7A-35. Repealed by Session Laws 1971, c. 377, s. 32.

§ 7A-36. Repealed by Session Laws 1969, c. 1190, s. 57.

§ 7A-37: Repealed by Session Laws 1993, c. 553, s. 1.

§ 7A-37.1. Statewide court-ordered, nonbinding arbitration in certain civil actions.

(a) The General Assembly finds that court-ordered, nonbinding arbitration may be a more economical, efficient and satisfactory procedure to resolve certain civil actions than by traditional civil litigation and therefore authorizes court-ordered nonbinding arbitration as an alternative civil procedure, subject to these provisions.

(b) The Supreme Court of North Carolina may adopt rules governing this procedure and may supervise its implementation and operation through the Administrative Office of the Courts. These rules shall ensure that no party is deprived of the right to jury trial and that any party dissatisfied with an arbitration award may have trial de novo.

(c)   Except as otherwise provided in rules promulgated by the Supreme Court of North Carolina pursuant to subsection (b) of this section, this procedure shall be employed in all civil actions in district court, unless all parties to the action waive arbitration under this section.

(c1)   Except as provided in subsection (c2) of this section, in cases referred to nonbinding arbitration as provided in this section, a fee of one hundred dollars ($100.00) shall be assessed per arbitration, to be divided equally among the parties, to cover the cost of providing arbitrators. Fees assessed under this section shall be paid to the clerk of superior court in the county where the case was filed and remitted by the clerk to the State Treasurer.

(c2)   In appeals in small claims actions under Article 19 of Chapter 7A of the General Statutes, if (i) the arbitrator finds in favor of the appellee, (ii) the arbitrator's decision is appealed for trial de novo under G.S. 7A-229, and (iii) the arbitrator's decision is affirmed on appeal, then the court shall consider the fact that the arbitrator's decision was affirmed as a significant factor in favor of assessing all court costs and attorneys' fees associated with the case in both the original action and the two appeals, including the arbitration fee assessed under subsection (c1) of this section, against the appellant.

(d)   This procedure may be implemented in a judicial district, in selected counties within a district, or in any court within a district, if the Director of the Administrative Office of the Courts, and the cognizant Senior Resident Superior Court Judge or the Chief District Court Judge of any court selected for this procedure, determine that use of this procedure may assist in the administration of justice toward achieving objectives stated in subsection (a) of this section in a judicial district, county, or court. The Director of the Administrative Office of the Courts, acting upon the recommendation of the cognizant Senior Resident Superior Court Judge or Chief District Court Judge of any court selected for this procedure, may terminate this procedure in any judicial district, county, or court upon a determination that its use has not accomplished objectives stated in subsection (a) of this section.

(e)   Arbitrators in this procedure shall have the same immunity as judges from civil liability for their official conduct. (1989, c. 301, s. 1; 2002-126, s. 14.3(a); 2003-284, s. 36A.1; 2013-159, s. 3; 2013-225, s. 1.)

§ 7A-38: Repealed by Session Laws 1995, c. 500, s. 3.

§ 7A-38.1. Mediated settlement conferences in superior court civil actions.

(a) Purpose. - The General Assembly finds that a system of court-ordered mediated settlement conferences should be established to facilitate the settlement of superior court civil actions and to make civil litigation more economical, efficient, and satisfactory to litigants and the State. Therefore, this section is enacted to require parties to superior court civil actions and their representatives to attend a pretrial, mediated settlement conference conducted pursuant to this section and pursuant to rules of the Supreme Court adopted to implement this section.

(b) Definitions. - As used in this section:

(1) "Mediated settlement conference" means a pretrial, court-ordered conference of the parties to a civil action and their representatives conducted by a mediator.

(2) "Mediation" means an informal process conducted by a mediator with the objective of helping parties voluntarily settle their dispute.

(3) "Mediator" means a neutral person who acts to encourage and facilitate a resolution of a pending civil action. A mediator does not make an award or render a judgment as to the merits of the action.

(c) Rules of procedure. - The Supreme Court may adopt rules to implement this section.

(d) Statewide implementation. - Mediated settlement conferences authorized by this section shall be implemented in all judicial districts as soon as practicable, as determined by the Director of the Administrative Office of the Courts.

(e) Cases selected for mediated settlement conferences. - The senior resident superior court judge of any participating district may order a mediated settlement conference for any superior court civil action pending in the district. The senior resident superior court judge may by local rule order all cases, not otherwise exempted by the Supreme Court rule, to mediated settlement conference.

(f) Attendance of parties. - The parties to a superior court civil action in which a mediated settlement conference is ordered, their attorneys and other persons or entities with authority, by law or by contract, to settle the parties' claims shall attend the mediated settlement conference unless excused by rules of the Supreme Court or by order of the senior resident superior court judge. Nothing in this section shall require any party or other participant in the conference to make a settlement offer or demand which it deems is contrary to its best interests.

(g) Sanctions. - Any person required to attend a mediated settlement conference or other settlement procedure under this section who, without good cause, fails to attend or fails to pay any or all of the mediator's or other neutral's fee in compliance with this section and the rules promulgated by the Supreme Court to implement this section is subject to the contempt powers of the court and monetary sanctions imposed by a resident or presiding superior court judge. The monetary sanctions may include the payment of fines, attorneys' fees, mediator and neutral fees, and the expenses and loss of earnings incurred by persons attending the procedure. A party seeking sanctions against another party or person shall do so in a written motion stating the grounds for the motion and the relief sought. The motion shall be served upon all parties and upon any person against whom the sanctions are being sought. The court may initiate sanction proceedings upon its own motion by the entry of a show cause order. If the court imposes sanctions, it shall do so, after notice and a hearing, in a written order, making findings of fact and conclusions of law. An order imposing sanctions shall be reviewable upon appeal where the entire record as submitted shall be reviewed to determine whether the order is supported by substantial evidence.

(h) Selection of mediator. - The parties to a superior court civil action in which a mediated settlement conference is to be held pursuant to this section shall have the right to designate a mediator. Upon failure of the parties to designate a mediator within the time established by the rules of the Supreme Court, a mediator shall be appointed by the senior resident superior court judge.

(i) Promotion of other settlement procedures. - Nothing in this section is intended to preclude the use of other dispute resolution methods within the superior court. Parties to a superior court civil action are encouraged to select other available dispute resolution methods. The senior resident superior court judge, at the request of and with the consent of the parties, may order the parties to attend and participate in any other settlement procedure authorized by rules of the Supreme Court or by the local superior court rules, in lieu of attending a mediated settlement conference. Neutral third parties acting pursuant to this section shall be selected and compensated in accordance with such rules or pursuant to agreement of the parties. Nothing in this section shall prohibit the parties from participating in, or the court from ordering, other dispute resolution procedures, including arbitration to the extent authorized under State or federal law.

(j) Immunity. - Mediator and other neutrals acting pursuant to this section shall have judicial immunity in the same manner and to the same extent as a judge of the General Court of Justice, except that mediators and other neutrals may be disciplined in accordance with enforcement procedures adopted by the Supreme Court pursuant to G.S. 7A-38.2.

(k) Costs of mediated settlement conference. - Costs of mediated settlement conferences shall be borne by the parties. Unless otherwise ordered by the court or agreed to by the parties, the mediator's fees shall be paid in equal shares by the parties. For purposes of this section, multiple parties shall be considered one party when they are represented by the same counsel. The rules adopted by the Supreme Court implementing this section shall set out a method whereby parties found by the court to be unable to pay the costs of the mediated settlement conference are afforded an opportunity to participate without cost. The rules adopted by the Supreme Court shall set the fees to be paid a mediator appointed by a judge upon the failure of the parties to designate a mediator.

(l) Inadmissibility of negotiations. - Evidence of statements made and conduct occurring in a mediated settlement conference or other settlement proceeding conducted under this section, whether attributable to a party, the mediator, other neutral, or a neutral observer present at the settlement proceeding, shall not be subject to discovery and shall be inadmissible in any proceeding in the action or other civil actions on the same claim, except:

(1) In proceedings for sanctions under this section;

(2) In proceedings to enforce or rescind a settlement of the action;

(3) In disciplinary proceedings before the State Bar or any agency established to enforce standards of conduct for mediators or other neutrals; or

(4) In proceedings to enforce laws concerning juvenile or elder abuse.

As used in this section, the term "neutral observer" includes persons seeking mediator certification, persons studying dispute resolution processes, and persons acting as interpreters.

No settlement agreement to resolve any or all issues reached at the proceeding conducted under this subsection or during its recesses shall be enforceable unless it has been reduced to writing and signed by the parties. No evidence otherwise discoverable shall be inadmissible merely because it is presented or discussed in a mediated settlement conference or other settlement proceeding.

No mediator, other neutral, or neutral observer present at a settlement proceeding shall be compelled to testify or produce evidence concerning statements made and conduct occurring in anticipation of, during, or as a follow-up to a mediated settlement conference or other settlement proceeding pursuant to this section in any civil proceeding for any purpose, including proceedings to enforce or rescind a settlement of the action, except to attest to the signing of any agreements, and except proceedings for sanctions under this section, disciplinary hearings before the State Bar or any agency established to enforce standards of conduct for mediators or other neutrals, and proceedings to enforce laws concerning juvenile or elder abuse.

(m)   Right to jury trial. - Nothing in this section or the rules adopted by the Supreme Court implementing this section shall restrict the right to jury trial. (1995, c. 500, s. 1; 1999-354, s. 5; 2005-167, s. 1; 2008-194, s. 8(a).)

§ 7A-38.2. Regulation of mediators and other neutrals.

(a)   The Supreme Court may adopt standards of conduct for mediators and other neutrals who are certified or otherwise qualified pursuant to G.S. 7A-38.1, 7A-38.3, 7A-38.3B, 7A-38.3D, 7A-38.3E, and 7A-38.4A, or who participate in proceedings conducted pursuant to those sections. The standards may also regulate mediator and other neutral training programs. The Supreme Court may adopt procedures for the enforcement of those standards.

(b)   The administration of the certification and qualification of mediators and other neutrals, and mediator and other neutral training programs shall be conducted through the Dispute Resolution Commission, established under the Judicial Department. The Supreme Court shall adopt rules and regulations governing the operation of the Commission. The Commission shall exercise all of its duties independently of the Director of the Administrative Office of the

Courts, except that the Commission shall consult with the Director regarding personnel and budgeting matters.

(c) The Dispute Resolution Commission shall consist of 16 members: five judges appointed by the Chief Justice of the Supreme Court, at least two of whom shall be superior court judges, and at least two of whom shall be district court judges; one clerk of superior court appointed by the Chief Justice of the Supreme Court; two mediators certified to conduct superior court mediated settlement conferences and two mediators certified to conduct equitable distribution mediated settlement conferences appointed by the Chief Justice of the Supreme Court; one certified district criminal court mediator who is a representative of a community mediation center appointed by the Chief Justice of the Supreme Court; two practicing attorneys who are not certified as mediators appointed by the President of the North Carolina State Bar, one of whom shall be a family law specialist; and three citizens knowledgeable about mediation, one of whom shall be appointed by the Governor, one by the General Assembly upon the recommendation of the Speaker of the House of Representatives in accordance with G.S. 120-121, and one by the General Assembly upon the recommendation of the President Pro Tempore of the Senate in accordance with G.S. 120-121. Members shall initially serve four-year terms, except that one judge, one mediator, one attorney, and the citizen member appointed by the Governor, shall be appointed for an initial term of two years. Incumbent members as of September 30, 1998 shall serve the remainder of the terms to which they were appointed. Members appointed to newly-created membership positions effective October 1, 1998 shall serve initial terms of two years. Thereafter, members shall serve three-year terms and shall be ineligible to serve more than two consecutive terms. The Chief Justice shall designate one of the members to serve as chair for a two-year term. Members of the Commission shall be compensated pursuant to G.S. 138-5.

Vacancies shall be filled for unexpired terms and full terms in the same manner as incumbents were appointed. Appointing authorities may receive and consider suggestions and recommendations of persons for appointment from the Dispute Resolution Commission, the Family Law, Litigation, and Dispute Resolution Sections of the North Carolina Bar Association, the North Carolina Association of Professional Family Mediators, the North Carolina Conference of Clerks of Superior Court, the North Carolina Conference of Court Administrators, the Mediation Network of North Carolina, the Dispute Resolution Committee of the Supreme Court, the Conference of Chief District Court Judges, the Conference of Superior Court Judges, the Director of the Administrative Office of the Courts, and the Child Custody Mediation Advisory Committee of the Administrative Office of the Courts.

(d) An administrative fee, not to exceed two hundred dollars ($200.00), may be charged by the Administrative Office of the Courts to applicants for certification and annual renewal of certification for mediators and mediation training programs operating under this Article. The fees collected may be used by the Director of the Administrative Office of the Courts to establish and maintain the operations of the Commission and its staff. Notwithstanding the provisions of G.S. 143C-1-2(b), certification and renewal fees collected by the Dispute Resolution Commission are nonreverting and are only to be used at the direction of the Commission.

(e) The chair of the Commission may employ an executive secretary and other staff as necessary to assist the Commission in carrying out its duties. The chair may also employ special counsel or call upon the Attorney General to furnish counsel to assist the Commission in conducting hearings pursuant to its certification or qualification and regulatory responsibilities. Special counsel or counsel furnished by the Attorney General may present the evidence in support of a denial or revocation of certification or qualification or a complaint against a mediator, other neutral, training program, or trainers or staff affiliated with a program. Special counsel or counsel furnished by the Attorney General may also represent the Commission when its final determinations are the subject of an appeal.

(f) In connection with any investigation or hearing conducted pursuant to an application for certification or qualification of any mediator, other neutral, or training program, or conducted pursuant to any disciplinary matter, the chair of the Dispute Resolution Commission or his/her designee, may:

(1) Administer oaths and affirmations;

(2) Sign and issue subpoenas in the name of the Dispute Resolution Commission or direct its executive secretary to issue such subpoenas on its behalf requiring attendance and the giving of testimony by witnesses and the production of books, papers, and other documentary evidence;

(3) Apply to the General Court of Justice, Superior Court Division, for any order necessary to enforce the power conferred in this section.

(g) The General Court of Justice, Superior Court Division, may enforce subpoenas issued in the name of the Dispute Resolution Commission and requiring attendance and the giving of testimony by witnesses and the production of books, papers, and other documentary evidence.

(h) The Commission shall keep confidential all information in its files pertaining to the certification of mediators, the qualification of other neutrals, the certification or qualification of training programs for mediators or other neutrals, and the renewal of such certifications and qualifications. However, disciplinary matters reported by an applicant for certification or qualification, a mediator, other neutral, trainer, or manager shall be treated as a complaint as set forth below. The Commission shall also keep confidential the identity of those persons requesting informal guidance or the issuance of formal advisory opinions from the Commission or its staff.

Unless an applicant, mediator, other neutral, or training program trainer or manager requests otherwise, all information in the Commission's disciplinary files pertaining to a complaint regarding the conduct of an applicant, mediator, other neutral, trainer, or manager shall remain confidential until such time as a preliminary investigation is completed and a determination is made that probable cause exists to believe that the applicant, mediator, neutral, trainer, or manager's words or actions:

(1) Violate standards for the conduct of mediators or other neutrals;

(2) Violate other standards of professional conduct to which the applicant, mediator, neutral, trainer, or manager is subject;

(3) Violate program rules; or

(4) Consist of conduct or actions that are inconsistent with good moral character or reflect a lack of fitness to serve as a mediator, other neutral, trainer, or manager.

The Commission may publish names, contact information, and biographical information for mediators, neutrals, and training programs that have been certified or qualified.

(i) The Commission shall conduct its initial review of all applications for certification and certification renewal or qualification and qualification renewal in private. The Commission shall also conduct its initial review of complaints regarding the qualifications of any certified mediator, other neutral, or training program, but not involving issues of ethics or conduct, in private. Appeals of denials of applications for certification, qualification, or renewal and appeals of revocations of certification or qualification for reasons that do not relate to ethics or conduct, shall be heard by the Commission in private unless the applicant, certified mediator, qualified neutral, or certified or qualified training program requests a public hearing.

(j)   The Commission shall conduct in private its initial review of all matters relating to the ethics or conduct of an applicant for certification, qualification, or renewal of certification or qualification or the ethics or conduct of a mediator, other neutral, trainer, or training program manager. If an applicant appeals the Commission's initial determination that sanctions be imposed, the hearing of such appeal by the Commission shall be open to the public, except that for good cause shown, the presiding officer may exclude from the hearing room all persons except the parties, counsel, and those engaged in the hearing. No hearing shall be closed to the public over the objection of an applicant, mediator, other neutral, trainer, or training program manager.

(k)   Appeals of final determinations by the Commission to deny certification or renewal of certification, to revoke certification, or to discipline a mediator, trainer, or training program manager shall be filed in the General Court of Justice, Wake County Superior Court Division. Notice of appeal shall be filed within 30 days of the date of the Commission's decision. (1995, c. 500, s. 1; 1998-212, s. 16.19(b), (c); 2005-167, ss. 2, 4; 2007-387, ss. 2, 3; 2010-169, s. 21(b); 2011-145, s. 15.5; 2011-411, s. 5.)

§ 7A-38.3. Prelitigation mediation of farm nuisance disputes.

(a)   Definitions. - As used in this section:

(1)   "Farm nuisance dispute" means a claim that the farming activity of a farm resident constitutes a nuisance.

(2)   "Farm resident" means a person holding an interest in fee, under a real estate contract, or under a lease, in land used for farming activity when that person manages the operations on the land.

(3)   "Farming activity" means the cultivation of farmland for the production of crops, fruits, vegetables, ornamental and flowering plants, and the utilization of

farmland for the production of dairy, livestock, poultry, and all other forms of agricultural products having a domestic or foreign market.

(4) "Mediator" means a neutral person who acts to encourage and facilitate a resolution of a farm nuisance dispute.

(5) "Nuisance" means an action that is injurious to health, indecent, offensive to the senses, or an obstruction to the free use of property.

(6) "Party" means any person having a dispute with a farm resident.

(7) "Person" means a natural person, or any corporation, trust, or limited partnership as defined in G.S. 59-102.

(b) Voluntary Mediation. - The parties to a farm nuisance dispute may agree at any time to mediation of the dispute under the provisions of this section.

(c) Mandatory Mediation. - Prior to bringing a civil action involving a farm nuisance dispute, a farm resident or any other party shall initiate mediation pursuant to this section. If a farm resident or any other party brings an action involving a farm nuisance dispute, this action shall, upon the motion of any party prior to trial, be dismissed without prejudice by the court unless any one or more of the following apply:

(1) The dispute involves a claim that has been brought as a class action.

(2) The nonmoving party has satisfied the requirements of this section and such is indicated in a mediator's certification issued under subsection (g) of this section.

(3) The court finds that a mediator improperly failed to issue a certification indicating that the nonmoving party satisfied the requirements of this section.

(4) The court finds good cause for a failure to attempt mediation. Good cause includes, but is not limited to, a determination that the time delay required for mediation would likely result in irreparable harm or that injunctive relief is otherwise warranted.

(d) Initiation of Mediation. - Prelitigation mediation of a farm nuisance dispute shall be initiated by filing a request for mediation with the clerk of superior court in a county in which the action may be brought. The

Administrative Office of the Courts shall prescribe a request for mediation form. The party filing the request for mediation also shall mail a copy of the request by certified mail, return receipt requested, to each party to the dispute. The clerk shall provide each party with a list of mediators certified by the Dispute Resolution Commission. If the parties agree in writing to the selection of a mediator from that list, the clerk shall appoint that mediator selected by the parties. If the parties do not agree on the selection of a mediator, the party filing the request for mediation shall bring the matter to the attention of the clerk, and a mediator shall be appointed by the senior resident superior court judge. The clerk shall notify the mediator and the parties of the appointment of the mediator.

(e) Mediation Procedure. - Except as otherwise expressly provided in this section, mediation under this section shall be conducted in accordance with the provisions for mediated settlement of civil cases in G.S. 7A-38.1 and G.S. 7A-38.2 and rules and standards adopted pursuant to those sections. The Supreme Court may adopt additional rules and standards to implement this section, including an exemption from the provisions of G.S. 7A-38.1 for cases in which mediation was attempted under this section.

(f) Waiver of Mediation. - The parties to the dispute may waive the mediation required by this section by informing the mediator of their waiver in writing. No costs shall be assessed to any party if all parties waive mediation prior to the occurrence of an initial mediation meeting.

(g) Certification That Mediation Concluded. - Immediately upon a waiver of mediation under subsection (f) of this section or upon the conclusion of mediation, the mediator shall prepare a certification stating the date on which the mediation was concluded and the general results of the mediation, including, as applicable, that the parties waived the mediation, that an agreement was reached, that mediation was attempted but an agreement was not reached, or that one or more parties, to be specified in the certification, failed or refused without good cause to attend one or more mediation meetings or otherwise participate in the mediation. The mediator shall file the original of the certification with the clerk and provide a copy to each party. Each party to the mediation has satisfied the requirements of this section upon the filing of the certification, except any party specified in the certification as having failed or refused to attend one or more mediation meetings or otherwise participate. The sanctions in G.S. 7A-38.1(g) do not apply to prelitigation mediation conducted under this section.

(h) Time Periods Tolled. - Any applicable statutes of limitations relating to a farm nuisance dispute shall be tolled upon the filing of a request for mediation under this section, until 30 days after the date on which the mediation is concluded as set forth in the mediator's certification, or if the mediator fails to set forth such date, until 30 days after the filing of the certification under subsection (g) of this section. The filing of a request for prelitigation mediation under subsection (d) of this section does not constitute the commencement or the bringing of an action involving a farm nuisance dispute. (1995, c. 500, s. 1; 2013-314, s. 2.)

§ 7A-38.3A. Prelitigation mediation of insurance claims.

(a) Initiation of Mediation. - Prelitigation mediation of an insurance claim may be initiated by an insurer that has provided the policy limits in accordance with G.S. 58-3-33 by filing a request for mediation with the clerk of superior court in a county in which the action may be brought. The insurer also shall mail a copy of the request by certified mail, return receipt requested, to the person who requested the information under G.S. 58-3-33.

(b) Costs of Mediation. - Costs of mediation, including the mediator's fees, shall be borne by the insurer and claimant equally. When an attorney represents a party to the mediation, that party shall pay his or her attorneys' fees.

(c) Mediation Procedure. - Except as otherwise expressly provided in this section, mediation under this section shall be conducted in accordance with the provisions for mediated settlement of civil cases in G.S. 7A-38.1 and G.S. 7A-38.2, and rules and standards adopted pursuant to those sections. The Supreme Court may adopt additional rules and standards to implement this section, including an exemption from the provisions of G.S. 7A-38.1 for cases in which mediation was attempted under this section.

(d) Certification That Mediation Concluded. - Upon the conclusion of mediation, the mediator shall prepare a certification stating the date on which the mediation was concluded and the general results of the mediation, including, as applicable, that an agreement was reached, that mediation was attempted but an agreement was not reached, or that one or more parties, to be specified in the certification, failed or refused without good cause to attend one or more mediation meetings or otherwise participate in the mediation. The mediator shall file the original of the certification with the clerk and provide a copy to each party. Each party to the mediation has satisfied the requirements of this section upon the filing of the certification, except any party specified in the certification as having failed or refused to attend one or more mediation meetings or otherwise participate. The sanctions in G.S. 7A-38.1(g) do not apply to prelitigation mediation conducted under this section.

(e) Time Periods Tolled. - Time periods relating to the filing of a claim or the taking of other action with respect to an insurance claim, including any applicable statutes of limitations, shall be tolled upon the filing of a request for mediation under this section, until 30 days after the date on which the mediation is concluded as set forth in the mediator's certification or, if the mediator fails to set forth such date, until 30 days after the filing of the certification under subsection (d) of this section.

(f) Medical Malpractice Claims Excluded. - This section does not apply to claims seeking recovery for medical malpractice. (2003-307, s. 2.)

§ 7A-38.3B. Mediation in matters within the jurisdiction of the clerk of superior court.

(a) Purpose. - The General Assembly finds that the clerk of superior court in the General Court of Justice should have the discretion and authority to order that mediation be conducted in matters within the clerk's jurisdiction in order to facilitate a more economical, efficient, and satisfactory resolution of those matters.

(b) Enabling Authority. - The clerk of superior court may order that mediation be conducted in any matter in which the clerk has exclusive or original jurisdiction, except for matters under Chapters 45 and 48 of the General Statutes and except in matters in which the jurisdiction of the clerk is ancillary. The Supreme Court may adopt rules to implement this section. Such mediations shall be conducted pursuant to this section and the Supreme Court rules as adopted.

(c) Attendance. - In those matters ordered to mediation pursuant to this section, the following persons or entities, along with their attorneys, may be ordered by the clerk to attend the mediation:

(1) Named parties.

(2) Interested persons, meaning persons or entities who have a right, interest, or claim in the matter; heirs or devisees in matters under Chapter 28A of the General Statutes, next of kin under Chapter 35A of the General Statutes, and other persons or entities as the clerk deems necessary for the adjudication of the matter. The meaning of "interested person" may vary according to the issues involved in the matter.

(3) Nonparty participants, meaning any other person or entity identified by the clerk as possessing useful information about the matter and whose attendance would be beneficial to the mediation.

(4) Fiduciaries, meaning persons or entities who serve as fiduciaries, as that term is defined by G.S. 36A-22.1, of named parties, interested persons, or nonparty participants.

Any person or entity ordered to attend a mediation shall be notified of its date, time, and location and shall attend unless excused by rules of the Supreme Court or by order of the clerk. No one attending the mediation shall be required to make a settlement offer or demand that it deems contrary to its best interests.

(d) Selection of Mediator. - Persons ordered to mediation pursuant to this section have the right to designate a mediator in accordance with rules promulgated by the Supreme Court implementing this section. Upon failure of those persons to agree upon a designation within the time established by rules of the Supreme Court, a mediator certified by the Dispute Resolution Commission pursuant to those rules shall be appointed by the clerk.

(e) Immunity. - Mediators acting pursuant to this section shall have judicial immunity in the same manner and to the same extent as a judge of the General Court of Justice, except that mediators may be disciplined in accordance with procedures adopted by the Supreme Court pursuant to G.S. 7A-38.2.

(f) Costs of Mediation. - Costs of mediation under this section shall be borne by the named parties, interested persons, and fiduciaries ordered to attend the mediation. The rules adopted by the Supreme Court implementing this section shall set out the manner in which costs shall be paid and a method by which an opportunity to participate without cost shall be afforded to persons found by the clerk to be unable to pay their share of the costs of mediation. Costs may only be assessed against the estate of a decedent, the estate of an adjudicated or alleged incompetent, a trust corpus, or against a fiduciary upon the entry of a written order making specific findings of fact justifying the taxing of costs.

(g) Inadmissibility of Negotiations. - Evidence of statements made or conduct occurring during a mediation conducted pursuant to this section, whether attributable to any participant, mediator, expert, or neutral observer, shall not be subject to discovery and shall be inadmissible in any proceeding in the matter or other civil actions on the same claim, except in:

(1) Proceedings for sanctions pursuant to this section;

(2) Proceedings to enforce or rescind a written and signed settlement agreement;

(3) Incompetency, guardianship, or estate proceedings in which a mediated agreement is presented to the clerk;

(4) Disciplinary proceedings before the North Carolina State Bar or any agency established to enforce standards of conduct for mediators or other neutrals; or

(5) Proceedings for abuse, neglect, or dependency of a juvenile, or for abuse, neglect, or exploitation of an adult, for which there is a duty to report under G.S. 7B-301 and Article 6 of Chapter 108A of the General Statutes, respectively.

No evidence otherwise discoverable shall be inadmissible merely because it is presented or discussed in mediation.

As used in this section, the term "neutral observer" includes persons seeking mediator certification, persons studying dispute resolution processes, and persons acting as interpreters.

(h) Testimony. - No mediator or neutral observer shall be compelled to testify or produce evidence concerning statements made and conduct occurring in anticipation of, during, or as a follow-up to the mediation in any civil proceeding for any purpose, including proceedings to enforce or rescind a settlement of the matter except to attest to the signing of any agreements reached in mediation, and except in:

(1) Proceedings for sanctions pursuant to this section;

(2) Disciplinary proceedings before the North Carolina State Bar or any agency established to enforce standards of conduct for mediators or other neutrals; or

(3) Proceedings for abuse, neglect, or dependency of a juvenile, or for abuse, neglect, or exploitation of an adult, for which there is a duty to report under G.S. 7B-301 and Article 6 of Chapter 108A of the General Statutes, respectively.

(i) Agreements. - In matters before the clerk in which agreements are reached in a mediation conducted pursuant to this section, or during one of its recesses, those agreements shall be treated as follows:

(1) Where as a matter of law, a matter may be resolved by agreement of the parties, a settlement is enforceable only if it has been reduced to writing and signed by the parties.

(2) In all other matters before the clerk, including guardianship and estate matters, all agreements shall be delivered to the clerk for consideration in deciding the matter.

(j) Sanctions. - Any person ordered to attend a mediation conducted pursuant to this section and rules of the Supreme Court who, without good cause, fails to attend the mediation or fails to pay any or all of the mediator's fee in compliance with this section and the rules promulgated by the Supreme Court to implement this section, is subject to the contempt powers of the clerk and monetary sanctions. The monetary sanctions may include the payment of fines, attorneys' fees, mediator fees, and the expenses and loss of earnings incurred by persons attending the mediation. If the clerk imposes sanctions, the clerk shall do so, after notice and a hearing, in a written order, making findings of fact and conclusions of law. An order imposing sanctions is reviewable by the superior court in accordance with G.S. 1-301.2 and G.S. 1-301.3, as applicable, and thereafter by the appellate courts in accordance with G.S. 7A-38.1(g).

(k) Authority to Supplement Procedural Details. - The clerk of superior court shall make all those orders just and necessary to safeguard the interests of all persons and may supplement all necessary procedural details not inconsistent with rules adopted by the Supreme Court implementing this section. (2005-67, s. 1; 2008-194, s. 8(b).)

§ 7A-38.3C: Repealed by Session Laws 2007-491, s. 4, effective August 21, 2007.

§ 7A-38.3D. Mediation in matters within the jurisdiction of the district criminal courts.

(a)   Purpose. - The General Assembly finds that it is in the public interest to promote high standards for persons who mediate matters in district criminal court. To that end, a program of certification for these mediators shall be established in judicial districts designated by the Dispute Resolution Commission and the Director of the Administrative Office of the Courts and in which the chief district court judge, the district attorney, and the community mediation center agree to participate. This section does not supersede G.S. 7A-38.5.

(b)   Enabling Authority. - In each district, the court may encourage mediation for any criminal district court action pending in the district, and the district attorney may delay prosecution of those actions so that the mediation may take place.

(c)   Program Administration. - A community mediation center established under G.S. 7A-38.5 and located in a district designated under subsection (a) of this section shall assist the court in administering a program providing mediation services in district criminal court cases. A community mediation center may assist in the screening and scheduling of cases for mediation and provide certified volunteer or staff mediators to conduct district criminal court mediations.

(d)   Rules of Procedure. - The Supreme Court shall adopt rules to implement this section. Each mediation shall be conducted pursuant to this section and the Supreme Court Rules as adopted.

(e)   Mediator Authority. - In the mediator's discretion, any person whose presence and participation may assist in resolving the dispute or addressing any issues underlying the mediation may be permitted to attend and participate. The mediator shall have discretion to exclude any individual who seeks to attend the mediation but whose participation the mediator deems would be counterproductive. Lawyers for the participants may attend and participate in the mediation.

(f) Mediator Qualification. - The Supreme Court shall establish requirements for the certification or qualification of mediators serving under this section. The Court shall also establish requirements for the qualification of training programs and trainers, including community mediation center staff, that train these mediators. The Court shall also adopt rules regulating the conduct of these mediators and trainers.

(g) Oversight and Evaluation. - The Supreme Court may require community mediation centers and their volunteer or staff mediators to collect and report caseload statistics, referral sources, fees collected, and any other information deemed essential for program oversight and evaluation purposes.

(h) Immunity. - A mediator under this section has judicial immunity in the same manner and to the same extent as a judge of the General Court of Justice, except that a mediator may be disciplined in accordance with procedures adopted by the Supreme Court. A community mediation center and its staff involved in supplying volunteer or staff mediators or other personnel to schedule cases or perform other duties under this section are immune from suit in any civil action, except in any case of willful or wanton misconduct.

(i) Confidentiality. - Any memorandum, work note, or product of the mediator and any case file maintained by a community mediation center acting under this section and any mediator certification application are confidential.

(j) Inadmissibility of Negotiations. - Evidence of any statement made and conduct occurring during a mediation under this section shall not be subject to discovery and shall be inadmissible in any proceeding in the action from which the mediation arises. Any participant in a mediation conducted under this section, including the mediator, may report to law enforcement personnel any statement made or conduct occurring during the mediation process that threatens or threatened the safety of any person or property. A mediator has discretion to warn a person whose safety or property has been threatened. No evidence otherwise discoverable is inadmissible for the reason it is presented or discussed in a mediated settlement conference or other settlement proceeding under this section.

(k) Testimony. - No mediator or neutral observer present at the mediation shall be compelled to testify or produce evidence concerning statements made and conduct occurring in or related to a mediation conducted under this section in any proceeding in the same action for any purpose, except in:

(1)   Proceedings for abuse, neglect, or dependency of a juvenile, or for abuse, neglect, or exploitation of an adult, for which there is a duty to report under G.S. 7B-301 and Article 6 of Chapter 108A of the General Statutes, respectively.

(2)   Disciplinary proceedings before the North Carolina State Bar or any agency established to enforce standards of conduct for mediators.

(3)   Proceedings in which the mediator acts as a witness pursuant to subsection (j) of this section.

(4)   Trials of a felony, during which a presiding judge may compel the disclosure of any evidence arising out of the mediation, excluding a statement made by the defendant in the action under mediation, if it is to be introduced in the trial or disposition of the felony and the judge determines that the introduction of the evidence is necessary to the proper administration of justice and the evidence cannot be obtained from any other source.

(l)   Written Agreements. - Any agreement reached in mediation shall be reduced to writing and signed by the parties. A non-attorney mediator may assist parties in reducing the agreement to writing.

(m)   Dismissal Fee. - Where an agreement has been reached in mediation and the case will be dismissed, the defendant shall pay to the clerk the dismissal fee of court set forth in G.S. 7A-38.7. By agreement, all or any portion of the fee may be paid by a person other than the defendant.

(n)   Definitions. - As used in this section, the following definitions apply:

(1)   Court. - A district court judge, a district attorney, or the designee of a district court judge or district attorney.

(2)   Neutral observer. - Includes any person seeking mediator certification, any person studying any dispute resolution process, and any person acting as an interpreter. (2007-387, s. 1; 2012-194, s. 63.3(b).)

§ 7A-38.3E. Mediation of public records disputes.

(a)   Voluntary Mediation. - The parties to a public records dispute under Chapter 132 of the General Statutes may agree at any time prior to filing a civil action under Chapter 132 of the General Statutes to mediation of the dispute under the provisions of this section. Mediation of a public records dispute shall be initiated by filing a request for mediation with the clerk of superior court in a county in which the action may be brought.

(b) Mandatory Mediation. - Subsequent to filing a civil action under Chapter 132 of the General Statutes, a person shall initiate mediation pursuant to this section. Such mediation shall be initiated no later than 30 days from the filing of responsive pleadings with the clerk in the county where the action is filed.

(c) Initiation of Mediation. - The Administrative Office of the Courts shall prescribe a request for mediation form. The party filing the request for mediation shall mail a copy of the request by certified mail, return receipt requested, to each party to the dispute. The clerk shall provide each party with a list of mediators certified by the Dispute Resolution Commission. If the parties agree in writing to the selection of a mediator from that list, the clerk shall appoint that mediator selected by the parties. If the parties do not agree on the selection of a mediator, the party filing the request for mediation shall bring the matter to the attention of the clerk, and a mediator shall be appointed by the senior resident superior court judge. The clerk shall notify the mediator and the parties of the appointment of the mediator.

(d) Mediation Procedure. - Except as otherwise expressly provided in this section, mediation under this section shall be conducted in accordance with the provisions for mediated settlement of civil cases in G.S. 7A-38.1 and G.S. 7A-38.2 and rules and standards adopted pursuant to those sections. The Supreme Court may adopt additional rules and standards to implement this section, including an exemption from the provisions of G.S. 7A-38.1 for cases in which mediation was attempted under this section.

(e) Waiver of Mediation. - The parties to the dispute may waive the mediation required by this section by informing the mediator of the parties' waiver in writing. No costs shall be assessed to any party if all parties waive mediation prior to the occurrence of an initial mediation meeting.

(f) Certification That Mediation Concluded. - Immediately upon a waiver of mediation under subsection (e) of this section or upon the conclusion of mediation, the mediator shall prepare a certification stating the date on which the mediation was concluded and the general results of the mediation, including, as applicable, that the parties waived the mediation, that an agreement was reached, that mediation was attempted but an agreement was not reached, or that one or more parties, to be specified in the certification, failed or refused without good cause to attend one or more mediation meetings or otherwise participate in the mediation. The mediator shall file the original of the certification with the clerk and provide a copy to each party.

(g) Time Periods Tolled. - Time periods relating to the filing of a claim or the taking of other action with respect to a public records dispute, including any applicable statutes of limitations, shall be tolled upon the filing of a request for mediation under this section, until 30 days after the date on which the mediation is concluded as set forth in the mediator's certification, or if the mediator fails to set forth such date, until 30 days after the filing of the certification under subsection (f) of this section.

(h) [Other Remedies Not Affected.] - Nothing in this section shall prevent a party seeking production of public records from seeking injunctive or other relief, including production of public records prior to any scheduled mediation. (2010-169, s. 21(a).)

§ 7A-38.3F. Prelitigation mediation of condominium and homeowners association disputes.

(a) Definitions. - The following definitions apply in this section:

(1) Association. - An association of unit or lot owners organized as allowed under North Carolina law, including G.S. 47C-3-101 and G.S. 47F-3-101.

(2) Dispute. - Any matter relating to real estate under the jurisdiction of an association about which the member and association cannot agree. The term "dispute" does not include matters expressly exempted in subsection (b) of this section.

(3) Executive board. - The body, regardless of name, designated in the declaration to act on behalf of an association.

(4) Mediator. - A neutral person who acts to encourage and facilitate a resolution of a dispute between an association and a member.

(5) Member. - A person who is a member of an association of unit or lot owners organized as allowed under North Carolina law, including G.S. 47C-3-101 and G.S. 47F-3-101.

(6) Party or parties. - An association or member who is involved in a dispute, as that term is defined in subdivision (2) of this subsection.

(b) Voluntary Prelitigation Mediation. - Prior to filing a civil action, the parties to a dispute arising under Chapter 47C of the General Statutes (North Carolina Condominium Act), Chapter 47F of the General Statutes (North Carolina Planned Community Act), or an association's declaration, bylaws, or rules and regulations are encouraged to initiate mediation pursuant to this section. However, disputes related solely to a member's failure to timely pay an association assessment or any fines or fees associated with the levying or collection of an association assessment are not covered under this section.

(c) Initiation of Mediation. - Either an association or a member may contact the North Carolina Dispute Resolution Commission or the Mediation Network of North Carolina for the name of a mediator or community mediation center. Upon contacting a mediator, either the association or member may supply to the mediator the physical address of the other party, or the party's representative, and the party's telephone number and e-mail address, if known. The mediator shall contact the party, or the party's representative, to notify him or her of the request to mediate. If the parties agree to mediate, they shall request in writing that the mediator schedule the mediation. The mediator shall then notify the parties in writing of the date, time, and location of the mediation, which shall be scheduled not later than 25 days after the mediator receives the written request from the parties.

(d) Mediation Procedure. - The following procedures shall apply to mediation under this section:

(1) Attendance. - The mediator shall determine who may attend mediation. The mediator may require the executive board or a large group of members to designate one or more persons to serve as their representatives in the mediation.

(2) All parties are expected to attend mediation. The mediator may allow a party to participate in mediation by telephone or other electronic means if the mediator determines that the party has a compelling reason to do so.

(3) If the parties cannot reach a final agreement in mediation because to do so would require the approval of the full executive board or the approval of a majority or some other percentage of the members of the association, the

mediator may recess the mediation meeting to allow the executive board or members to review and vote on the agreement.

(e) Decline Mediation. - Either party to a dispute may decline mediation under this section. If either party declines mediation after mediation has been initiated under subsection (c) of this section but mediation has not been held, the party declining mediation shall inform the mediator and the other party in writing of his or her decision to decline mediation. No costs shall be assessed to any party if either party declines mediation prior to the occurrence of an initial mediation meeting.

(f) Costs of Mediation. - The costs of mediation, including the mediator's fees, shall be shared equally by the parties unless otherwise agreed to by the parties. Fees shall be due and payable at the end of each mediation meeting. When an attorney represents a party to the mediation, that party shall pay his or her attorneys' fees.

(g) Certification That Mediation Concluded. - Upon the conclusion of mediation, the mediator shall prepare a certification stating the date on which the mediation was concluded and a statement that an agreement was reached or that mediation was attempted but an agreement was not reached. If both parties participate in mediation and a cause of action involving the dispute mediated is later filed, either party may file the certificate with the clerk of court, and the parties shall not be required to mediate again under any provision of law.

(h) Inadmissibility of Evidence. - Evidence of statements made and conduct occurring during mediation under this section shall not be subject to discovery and shall be inadmissible in any proceeding in a civil action arising from the dispute which was the subject of that mediation; except proceedings to enforce or rescind a settlement agreement reached at that mediation, disciplinary proceedings before the State Bar or Dispute Resolution Commission, or proceedings to enforce laws concerning juvenile or elder abuse. No evidence otherwise discoverable shall be inadmissible merely because it is presented or discussed in a mediation under this section.

No mediator shall be compelled to testify or produce evidence concerning statements made and conduct occurring in anticipation of, during, or as a follow-up to a mediation pursuant to this section in any civil proceeding for any purpose, including proceedings to enforce or rescind the settlement agreement; except in disciplinary hearings before the State Bar or Dispute Resolution

Commission and proceedings to enforce laws concerning juvenile or elder abuse, and except in proceedings to enforce or rescind an agreement reached in a mediation under this section, but only to attest to the signing of the agreement.

(i) Time Periods Tolled. - Time periods relating to the filing of a civil action, including any applicable statutes of limitations or statutes of repose, with respect to a dispute described in subsection (a) of this section, shall be tolled upon the initiation of mediation under this section until 30 days after the date on which the mediation is concluded as set forth in the mediator's certification. For purposes of this section, "initiation of mediation" shall be defined as the date upon which both parties have signed the written request to schedule the mediation.

(j) Association Duty to Notify. - Each association shall, in writing, notify the members of the association each year that they may initiate mediation under this section to try to resolve a dispute with the association. The association shall publish the notice required in this subsection on the association's Web site; but if the association does not have a Web site, the association shall publish the notice at the same time and in the same manner as the names and addresses of all officers and board members of the association are published as provided in G.S. 47C-3-103 and G.S. 47F-3-103. (2013-127, s. 1.)

§ 7A-38.4: Repealed by Session Laws 2001-320, s. 1.

§ 7A-38.4A. Settlement procedures in district court actions.

(a) The General Assembly finds that a system of settlement events should be established to facilitate the settlement of district court actions involving equitable distribution, alimony, or support and to make that litigation more economical, efficient, and satisfactory to the parties, their representatives, and the State. District courts should be able to require parties to those actions and their representatives to attend a pretrial mediated settlement conference or other settlement procedure conducted under this section and rules adopted by the Supreme Court to implement this section.

(b) The definitions in G.S. 7A-38.1(b)(2) and (b)(3) apply in this section.

(c) Any chief district court judge in a judicial district may order a mediated settlement conference or another settlement procedure, as provided under subsection (g) of this section, for any action pending in that district involving issues of equitable distribution, alimony, child or post separation support, or claims arising out of contracts between the parties under G.S. 52-10, G.S. 52-10.1, or Chapter 52B of the General Statutes. The chief district court judge may adopt local rules that order settlement procedures in all of the foregoing actions and designate other district court judges or administrative personnel to issue orders implementing those settlement procedures. However, local rules adopted by a chief district court judge shall not be inconsistent with any rules adopted by the Supreme Court.

(d)   The parties to a district court action where a mediated settlement conference or other settlement procedure is ordered, their attorneys, and other persons or entities with authority, by law or contract, to settle a party's claim, shall attend the mediated settlement conference or other settlement procedure, unless the rules ordering the settlement procedure provide otherwise. No party or other participant in a mediated settlement conference or other settlement procedure is required to make a settlement offer or demand that the party or participant deems contrary to that party's or participant's best interests. Parties who have been victims of domestic violence may be excused from physically attending or participating in a mediated settlement conference or other settlement procedure.

(e)   Any person required to attend a mediated settlement conference or other settlement procedure under this section who, without good cause fails to attend or fails to pay any or all of the mediator or other neutral's fee in compliance with this section is subject to the contempt powers of the court and monetary sanctions imposed by a district court judge. A party seeking sanctions against another party or person shall do so in a written motion stating the grounds for the motion and the relief sought. The motion shall be served upon all parties and upon any person against whom sanctions are being sought. The court may initiate sanction proceedings upon its own motion by the entry of a show cause order. If the court imposes sanctions, it shall do so, after notice and hearing, in a written order making findings of fact and conclusions of law. An order imposing sanctions is reviewable upon appeal, and the entire record shall be reviewed to determine whether the order is supported by substantial evidence.

(f)   The parties to a district court action in which a mediated settlement conference is to be held under this section shall have the right to designate a mediator. Upon failure of the parties to designate within the time established by the rules adopted by the Supreme Court, a mediator shall be appointed by a district court judge.

(g) A chief district court judge or that judge's designee, at the request of a party and with the consent of all parties, may order the parties to attend and participate in any other settlement procedure authorized by rules adopted by the Supreme Court or adopted by local district court rules, in lieu of attending a mediated settlement conference. Neutrals acting under this section shall be selected and compensated in accordance with rules adopted by the Supreme Court. Nothing herein shall prohibit the parties from participating in other dispute resolution procedures, including arbitration, to the extent authorized under State or federal law. Nothing herein shall prohibit the parties from participating in mediation at a community mediation center operating under G.S. 7A-38.5.

(h) Mediators and other neutrals acting under this section shall have judicial immunity in the same manner and to the same extent as a judge of the General Court of Justice, except that mediators and other neutrals may be disciplined in accordance with enforcement procedures adopted by the Supreme Court under G.S. 7A-38.2.

(i) Costs of mediated settlement conferences and other settlement procedures shall be borne by the parties. Unless otherwise ordered by the court or agreed to by the parties, the mediator's fees shall be paid in equal shares by the parties. The rules adopted by the Supreme Court shall set out a method whereby a party found by the court to be unable to pay the costs of settlement procedures is afforded an opportunity to participate without cost to that party and without expenditure of State funds.

(j) Evidence of statements made and conduct occurring in a mediated settlement conference or other settlement proceeding conducted under this section, whether attributable to a party, the mediator, other neutral, or a neutral observer present at the settlement proceeding, shall not be subject to discovery and shall be inadmissible in any proceeding in the action or other civil actions on the same claim, except:

(1) In proceedings for sanctions under this section;

(2) In proceedings to enforce or rescind a settlement of the action;

(3) In disciplinary proceedings before the State Bar or any agency established to enforce standards of conduct for mediators or other neutrals; or

(4) In proceedings to enforce laws concerning juvenile or elder abuse.

As used in this subsection, the term "neutral observer" includes persons seeking mediator certification, persons studying dispute resolution processes, and persons acting as interpreters.

No settlement agreement to resolve any or all issues reached at the proceeding conducted under this section or during its recesses shall be enforceable unless it has been reduced to writing and signed by the parties and in all other respects complies with the requirements of Chapter 50 of the General Statutes. No evidence otherwise discoverable shall be inadmissible merely because it is presented or discussed in a settlement proceeding.

No mediator, other neutral, or neutral observer present at a settlement proceeding under this section, shall be compelled to testify or produce evidence concerning statements made and conduct occurring in anticipation of, during, or as a follow-up to a mediated settlement conference or other settlement proceeding pursuant to this section in any civil proceeding for any purpose, including proceedings to enforce or rescind a settlement of the action, except to attest to the signing of any agreements, and except proceedings for sanctions under this section, disciplinary hearings before the State Bar or any agency established to enforce standards of conduct for mediators or other neutrals, and proceedings to enforce laws concerning juvenile or elder abuse.

(k)   The Supreme Court may adopt standards for the certification and conduct of mediators and other neutrals who participate in settlement procedures conducted under this section. The standards may also regulate mediator training programs. The Supreme Court may adopt procedures for the enforcement of those standards. The administration of mediator certification, regulation of mediator conduct, and decertification shall be conducted through the Dispute Resolution Commission.

(l)   An administrative fee not to exceed two hundred dollars ($200.00) may be charged by the Administrative Office of the Courts to applicants for certification and annual renewal of certification for mediators and mediator training programs operating under this section. The fees collected may be used by the Director of the Administrative Office of the Courts to establish and maintain the operations of the Commission and its staff. The administrative fee shall be set by the Director of the Administrative Office of the Courts in consultation with the Dispute Resolution Commission.

(m) The Administrative Office of the Courts, in consultation with the Dispute Resolution Commission, may require the chief district court judge of any district to report statistical data about settlement procedures conducted under this section for administrative purposes.

(n) Nothing in this section or in rules adopted by the Supreme Court implementing this section shall restrict a party's right to a trial by jury.

(o) The Supreme Court may adopt rules to implement this section. (1997-229, s. 1; 1998-212, s. 16.19(a); 1999-354, s. 6; 2000-140, s. 1; 2001-320, s. 2; 2001-487, s. 39; 2005-167, s. 3; 2008-194, s. 8(c).)

§ 7A-38.5. Community mediation centers.

(a) The General Assembly finds that it is in the public interest to encourage the establishment of community mediation centers, also known as dispute settlement centers or dispute resolution centers, to support the work of these centers in facilitating communication, understanding, reconciliation, and settlement of conflicts in communities, courts, and schools, and to promote the widest possible use of these centers by the courts and law enforcement officials across the State. A center may establish and charge fees for its services.

(b) Community mediation centers, functioning as or within nonprofit organizations and local governmental entities, may receive referrals from courts, law enforcement agencies, and other public entities for the purpose of facilitating communication, understanding, reconciliation, and settlement of conflicts.

(c) Each chief district court judge and district attorney shall encourage mediation for any criminal district court action pending in the district when the judge and district attorney determine that mediation is an appropriate alternative.

(d) Each chief district court judge shall encourage mediation for any civil district court action pending in the district when the judge determines that mediation is an appropriate alternative.

(e) Except as provided in this subsection and subsection (f) of this section, each chief district court judge and district attorney shall refer any misdemeanor criminal action in district court that is generated by a citizen-initiated arrest warrant to the local mediation center for resolution, except for (i) any case involving domestic violence; (ii) any case in which the judge or the district attorney determine that mediation would be inappropriate; or (iii) any case being tried in a county in which mediation services are not available. The mediation center shall have 30 days to resolve each case and report back to the court with a resolution. The district attorney shall delay prosecution in order for the mediation to occur. If the case is not resolved through mediation within 30 days of referral, the court may proceed with the case as a criminal action. For purposes of this section, the term "citizen-initiated arrest warrant" means a warrant issued pursuant to G.S. 15A-304 by a magistrate or other judicial official based upon information supplied through the oath or affirmation of a private citizen.

(f) Any prosecutorial district may opt out of the mandatory mediation under subsection (e) of this section if the district attorney files a statement with the chief district court judge declaring that subsection shall not apply within the prosecutorial district. (1999-354, s. 1; 2011-145, s. 31.24(b); 2012-194, s. 63.3(a).)

§ 7A-38.6. Report on community mediation centers.

(a) All community mediation centers shall report annually to the Mediation Network of North Carolina on the program's funding and activities, including:

(1) Types of dispute settlement services provided;

(2) Clients receiving each type of dispute settlement service;

(3) Number and type of referrals received, cases actually mediated (identified by docket number), cases resolved in mediation, and total clients served in the cases mediated;

(4) Total program funding and funding sources;

(5) Itemization of the use of funds, including operating expenses and personnel;

(6) Itemization of the use of State funds appropriated to the center;

(7) Level of volunteer activity; and

(8)   Identification of future service demands and budget requirements.

(a1)   The Mediation Network of North Carolina shall compile and summarize the information provided pursuant to subsection (a) of this section and shall provide the information to the Chairs of the House of Representatives and Senate Appropriations Committees and the Chairs of the House of Representatives and Senate Appropriations Subcommittees on Justice and Public Safety by February 1 of each year.

The Mediation Network of North Carolina shall also submit a copy of its report to the Administrative Office of the Courts. The receipt and review of this report by the Administrative Office of the Courts shall satisfy any program monitoring, evaluation, and contracting requirements imposed on the Administrative Office of the Courts by Part 3 of Article 6 of Chapter 143C of the General Statutes and any rules adopted under that Part.

(b)   A community mediation center requesting State funds for the first time shall provide the General Assembly with the information enumerated in subsection (a) of this section, or projections where historical data are not available, as well as a detailed statement justifying the need for State funding.

(c)   Each community mediation center receiving State funds for the first time shall document in the information provided pursuant to this section that, after the second year of receiving State funds, at least ten percent (10%) of total funding comes from non-State sources.

(d)   Each community mediation center receiving State funds for the third, fourth, or fifth year shall document that at least twenty percent (20%) of total funding comes from non-State sources.

(e)   Each community mediation center receiving State funds for six or more years shall document that at least fifty percent (50%) of total funding comes from non-State sources.

(f)   Each community mediation center currently receiving State funds that has achieved a funding level from non-State sources greater than that provided for that center by subsection (c), (d), or (e) of this section shall make a good faith effort to maintain that level of funding.

(g) The percentage that State funds comprise of the total funding of each community mediation center shall be determined at the conclusion of each fiscal year with the information provided pursuant to this section and is intended as a funding ratio and not a matching funds requirement. Community mediation centers may include the market value of donated office space, utilities, and professional legal and accounting services in determining total funding.

(h) A community mediation center having difficulty meeting the funding ratio provided for that center by subsection (c), (d), or (e) of this section may request a waiver or special consideration through the Mediation Network of North Carolina for consideration by the Senate and House of Representatives Appropriations Subcommittees on Justice and Public Safety.

(i) The provisions of G.S. 143C-4-5 do not apply to community mediation centers receiving State funds.

(j) Each community mediation center receiving State funds shall function as, or as part of, a nonprofit organization or local government entity. A community mediation center functioning as a nonprofit organization shall have a governing board of directors that consists of a significant number of citizens from the surrounding community. State funds may not be used for indirect costs associated with contracts between the community mediation center and another entity for the provision of management-related services. (2001-424, s. 22.2; 2003-284, s. 13.15(c); 2006-66, s. 14.12; 2006-203, s. 10; 2009-570, s. 28; 2011-145, s. 31.24(c).)

§ 7A-38.7. Dispute resolution fee for cases resolved in mediation.

(a) In each criminal case filed in the General Court of Justice that is resolved through referral to a community mediation center, a dispute resolution fee shall be assessed in the sum of sixty dollars ($60.00) per mediation to support the services provided by the community mediation centers and the Mediation Network of North Carolina. Fees assessed under this section shall be paid to the clerk of superior court in the county where the case was filed and remitted by the clerk to the Mediation Network of North Carolina. The Mediation Network may retain up to three dollars ($3.00) of this amount as an allowance for its administrative expenses. The Mediation Network must remit the remainder of this amount to the community mediation center that mediated the case. The court may waive or reduce a fee assessed under this section only upon entry of a written order, supported by findings of fact and conclusions of law, determining there is just cause to grant the waiver or reduction.

(b) Before providing the district attorney with a dismissal form, the community mediation center shall require proof that the defendant has paid the dispute resolution fee as required by subsection (a) of this section and shall attach the receipt to the dismissal form. (2002-126, s. 29A.11(a); 2003-284, s. 13.13; 2011-145, s. 31.24(d); 2012-142, s. 16.6(a).)

§ 7A-39. Cancellation of court sessions and closing court offices; extension of statutes of limitations and other emergency orders in catastrophic conditions.

(a) Cancellation of Court Sessions, Closing Court Offices. - In response to adverse weather or other emergency situations, including catastrophic conditions, any session of any court of the General Court of Justice may be cancelled, postponed, or altered by judicial officials, and court offices may be closed by judicial branch hiring authorities, pursuant to uniform statewide guidelines prescribed by the Director of the Administrative Office of the Courts. As used in this section, "catastrophic conditions" means any set of circumstances that makes it impossible or extremely hazardous for judicial officials, employees, parties, witnesses, or other persons with business before the courts to reach a courthouse, or that creates a significant risk of physical harm to persons in a courthouse, or that would otherwise convince a reasonable person to avoid traveling to or being in a courthouse.

(b) Authority of Chief Justice. - When the Chief Justice of the North Carolina Supreme Court determines and declares that catastrophic conditions exist or have existed in one or more counties of the State, the Chief Justice may by order entered pursuant to this subsection:

(1) Extend, to a date certain no fewer than 10 days after the effective date of the order, the time or period of limitation within which pleadings, motions, notices, and other documents and papers may be timely filed and other acts may be timely done in civil actions, criminal actions, estates, and special proceedings in each county named in the order. The Chief Justice may enter an order under this subsection during the catastrophic conditions or at any time after such conditions have ceased to exist. The order shall be in writing and shall become effective for each affected county upon the date set forth in the order, and if no date is set forth in the order, then upon the date the order is signed by the Chief Justice.

(2) Issue any emergency directives that, notwithstanding any other provision of law, are necessary to ensure the continuing operation of essential trial or appellate court functions, including the designation or assignment of judicial officials who may be authorized to act in the general or specific matters stated in the emergency order, and the designation of the county or counties and specific locations within the State where such matters may be heard, conducted, or otherwise transacted. The Chief Justice may enter such emergency orders under this subsection in response to existing or impending catastrophic conditions or their consequences. An emergency order under this subsection shall expire the sooner of the date stated in the order, or 30 days from issuance of the order, but the order may be extended in whole or in part by the Chief Justice for additional 30-day periods if the Chief Justice determines that the directives remain necessary.

(c) In Chambers Jurisdiction Not Affected. - Nothing in this section prohibits a judge or other judicial officer from exercising, during adverse weather or other emergency situations, including catastrophic conditions, any in chambers or ex parte jurisdiction conferred by law upon that judge or judicial officer, as provided by law. The effectiveness of any such exercise shall not be affected by a determination by the Chief Justice that catastrophic conditions existed at the time it was exercised.

(d) Nothing in this section shall be construed to abrogate or diminish the inherent judicial powers of the Chief Justice or the Judicial Branch. (2000-166, s. 1; 2006-187, s. 6; 2009-516, s. 11.)

Article 6.

Retirement of Justices and Judges of the Appellate Division; Retirement Compensation; Recall to Emergency Service; Disability Retirement.

§ 7A-39.1. Justice, emergency justice, judge and emergency judge defined.

(a) As herein used "justice of the Supreme Court" includes the Chief Justice of the Supreme Court and "judge of the Court of Appeals" includes the Chief Judge of the Court of Appeals, unless the context clearly indicates a contrary intent.

(b)   As used herein, "emergency justice", "emergency judge", or "emergency recall judge" means any justice of the Supreme Court or any judge of the Court of Appeals, respectively, who has retired subject to recall for temporary service. (1967, c. 108, s. 1; 1985, c. 698, s. 16(a); 1995, c. 108, s. 2.)

§ 7A-39.2. Age and service requirements for retirement of justices of the Supreme Court and judges of the Court of Appeals.

(a)   Any justice of the Supreme Court or judge of the Court of Appeals who has attained the age of 65 years, and who has served for a total of 15 years, whether consecutive or not, on the Supreme Court, the Court of Appeals, or the superior court, or as Administrative Officer of the Courts, or in any combination of these offices, may retire from his present office and receive for life compensation equal to two thirds of the total annual compensation, including longevity, but excluding any payments in the nature of reimbursement for expenses, from time to time received by the occupant or occupants of the office from which he retired.

(b)   Any justice of the Supreme Court or judge of the Court of Appeals who has attained the age of 65 years, and who has served as justice or judge, or both, in the Appellate Division for 12 consecutive years may retire and receive for life compensation equal to two thirds of the total annual compensation, including longevity, but excluding any payments in the nature of reimbursement for expenses, from time to time received by the occupant or occupants of the office from which he retired.

(c)   Any justice or judge of the Appellate Division, who has served for a total of 24 years, whether continuously or not, as justice of the Supreme Court, judge of the Court of Appeals, judge of the superior court, or Administrative Officer of the Courts, or in any combination of these offices, may retire, regardless of age, and receive for life compensation equal to two thirds of the total annual compensation, including longevity, but excluding any payments in the nature of reimbursement for expenses, from time to time received by the occupant or occupants of the office from which he retired. In determining eligibility for retirement under this subsection, time served as a district solicitor of the superior court prior to January 1, 1971, may be included, provided the person has served at least eight years as a justice, judge, or Administrative Officer of the Courts, or in any combination of these offices.

(d) For purposes of this section, the "occupant or occupants of the office from which" the retired judge retired will be deemed to be a judge or justice of the Appellate Division holding the same office and with the same service as the retired judge had immediately prior to retirement. (1967, c. 108, s. 1; 1971, c. 508, s. 2; 1983 (Reg. Sess., 1984), c. 1109, ss. 13.6-13.9.)

§ 7A-39.3. Retired justices and judges may become emergency justices and judges subject to recall to active service; compensation for emergency justices and judges on recall.

(a) Justices of the Supreme Court and judges of the Court of Appeals who have not reached the mandatory retirement age specified in G.S. 7A-4.20, but who have retired under the provisions of G.S. 7A-39.2, or under the Uniform Judicial Retirement Act after having completed 12 years of creditable service, may apply as provided in G.S. 7A-39.6 to become emergency justices or judges and upon being commissioned as an emergency justice or emergency judge shall be subject to temporary recall to active service in place of a justice or judge who is temporarily incapacitated as provided in G.S. 7A-39.5.

(b) In addition to the compensation or retirement allowance he would otherwise be entitled to receive by law, each emergency justice or emergency judge recalled for temporary active service shall be paid by the State his actual expenses, plus three hundred dollars ($300.00) for each day of active service rendered upon recall. No recalled retired or emergency justice or judge shall receive from the State total annual compensation for judicial services in excess of that received by an active justice or judge of the bench to which the justice or judge is being recalled. (1967, c. 108, s. 1; 1973, c. 640, s. 3; 1977, c. 736, s. 1; 1979, c. 884, s. 1; 1981, c. 455, s. 3; c. 859, s. 46; 1981 (Reg. Sess., 1982), c. 1253, s. 2; 1983, c. 784; 1985, c. 698, ss. 9(a), 16(b); 1987 (Reg. Sess., 1988), c. 1086, s. 31(a); 2002-159, s. 25.)

§ 7A-39.4. Retirement creates vacancy.

The retirement of any justice of the Supreme Court or any judge of the Court of Appeals under the provisions of this Article shall create a vacancy in his office to be filled as provided by law. (1967, c. 108, s. 1.)

§ 7A-39.5. Recall of emergency justice or emergency judge upon temporary incapacity of a justice or judge.

(a) Upon the request of any justice of the Supreme Court who has been advised in writing by a reputable and competent physician that he is temporarily incapable of performing efficiently and promptly all the duties of his office, the Chief Justice may recall any emergency justice who, in his opinion, is competent to perform the duties of an associate justice, to serve temporarily in the place of the justice in whose behalf he is recalled; provided, that when the incapacity of a justice of the Supreme Court is such that he cannot request the recall of an emergency justice to serve in his place, an order of recall may be issued by the Chief Justice upon satisfactory medical proof of the facts upon which the order of recall must be based. Orders of recall shall be in writing and entered upon the minutes of the court.

(b) Upon the request of any judge of the Court of Appeals who has been advised in writing by a reputable and competent physician that he is temporarily incapable of performing efficiently and promptly all the duties of his office, the Chief Judge may recall any emergency judge who, in his opinion, is competent to perform the duties of a judge of the Court of Appeals, to serve temporarily in the place of the judge in whose behalf he is recalled; provided, that when the incapacity of a judge of the Court of Appeals is such that he cannot request the recall of an emergency judge to serve in his place, an order of recall may be issued by the Chief Judge upon satisfactory medical proof of the facts upon which the order of recall must be based. If the Chief Judge does not recall an emergency judge to serve in the place of the temporarily incapacitated judge, the Chief Justice may recall an emergency justice who, in his opinion, is competent to perform the duties of a judge of the Court of Appeals, to serve temporarily in the place of the judge in whose behalf he is recalled. In no case, however, may more than one emergency justice or emergency judge serve on one panel of the Court of Appeals at any given time. Orders of recall shall be in writing and entered upon the minutes of the court. (1967, c. 108, s. 1; 1985, c. 698, s. 16(c).)

§ 7A-39.6. Application to the Governor; commission as emergency justice or emergency judge.

No retired justice of the Supreme Court or retired judge of the Court of Appeals may become an emergency justice or emergency judge except upon his written application to the Governor certifying his desire and ability to serve as an emergency justice or emergency judge. If the Governor is satisfied that the applicant qualifies under G.S. 7A-39.3(a) to become an emergency justice or emergency judge and that he is physically and mentally able to perform the official duties of an emergency justice or emergency judge, he shall issue to such applicant a commission as an emergency justice or emergency judge of the court from which he retired. The commission shall be effective upon the date of its issue and shall terminate when the judge to whom it is issued reaches the maximum age for judicial service under G.S. 7A-4.20(a). (1967, c. 108, s. 1; 1977, c. 736, s. 2; 1979, c. 884, s. 2.)

§ 7A-39.7. Jurisdiction and authority of emergency justices and emergency judges.

An emergency justice or emergency judge shall not have or possess any jurisdiction or authority to hear arguments or participate in the consideration and decision of any cause or perform any other duty or function of a justice of the Supreme Court or judge of the Court of Appeals, respectively, except while serving under an order of recall and in respect to appeals, motions, and other matters heard, considered, and decided by the court during the period of his temporary service under such order; and the justice of the Supreme Court or judge of the Court of Appeals in whose behalf an emergency justice or emergency judge is recalled to active service shall be disqualified to participate in the consideration and decision of any question presented to the court by appeal, motion or otherwise in which any emergency justice or emergency judge recalled in his behalf participated. (1967, c. 108, s. 1.)

§ 7A-39.8. Court authorized to adopt rules.

The Supreme Court shall prescribe rules respecting the filing of opinions prepared by an emergency justice or an emergency judge after his period of temporary service has expired, and any other matter deemed necessary and consistent with the provisions of this Article. (1967, c. 108, s. 1.)

§ 7A-39.9. Chief Justice and Chief Judge may recall and terminate recall of justices and judges; procedure when Chief Justice or Chief Judge incapacitated.

(a) Decisions of the Chief Justice and the Chief Judge regarding recall of emergency justices and emergency judges, when not in conflict with the provisions of this Article, are final.

(b) The Chief Justice or Chief Judge, may, at any time, in his discretion, cancel any order of recall issued by him or fix the termination date thereof.

(c) Whenever the Chief Justice is the justice in whose behalf an emergency justice is recalled to temporary service, the powers vested in him as Chief Justice by this article shall be exercised by the associate justice senior in point of time served on the Supreme Court. Whenever the Chief Judge is the judge in whose behalf an emergency judge or justice is recalled to temporary service the powers vested in him as Chief Judge by this article shall be exercised by the associate judge senior in point of time served on the Court of Appeals. If two or more judges have served the same length of time on the Court of Appeals, the eldest shall be deemed the senior judge. (1967, c. 108, s. 1; 1985, c. 698, s. 16(d), (e).)

§ 7A-39.10. Article applicable to previously retired justices.

All provisions of this Article shall apply to every justice of the Supreme Court who has heretofore retired and is receiving compensation as an emergency justice. (1967, c. 108, s. 1.)

§ 7A-39.11. Retirement on account of total and permanent disability.

Every justice of the Supreme Court or judge of the Court of Appeals who has served for eight years or more on the Supreme Court, the Court of Appeals, or the superior court, or as Administrative Officer of the Courts, or in any combination of these offices, and who while in active service becomes totally and permanently disabled so as to be unable to perform efficiently the duties of his office, and who retires by reason of such disability, shall receive for life compensation equal to two thirds of the annual salary from time to time received by the occupant or occupants of the office from which he retired. In determining whether a judge is eligible for retirement under this section, time served as district solicitor of the superior court prior to January 1, 1971, may be included. Whenever any justice or judge claims retirement benefits under this section on account of total and permanent disability, the Governor and Council of State, acting together, shall, after notice and an opportunity to be heard is given the applicant, by a majority vote of said body, make findings of fact from the evidence offered. Such findings of fact shall be reduced to writing and entered upon the minutes of the Council of State. The findings so made shall be conclusive as to such matters and determine the right of the applicant to retirement benefits under this section. Justices and judges retired under the provisions of this section are not subject to recall as emergency justices or judges. (1967, c. 108, s. 1.)

§ 7A-39.12. Applicability of §§ 7A-39.2 and 7A-39.11.

The provisions of G.S. 7A-39.2 and 7A-39.11 shall apply only to justices and judges who entered into office prior to January 1, 1974. The extent of such application is specified in Chapter 135, Article 4 (Uniform Judicial Retirement Act). (1973, c. 640, s. 5.)

§ 7A-39.13. Recall of active and emergency justices and judges who have reached mandatory retirement age.

Justices and judges retired because they have reached the mandatory retirement age, and emergency justices and judges whose commissions have expired because they have reached the mandatory retirement age, may be temporarily recalled to active service under the following circumstances:

(1) The justice or judge must consent to the recall.

(2) The Chief Justice may recall retired justices to serve on the Supreme Court or on the Court of Appeals, and the Chief Judge may recall retired judges of the Court of Appeals to serve on that court.

(3) The period of recall shall not exceed six months, but it may be renewed for an additional six months if the emergency for which the recall was ordered continues.

(4) Prior to recall, the Chief Justice or the Chief Judge, as the case may be, shall satisfy himself that the justice or judge being recalled is capable of efficiently and promptly performing the duties of the office to which recalled.

(5) Recall is authorized only to replace an active justice or judge who is temporarily incapacitated.

(6) Jurisdiction and authority of a recalled justice or judge is as specified in G.S. 7A-39.7.

(7) The Supreme Court and the Court of Appeals, as the case may be, shall prescribe rules respecting the filing of opinions prepared by a retired justice or judge after his period of temporary service has expired, and respecting any other matter deemed necessary and consistent with this section.

(8) Compensation of recalled retired justices and judges is the same as for recalled emergency justices and judges under G.S. 7A-39.3(b).

(9) Recall shall be evidenced by a commission signed by the Chief Justice or Chief Judge, as the case may be. (1981, c. 455, s. 2; 1985, c. 698, s. 16(f).)

§ 7A-39.14. Recall by Chief Justice of retired or emergency justices or judges for temporary vacancy.

(a) In addition to the authority granted to the Chief Justice under G.S. 7A-39.5 to recall emergency justices and under G.S. 7A-39.13 to recall retired justices, the Chief Justice may recall not more than one retired or emergency justice or retired emergency judge of the Court of Appeals, including an emergency justice or judge whose commission has expired because he has reached the mandatory retirement age, in the following circumstances:

(1) If a vacancy exists on the Supreme Court, he may recall an emergency or retired justice to serve on that court until the vacancy is filled in accordance with law.

(2) If a vacancy exists on the Court of Appeals, he may recall an emergency or retired justice of the Supreme Court or judge of the Court of Appeals to serve on the Court of Appeals until the vacancy is filled in accordance with law.

(3) With the concurrence of a majority of the Supreme Court, he may recall an emergency or retired justice to serve on the Supreme Court in place of a sitting justice who, as determined by the Chief Justice, is temporarily unable to perform all of the duties of his office.

(4) With the concurrence of a majority of the Supreme Court, he may recall an emergency or retired justice of the Supreme Court or judge of the Court of

Appeals to serve on the Court of Appeals in place of a sitting judge who, as determined by the Chief Justice, is temporarily unable to perform all of the duties of his office.

(b)   No judge or justice may be recalled unless he consents to the recall. Orders of recall issued pursuant to this section must be in writing and entered on the minutes of the court. In addition, if the judge or justice is recalled pursuant to subdivision (a)(3) or (a)(4), the order shall contain a finding by the Chief Justice setting out, in detail, the reason for the recall.

(c)   A judge or justice recalled pursuant to subdivision (a)(1) or (a)(2) of this section:

(1)   Has the same authority and jurisdiction granted to emergency justices and judges under G.S. 7A-39.7;

(2)   Is subject to rules adopted pursuant to G.S. 7A-39.8 regarding filing of opinions and other matters; and

(3)   Is compensated as are other retired or emergency justices or judges recalled for service pursuant to G.S. 7A-39.5 or G.S. 7A-39.13.

(d)   A judge or justice recalled pursuant to subdivision (a)(3) or (a)(4) of this section:

(1)   Has the same authority and jurisdiction granted to emergency justices and judges under G.S. 7A-39.7;

(2)   Is subject to rules adopted pursuant to G.S. 7A-39.8 regarding filing of opinions and other matters;

(3)   May, after the return of the judge or justice in whose place he was sitting, complete the duties assigned to him before the return of that judge or justice; and

(4)   Is compensated as are other retired or emergency justices or judges recalled for service pursuant to G.S. 7A-39.5 or G.S. 7A-39.13.

(e)   A retired or emergency justice or judge may serve on the Supreme Court or Court of Appeals pursuant to subdivision (a)(3) or (a)(4) only if he is recalled to serve temporarily in place of a sitting justice or judge who is not temporarily incapacitated under circumstances that would permit temporary service of the retired or emergency justice or judge pursuant to G.S. 7A-39.5 or G.S. 7A-39.13. This section does not authorize more than seven justices to serve on the Supreme Court at any given time, nor does it authorize more than 15 justices and judges to serve on the Court of Appeals at any given time. In no case may more than one emergency justice or emergency judge serve on one panel of the Court of Appeals at any given time.

(f)   Repealed by Session Laws 1989, c. 795, s. 27.1. (1985, c. 698, s. 15(a), (b); 1985 (Reg. Sess., 1986), c. 851, s. 3; c. 1014, s. 225; 1987, c. 703, s. 5; c. 738, ss. 131(a), (b); 1989, c. 795, s. 27.1; 2009-570, s. 1.)

§ 7A-39.15. Emergency recall judges of the Court of Appeals.

(a)   A retired justice or judge of the Appellate Division of the General Court of Justice is eligible to be appointed as an emergency recall judge of the Court of Appeals under the following circumstances:

(1)   The justice or judge has retired under the provisions of the Consolidated Judicial Retirement Act, Article 4 of Chapter 135 of the General Statutes, or is eligible to receive a retirement allowance under that act;

(2)   The justice or judge has not reached the mandatory retirement age specified in G.S. 7A-4.20;

(3)   The justice or judge has served a total of at least five years as a judge or justice of the General Court of Justice, provided that at least six months was served in the Appellate Division, whether or not otherwise eligible to serve as an emergency justice or judge of the Appellate Division of the General Court of Justice;

(4)   The judicial service of the justice or judge ended within the preceding 15 years; and

(5)   The justice or judge has applied to the Governor for appointment as an emergency recall judge of the Court of Appeals in the same manner as is provided for application in G.S. 7A-53. If the Governor is satisfied that the applicant meets the requirements of this section and is physically and mentally able to perform the duties of a judge of the Court of Appeals, the Governor shall issue a commission appointing the applicant as an emergency recall judge of

the Court of Appeals until the applicant reaches the mandatory retirement age for judges of the Court of Appeals specified in G.S. 7A-4.20.

Any former justice or judge of the Appellate Division of the General Court of Justice who otherwise meets the requirements of this section to be appointed an emergency recall judge of the Court of Appeals, but who has already reached the mandatory retirement age for judges of the Court of Appeals set forth in G.S. 7A-4.20, may apply to the Governor to be appointed as an emergency recall judge of the Court of Appeals as provided in this section. If the Governor issues a commission to the applicant, the retired justice or judge is subject to recall as an emergency recall judge of the Court of Appeals as provided in this section.

(b)   Notwithstanding any other provision of law, the Chief Judge of the Court of Appeals may recall and assign one or more emergency recall judges of the Court of Appeals, not to exceed three at any one time, provided funds are available, if the Chief Judge determines that one or more emergency recall judges of the Court of Appeals are necessary to discharge the court's business expeditiously.

(c)   Any emergency recall judge of the Court of Appeals appointed as provided in this section shall be subject to recall in the following manner:

(1)   The judge shall consent to the recall;

(2)   The Chief Judge of the Court of Appeals may order the recall;

(3)   Prior to ordering recall, the Chief Judge of the Court of Appeals shall be satisfied that the recalled judge is capable of efficiently and promptly discharging the duties of the office to which recalled;

(4)   Orders of recall and assignment shall be in writing, evidenced by a commission signed by the Chief Judge of the Court of Appeals, and entered upon the minutes of the permanent records of the Court of Appeals;

(5)   Compensation, expenses, and allowances of emergency recall judges of the Court of Appeals are the same as for recalled emergency superior court judges under G.S. 7A-52(b);

(6)   Emergency recall judges assigned under those provisions shall have the same powers and duties, when duly assigned to hold court, as provided for by law for judges of the Court of Appeals;

(7) Emergency recall judges of the Court of Appeals are subject to assignment in the same manner as provided for by G.S. 7A-16 and G.S. 7A-19;

(8) Emergency recall judges of the Court of Appeals shall be subject to rules adopted pursuant to G.S. 7A-39.8 regarding the filing of opinions and other matters;

(9) Emergency recall judges of the Court of Appeals shall be subject to the provisions and requirements of the Canons of Judicial Conduct during the term of assignment; and

(10) An emergency recall judge of the Court of Appeals shall not engage in the practice of law during any period for which the emergency recall Court of Appeals judgeship is commissioned. However, this subdivision shall not be construed to prohibit an emergency recall judge of the Court of Appeals appointed pursuant to this section from serving as a referee, arbitrator, or mediator during service as an emergency recall judge of the Court of Appeals so long as the service does not conflict with or interfere with the judge's service as an emergency recall judge of the Court of Appeals.

(d) A justice or judge commissioned as an emergency recall judge of the Court of Appeals is also eligible to receive a commission as an emergency special superior court judge. However, no justice or judge who has been recalled as provided in this section shall, during the period so recalled and assigned, contemporaneously serve as an emergency special superior court judge or emergency justice of the General Court of Justice. (1995, c. 108, s. 1.)

SUBCHAPTER III. SUPERIOR COURT DIVISION OF THE GENERAL COURT OF JUSTICE.

Article 7.

Organization.

§ 7A-40. Composition; judicial powers of clerk.

The Superior Court Division of the General Court of Justice consists of the several superior courts of the State. The clerk of superior court in the exercise of the judicial power conferred upon him as ex officio judge of probate, and in the exercise of other judicial powers conferred upon him by law in respect of special proceedings and the administration of guardianships and trusts, is a judicial officer of the Superior Court Division, and not a separate court. (1965, c. 310, s. 1; 1967, c. 691, s. 1; 1969, c. 1190, s. 4; 1971, c. 377, s. 4.)

§ 7A-41. Superior court divisions and districts; judges.

(a) (Effective until January 1, 2015) The counties of the State are organized into judicial divisions and superior court districts, and each superior court district has the counties, and the number of regular resident superior court judges set forth in the following table, and for districts of less than a whole county, as set out in subsection (b) of this section:

Superior

Judicial Division	Court District	Counties	No. of Resident Judges
First	1	Camden, Chowan, Currituck, Dare, Gates, Pasquotank, Perquimans	2
First	2	Beaufort, Hyde, Martin, Tyrrell, Washington	1
First	3A	Pitt	2
Second	3B	Carteret, Craven, Pamlico	3
Second	4A	Duplin, Jones, Sampson	1

Second	4B	Onslow	1
Second	5A	(part of New Hanover, part of Pender see subsection (b))	1
	5B	(part of New Hanover, part of Pender see subsection (b))	1
	5C	(part of New Hanover, see subsection (b))	1
First	6A	Halifax	1
First	6B	Bertie, Hertford, Northampton	1
First	7A	Nash	1
First	7B	(part of Wilson, part of Edgecombe, see subsection (b))	1
First	7C	(part of Wilson, part of Edgecombe, see subsection (b))	1
Second	8A	Lenoir and Greene	1
Second	8B	Wayne	1
Third	9	Franklin, Granville, Vance, Warren	2
Third	9A	Person, Caswell	1
Third	10A	(part of Wake,	1

		see subsection (b))	
Third	10B	(part of Wake,	1
		see subsection (b))	
Third	10C	(part of Wake,	1
		see subsection (b))	
Third	10D	(part of Wake,	1
		see subsection (b))	
Third	10E	(part of Wake,	1
		see subsection (b))	
Third	10F	(part of Wake,	1
		see subsection (b))	
Fourth	11A	Harnett, Lee	1
Fourth	11B	Johnston	1
Fourth	12A	(part of Cumberland,	1
		see subsection (b))	
Fourth	12B	(part of Cumberland,	1
		see subsection (b))	
Fourth	12C	(part of Cumberland,	2
		see subsection (b))	
Fourth	13A	Bladen, Columbus	1
Fourth	13B	Brunswick	1
Third	14A	(part of Durham,	1
		see subsection (b))	
Third	14B	(part of Durham,	3
		see subsection (b))	

Third	15A	Alamance	2
Third	15B	Orange, Chatham	2
Fourth	16A	Scotland, Hoke	1
Fourth	16B	Robeson	2
Fifth	17A	Rockingham	2
Fifth	17B	Stokes, Surry	2
Fifth	18A	(part of Guilford, see subsection (b))	1
Fifth	18B	(part of Guilford, see subsection (b))	1
Fifth	18C	(part of Guilford, see subsection (b))	1
Fifth	18D	(part of Guilford, see subsection (b))	1
Fifth	18E	(part of Guilford, see subsection (b))	1
Sixth	19A	Cabarrus	1
Fifth	19B	Montgomery, Randolph	1
Sixth	19C	Rowan	1
Fifth	19D	Moore	1
Sixth	20A	Anson, Richmond, Stanley	2
Sixth	20B	Union	2
Fifth	21A	(part of Forsyth, see subsection (b))	1

Fifth	21B	(part of Forsyth, see subsection (b))	1
Fifth	21C	(part of Forsyth, see subsection (b))	1
Fifth	21D	(part of Forsyth, see subsection (b))	1
Sixth	22A	Alexander, Iredell	2
Sixth	22B	Davidson, Davie	2
Fifth	23	Alleghany, Ashe, Wilkes, Yadkin	1
Eighth	24	Avery, Madison, Mitchell, Watauga, Yancey	2
Seventh	25A	Burke, Caldwell	2
Seventh	25B	Catawba	2
Seventh	26A	(part of Mecklenburg, see subsection (b))	2
Seventh	26B	(part of Mecklenburg, see subsection (b))	3
Seventh	26C	(part of Mecklenburg, see subsection (b))	2
Seventh	27A	Gaston	2
Seventh	27B	Cleveland, Lincoln	2
Eighth	28	Buncombe	2
Eighth	29A	McDowell, Rutherford	1

Eighth	29B	Henderson, Polk, Transylvania	1
Eighth	30A	Cherokee, Clay, Graham, Macon, Swain	1
Eighth	30B	Haywood, Jackson	1.

(a) (Effective January 1, 2015) The counties of the State are organized into judicial divisions and superior court districts, and each superior court district has the counties, and the number of regular resident superior court judges set forth in the following table, and for districts of less than a whole county, as set out in subsection (b) of this section:

Judicial Division	Superior Court District	Counties	No. of Resident Judges
First	1	Camden, Chowan, Currituck, Dare, Gates, Pasquotank, Perquimans	2
First	2	Beaufort, Hyde, Martin, Tyrrell, Washington	1
First	3A	Pitt	2
Second	3B	Carteret, Craven, Pamlico	3

Second	4A	Duplin, Jones, Sampson	1
Second	4B	Onslow	1
Second	5A	(part of New Hanover, part of Pender see subsection (b))	1
	5B	(part of New Hanover, part of Pender see subsection (b))	1
	5C	(part of New Hanover, see subsection (b))	1
First	6A	Halifax	1
First	6B	Bertie, Hertford, Northampton	1
First	7A	Nash	1
First	7B	(part of Wilson, part of Edgecombe, see subsection (b))	1
First	7C	(part of Wilson, part of Edgecombe, see subsection (b))	1
Second	8A	Lenoir and Greene	1
Second	8B	Wayne	1
Third	9	Franklin, Granville, Vance, Warren	2
Third	9A	Person, Caswell	1

Third	10A	(part of Wake, see subsection (b))	1
Third	10B	(part of Wake, see subsection (b))	1
Third	10C	(part of Wake, see subsection (b))	1
Third	10D	(part of Wake, see subsection (b))	1
Third	10E	(part of Wake, see subsection (b))	1
Third	10F	(part of Wake, see subsection (b))	1
Fourth	11A	Harnett, Lee	1
Fourth	11B	Johnston	1
Fourth	12A	(part of Cumberland, see subsection (b))	1
Fourth	12B	(part of Cumberland, see subsection (b))	1
Fourth	12C	(part of Cumberland, see subsection (b))	2
Fourth	13A	Bladen, Columbus	1
Fourth	13B	Brunswick	1
Third	14A	(part of Durham, see subsection (b))	1

Third	14B	(part of Durham, see subsection (b))	3
Third	15A	Alamance	2
Third	15B	Orange, Chatham	2
Fourth	16A	Anson, Richmond, Scotland, Hoke	2
Fourth	16B	Robeson	2
Fifth	17A	Rockingham	2
Fifth	17B	Stokes, Surry	2
Fifth	18A	(part of Guilford, see subsection (b))	1
Fifth	18B	(part of Guilford, see subsection (b))	1
Fifth	18C	(part of Guilford, see subsection (b))	1
Fifth	18D	(part of Guilford, see subsection (b))	1
Fifth	18E	(part of Guilford, see subsection (b))	1
Sixth	19A	Cabarrus	1
Fifth	19B	Montgomery, Randolph	1
Sixth	19C	Rowan	1
Fourth	19D	Moore	1
Sixth	20A	Stanly	1
Sixth	20B	Union	2
Fifth	21A	(part of Forsyth,	1

		see subsection (b))	
Fifth	21B	(part of Forsyth, see subsection (b))	1
Fifth	21C	(part of Forsyth, see subsection (b))	1
Fifth	21D	(part of Forsyth, see subsection (b))	1
Sixth	22A	Alexander, Iredell	2
Sixth	22B	Davidson, Davie	2
Fifth	23	Alleghany, Ashe, Wilkes, Yadkin	1
Eighth	24	Avery, Madison, Mitchell, Watauga, Yancey	2
Seventh	25A	Burke, Caldwell	2
Seventh	25B	Catawba	2
Seventh	26A	(part of Mecklenburg, see subsection (b))	2
Seventh	26B	(part of Mecklenburg, see subsection (b))	3
Seventh	26C	(part of Mecklenburg, see subsection (b))	2
Seventh	27A	Gaston	2
Seventh	27B	Cleveland, Lincoln	2
Eighth	28	Buncombe	2

Eighth	29A	McDowell, Rutherford	1
Eighth	29B	Henderson, Polk, Transylvania	1
Eighth	30A	Cherokee, Clay, Graham, Macon, Swain	1
Eighth	30B	Haywood, Jackson	1.

(b) For superior court districts of less than a whole county, or with part of one county with part of another, the composition of the district and the number of judges is as follows:

(1) District 5A: New Hanover County: VTD: CF01, VTD: CF02, VTD: H01, VTD: H04, VTD: H06, VTD: H07: Block(s) 1290116072000, 1290116072001, 1290116072002, 1290116072003, 1290116072004, 1290116072005, 1290116072006, 1290116072007, 1290116072008, 1290116072009, 1290116072010, 1290116072011, 1290116072012, 1290116072013, 1290116072014, 1290116072015, 1290116072016, 1290116072017, 1290116072018, 1290116072019, 1290116072020, 1290116072021, 1290116072022, 1290116073000, 1290116073001, 1290116073002, 1290116073003, 1290116073004, 1290116073005, 1290116073006, 1290116073007, 1290116073008, 1290116073009, 1290116073010, 1290116073012, 1290116073013, 1290116073014, 1290116073016, 1290116073017, 1290116073018, 1290116073019, 1290116073020, 1290116073021, 1290116073022, 1290116073023, 1290116073024, 1290116073025, 1290116073026, 1290116073027, 1290116073028, 1290116073029, 1290116073030, 1290116073031, 1290116073032, 1290116073033, 1290116073034, 1290116073035, 1290116073036, 1290116073037, 1290116073038, 1290116073039, 1290116073040, 1290116073041, 1290116073042, 1290116073043, 1290116073044, 1290116073045, 1290116073046, 1290116073047, 1290116073048, 1290116073049, 1290116073050, 1290116081021, 1290116081022, 1290116081023, 1290116081024, 1290116081025, 1290116081026, 1290116081027, 1290116081028, 1290116081029, 1290116081030, 1290116081031, 1290116081032, 1290116081033, 1290116081034, 1290116081035, 1290116081036, 1290116081037, 1290116081038, 1290116081039, 1290116081040, 1290116081041, 1290116081042, 1290116081049; VTD: W03, VTD: W08, VTD: W15, VTD: W25, VTD: W26, VTD: W27, VTD: W29; Pender County: VTD: CL05, VTD: CS04, VTD: CT03, VTD: GR06, VTD: UH08, VTD: UU17. It has one judge.

(2) District 5B: New Hanover County: VTD: CF03, VTD: H02, VTD: H03: Block(s) 1290119024001, 1290119024002, 1290119024003, 1290119024005, 1290119024008, 1290119024009, 1290119024010, 1290119035012, 1290119035013, 1290119035016, 1290119042006, 1290119042007, 1290119042008, 1290119042009, 1290119042010, 1290119042011, 1290119042012, 1290119042013, 1290119042014, 1290119042015, 1290119042016, 1290119042017, 1290119042018, 1290119042019, 1290119042020, 1290119042021, 1290119042022, 1290119042023, 1290119042024, 1290119042025, 1290119042027, 1290119042028, 1290119042029, 1290119042030, 1290119042031,

1290119042032, 1290119042033, 1290119042034, 1290119042035, 1290119042036, 1290119042037, 1290119042038, 1290119042039, 1290120013000, 1290120013001, 1290120013002, 1290120013003, 1290120013004, 1290120013005, 1290120013006, 1290120013007, 1290120013008, 1290120013009, 1290120013010, 1290120013011, 1290120013012, 1290120013013, 1290120013014, 1290120013015, 1290120013016; VTD: H05, VTD: H07: Block(s) 1290116071000, 1290116071001, 1290116071002, 1290116071003, 1290116071004, 1290116071005, 1290116071006, 1290116071007, 1290116071009, 1290116071010, 1290116071011, 1290116071012, 1290116071013, 1290116071014, 1290116071015, 1290116071016, 1290116071017, 1290116071018, 1290116071019, 1290116071020, 1290116071021, 1290116071022, 1290116071023, 1290116071024, 1290116071025, 1290116073015, 1290116081046, 1290116082017, 1290116082018, 1290116082019, 1290116082020, 1290116082021, 1290116082022, 1290116082023, 1290116082024, 1290116082026, 1290116082027, 1290116082028, 1290116082029, 1290116082030, 1290116082031, 1290116082032, 1290116082033, 1290116082058, 1290116082060, 1290116082079, 1290116082081, 1290116082082, 1290116082084, 1290116082085, 1290116082086, 1290116082087, 1290116082088, 1290116082090, 1290116083001, 1290116083002, 1290116083010; VTD: H08, VTD: H09, VTD: W12, VTD: W13, VTD: W24, VTD: W28, VTD: W31: Block(s) 1290104003015, 1290104003018, 1290104003019, 1290104003020, 1290104003021, 1290104003027, 1290104003028, 1290104003029, 1290104003030, 1290104003031, 1290104003032, 1290104003033, 1290104003034, 1290104003035, 1290104003036, 1290104003037, 1290104003038, 1290104003039, 1290104003040, 1290104003041, 1290104003042, 1290104003043, 1290106001000, 1290106001001, 1290106001002, 1290106001003, 1290106001004, 1290106001005, 1290106001006, 1290106001007, 1290106001008, 1290106001009, 1290106001010, 1290106001011, 1290106001012, 1290106001013, 1290106001014, 1290106001015, 1290106001016, 1290106001017, 1290106001018, 1290106001019, 1290106001020, 1290106001021, 1290106001022, 1290106001023, 1290106001024, 1290106001025, 1290106001026, 1290106002000, 1290106002001, 1290106002002, 1290106002003, 1290106002004, 1290106002005, 1290106002006, 1290106002007, 1290106002008, 1290106002009, 1290106002010, 1290106002011, 1290106002012, 1290106002013, 1290106002014, 1290106002015, 1290106002016, 1290106002017, 1290106002018, 1290106002019, 1290106002020, 1290106002021, 1290106002022, 1290106002023, 1290106002024, 1290106002025, 1290106002026, 1290106002027, 1290106002028, 1290106002029, 1290106002030, 1290106002031, 1290106002032, 1290106002033, 1290106002034, 1290106002035, 1290106002036, 1290106002037, 1290106002040, 1290106002039, 1290106002040, 1290106002041, 1290106002042, 1290106002043, 1290106002044, 1290106002045, 1290106002046, 1290106002047, 1290106002048, 1290106002049, 1290106002050, 1290106002051, 1290106002052, 1290106002053, 1290106002054, 1290107001021, 1290107001032, 1290107001036, 1290107001037, 1290107002000, 1290107002017, 1290107002018; VTD: WB; Pender County: VTD: CF11, VTD: LC09, VTD: LT18, VTD: LU16, VTD: MH07, VTD: MT19, VTD: NB01, VTD: PL10, VTD: RP20, VTD: SB02, VTD: SC13, VTD: SH12, VTD: SP15, VTD: UT14. It has one judge.

(3) District 5C: New Hanover County: VTD: FP01, VTD: FP02, VTD: FP03, VTD: FP04, VTD: FP05, VTD: H03: Block(s) 1290118001000, 1290119023000, 1290119023001, 1290119023002, 1290119023003, 1290119023004, 1290119023005, 1290119023006, 1290119023019, 1290119023020, 1290119023023, 1290119023024, 1290119023025, 1290119023026, 1290119023027, 1290119023028, 1290119023029, 1290119023030, 1290119023031, 1290119023032, 1290119023033, 1290119023034, 1290119023035, 1290119023036, 1290119024000, 1290119024006, 1290119024007, 1290120012000, 1290120012001, 1290120012002, 1290120012003, 1290120012004, 1290120012005, 1290120012006,

1290120012007, 1290120012008, 1290120012009, 1290120012010, 1290120012011, 1290120012012, 1290120012013, 1290120012014, 1290120012015, 1290120012016, 1290120012017, 1290120012018, 1290120012019, 1290120012020, 1290120012021, 1290120012022, 1290120012023, 1290120012034, 1290120012035, 1290120012036, 1290120012037, 1290120013017, 1290120013018, 1290120013019, 1290120013020, 1290120013021, 1290120013022, 1290120013023, 1290120013024, 1290120013025, 1290120013026, 1290120013027, 1290120013028, 1290120013029, 1290120013030, 1290120013031, 1290120013032, 1290120013033, 1290120013034, 1290120013035, 1290120013036, 1290120013037, 1290120013038, 1290120013039, 1290120014000, 1290120014001, 1290120014002, 1290120014003, 1290120014004, 1290120014005, 1290120014013, 1290120014014, 1290120014015, 1290120014016, 1290120014017, 1290120014018, 1290120014019, 1290120014020, 1290120014021, 1290120014022, 1290120014023, 1290120014024; VTD: M02, VTD: M03, VTD: M04, VTD: M05, VTD: W16, VTD: W17, VTD: W18, VTD: W21, VTD: W30, VTD: W31: Block(s) 1290105023010, 1290105023020, 1290105023021, 1290105023022, 1290105023023, 1290105023024, 1290105023025, 1290105023026, 1290105023027, 1290105023028, 1290105023029, 1290105023030, 1290105023031, 1290105023032, 1290105023033, 1290105023034, 1290105023035, 1290105024024, 1290105024025, 1290105024026, 1290105024032, 1290105024033, 1290105024034, 1290105024035, 1290106003000, 1290106003001, 1290106003002, 1290106003003, 1290106003004, 1290106003005, 1290106003006, 1290106003007, 1290106003008, 1290106003009, 1290106003010, 1290106003011, 1290106003012, 1290106003013, 1290106003014, 1290106003015, 1290106003016, 1290106003017, 1290106003018, 1290106003019, 1290106003020, 1290106003021, 1290106003022, 1290106003023, 1290106003024, 1290106003025, 1290106003026, 1290106003027, 1290106003028, 1290106003029, 1290106003030, 1290106003031, 1290106003032, 1290106003033, 1290106003034, 1290106003035, 1290106003036, 1290106003037, 1290106003038, 1290106003039, 1290106003040, 1290106003041, 1290106003042, 1290106003043, 1290106003044, 1290106003045, 1290106003046, 1290106003047, 1290106003048, 1290106003049, 1290106003050, 1290106003051, 1290106003052, 1290106003053, 1290106003054, 1290106003055, 1290106003056. It has one judge.

(4) District 7B: Edgecombe County: VTD: 1101: Block(s) 0650213001035; VTD: 1201, VTD: 1202, VTD: 1203, VTD: 1204, VTD: 1205: Block(s) 0650203001005, 0650203001006, 0650203001007, 0650203001008, 0650203001009, 0650203001010, 0650203001011, 0650203001012, 0650203001013, 0650203001014, 0650203001015, 0650203001016, 0650203001017, 0650204001000, 0650204001001, 0650204001002, 0650204001003, 0650204001004, 0650204001005, 0650204001006, 0650204001007, 0650204001008, 0650204001009, 0650204001010, 0650204001011, 0650204001012, 0650204001013, 0650204001014, 0650204001015, 0650204001016, 0650204001017, 0650204001018, 0650204001019, 0650204001020, 0650204001021, 0650204001022, 0650204001023, 0650204001024, 0650204001025, 0650204001026, 0650204001027, 0650204001028, 0650204001029, 0650204001030, 0650204001031, 0650204001032, 0650204001033, 0650204001034, 0650204001035, 0650204001036, 0650204001037, 0650204001038, 0650204001039, 0650204001040, 0650204001041, 0650204001042, 0650204001043, 0650204001044, 0650204001045, 0650204001046, 0650204001047, 0650204001048, 0650204001049, 0650204002000, 0650204002001, 0650204002002, 0650204002003, 0650204002004, 0650204002005, 0650204002006, 0650204002007, 0650204002008, 0650204002009, 0650204002010, 0650204002011, 0650204002012, 0650204002013, 0650204002014, 0650204002015, 0650204002016, 0650204002017, 0650204002018, 0650204002019, 0650204002020, 0650204002021, 0650204002022, 0650204002023, 0650204002024, 0650204002025; VTD: 1301: 0650214002017; VTD: 1401; Wilson County: VTD:

PRBL: Block(s) 1950009001045, 1950009001046; VTD: PRGA: 1950007001065, 1950007001066, 1950007001067, 1950012001000, 1950012001001, 1950012001002, 1950012001003, 1950012001012, 1950012001013, 1950012001014, 1950012001015, 1950012001016, 1950012001017, 1950012001018, 1950012001019, 1950012001020, 1950012001021, 1950012001022, 1950012001023, 1950012001025, 1950012001026, 1950012001031, 1950012001032, 1950012001033, 1950012001034, 1950012001035, 1950012001036, 1950012001038, 1950012002000, 1950012002001, 1950012002002, 1950012002003, 1950012002004, 1950012002005, 1950012002006, 1950012002007, 1950012002008, 1950012002009, 1950012002010, 1950012002011, 1950012002012, 1950012002013, 1950012002014, 1950012002016, 1950012003000, 1950012003001, 1950012003002, 1950012003003, 1950012003004, 1950012003005, 1950012003006, 1950012003007, 1950012003008, 1950012003009, 1950012003010, 1950012003011, 1950012003012, 1950012003013, 1950012003014, 1950012003015, 1950012003016, 1950012003017, 1950012003018, 1950012003019, 1950012003020, 1950012003021; VTD: PRSA: 1950011001025, 1950011001028, 1950011001030, 1950011002000; VTD: PRST: 1950008022045, 1950008022047, 1950008022055, 1950008022059, 1950008022060, 1950008022061, 1950008022063, 1950008023031, 1950008023032, 1950008023033, 1950008023034, 1950008023035, 1950008023039; VTD: PRTO: 1950012001004, 1950012001005, 1950012001006, 1950012001007, 1950012001008, 1950012001009, 1950012001010, 1950012001011, 1950012001024, 1950013001000, 1950013001001, 1950013001002, 1950013001003, 1950013001004, 1950013001005, 1950013001006, 1950013001007, 1950013001008, 1950013001009, 1950013001010, 1950013001011, 1950013001012, 1950013001013, 1950013001014, 1950013001015, 1950013001016, 1950013001017, 1950013001018, 1950013001019, 1950013001020, 1950013001021, 1950013001022, 1950013001023, 1950013001024, 1950013001025, 1950013001026, 1950013001027, 1950013001028, 1950013001029, 1950013001030, 1950013001031, 1950013001032, 1950013001033, 1950013001034, 1950013001035, 1950013001036, 1950013001037, 1950013001038, 1950013001039, 1950013001040, 1950013001041, 1950013001042, 1950013001043, 1950013001044, 1950013001045, 1950013002000, 1950013002001, 1950013002002, 1950013002003, 1950013002004, 1950013002005, 1950013002006, 1950013002007, 1950013002008, 1950013002009, 1950013002010, 1950013002011, 1950013002012, 1950013002013, 1950013002014, 1950013002015, 1950013002016, 1950013002017, 1950013002018, 1950013002019, 1950013002020, 1950013002021, 1950013002022, 1950013002023, 1950013002024, 1950013002025, 1950013002026, 1950013002027, 1950013002028, 1950013002029, 1950013002030, 1950013002031, 1950013002032, 1950013002033, 1950013002034, 1950013002035, 1950013002036, 1950013002037, 1950013002038, 1950013002039, 1950013002040, 1950013002041, 1950013002042, 1950013002043, 1950013002044, 1950013002045, 1950013002046, 1950013002047, 1950013002048, 1950013002049, 1950013002050, 1950013002051, 1950013002052, 1950013002053, 1950013002054, 1950013002055, 1950013002056, 1950013002057, 1950013002058, 1950013002059, 1950013002060, 1950013002061, 1950013002062, 1950013002063, 1950013002064, 1950013002065, 1950013002066, 1950013002067, 1950013002068, 1950013002069, 1950013002070, 1950013002074, 1950013002075, 1950013002078, 1950013002079, 1950013002080, 1950013002081, 1950013002082, 1950013002083, 1950013002084, 1950013002087, 1950013002088; VTD: PRWA, VTD: PRWB: Block(s) 1950002001000, 1950002001001, 1950002001002, 1950002001003, 1950002001004, 1950002001005, 1950002001006, 1950002001007, 1950002001008, 1950002001009, 1950002001010, 1950002001011, 1950002001012, 1950002001013, 1950002001014, 1950002001015, 1950002001016, 1950002001017, 1950002001018, 1950002001019, 1950002001020, 1950002001021, 1950002001022, 1950002001023, 1950002001024, 1950002001025, 1950002001026, 1950002001027, 1950002001028,

1950002001029, 1950002001030, 1950002001031, 1950002001032, 1950002001033,
1950002001034, 1950002001035, 1950002001036, 1950002001037, 1950002001038,
1950002001039, 1950002001040, 1950002001041, 1950002001042, 1950002001043,
1950002001044, 1950002001045, 1950002001046, 1950002001052, 1950002001053,
1950002001054, 1950002001055, 1950002001056, 1950002001057, 1950002001058,
1950002001059, 1950002001060, 1950002001062, 1950002001063, 1950002001064,
1950002001065, 1950003002000, 1950003002001, 1950003002002, 1950003002003,
1950003002004, 1950003002005, 1950003002006, 1950003002013, 1950003002017,
1950003002018, 1950003002019, 1950003002020, 1950003002021, 1950003002022,
1950003002023, 1950003002025, 1950003002026, 1950003002027, 1950003002028,
1950003002029, 1950003002030, 1950003002031, 1950003002032, 1950003002033,
1950003002034, 1950003002035, 1950003002036, 1950003002037, 1950003002038,
1950003002039, 1950008011000, 1950008011001, 1950008012000, 1950008012001,
1950008012002, 1950008012003; VTD: PRWC: 1950001003004, 1950001003005,
1950001003006, 1950001003007, 1950001003008, 1950001003015, 1950001003020,
1950001003021, 1950001004005, 1950001004006, 1950001004007, 1950001004008,
1950001004009, 1950001004017, 1950001004019, 1950001004021, 1950001004022,
1950001004023, 1950001004024, 1950001004025, 1950001004026; VTD: PRWE:
1950001002003, 1950001002004, 1950001002005, 1950001002024, 1950001002025; VTD:
PRWH, VTD: PRWN, VTD: PRWQ, VTD: PRWR. It has one judge.

(5) District 7C: Edgecombe County: VTD: 0101, VTD: 0102, VTD: 0103, VTD: 0104, VTD: 0201,
VTD: 0301, VTD: 0401, VTD: 0501, VTD: 0601, VTD: 0701, VTD: 0801, VTD: 0901, VTD: 1001,
VTD: 1101: Block(s) 0650213001009, 0650213001034, 0650213002000, 0650213002001,
0650213002002, 0650213002003, 0650213002004, 0650213002005, 0650213002006,
0650213002007, 0650213002008, 0650213002009, 0650213002010, 0650213002011,
0650213002012, 0650213002013, 0650213002014, 0650213002015, 0650213002016,
0650213002017, 0650213002018, 0650213002019, 0650213002022, 0650213002025,
0650213002026, 0650213002027, 0650213002028, 0650213002029, 0650213002035,
0650213002036, 0650213002037, 0650213002038, 0650213002039, 0650213002040,
0650213002041, 0650213002042, 0650213002043, 0650213002044, 0650213002045,
0650213002046, 0650213002048, 0650213002049, 0650213002050, 0650213002051,
0650213002052, 0650213002053, 0650213002054, 0650213002055, 0650213002056,
0650213002057, 0650213002058, 0650213002059, 0650213002060, 0650213002061,
0650213002062, 0650213002063, 0650213002064, 0650213002065, 0650213002066,
0650213002067, 0650213002068, 0650213002069, 0650213002070, 0650213002071,
0650213002072, 0650213002073, 0650213002074, 0650213002075, 0650213002076,
0650213002077, 0650213002078, 0650213002079, 0650213002080, 0650213002081,
0650213002082, 0650213002087, 0650213002088; VTD: 1205: 0650206001083, 0650206001084,
0650206001085, 0650206001086, 0650206001087, 0650206001089, 0650206001090,
0650206001091, 0650206001092; VTD: 1301: 0650214002000, 0650214002001, 0650214002002,
0650214002003, 0650214002004, 0650214002005, 0650214002006, 0650214002007,
0650214002008, 0650214002009, 0650214002010, 0650214002011, 0650214002012,
0650214002013, 0650214002014, 0650214002015, 0650214002016, 0650214002018,
0650214002019, 0650214002020, 0650214002021, 0650214002022, 0650214002023,
0650214002025, 0650214002026, 0650214002027, 0650214002028, 0650214002029,
0650214002030, 0650214002031, 0650214002032, 0650214002033, 0650214002034,
0650214002035, 0650214002036, 0650214002037, 0650214002038, 0650214002039,
0650214002040, 0650214002041, 0650214002042, 0650214002043; Wilson County: VTD: PRBL:
Block(s) 1950009001000, 1950009001001, 1950009001002, 1950009001003, 1950009001004,
1950009001005, 1950009001006, 1950009001007, 1950009001008, 1950009001009,

1950009001010, 1950009001011, 1950009001012, 1950009001013, 1950009001014, 1950009001015, 1950009001016, 1950009001017, 1950009001018, 1950009001019, 1950009001020, 1950009001021, 1950009001022, 1950009001023, 1950009001024, 1950009001025, 1950009001026, 1950009001027, 1950009001028, 1950009001029, 1950009001030, 1950009001031, 1950009001032, 1950009001033, 1950009001034, 1950009001035, 1950009001036, 1950009001037, 1950009001038, 1950009001039, 1950009001040, 1950009001041, 1950009001042, 1950009001043, 1950009001044, 1950009001047, 1950009001048, 1950009001049, 1950009001050, 1950009001051, 1950009001052, 1950009001053, 1950009001054, 1950009001055, 1950009001056, 1950009001057, 1950009001058, 1950009001059, 1950009001060, 1950009001061, 1950009001062, 1950009001063, 1950009001064, 1950009001065, 1950009001066, 1950009001067, 1950009001068, 1950009001069, 1950009001070, 1950009001071, 1950009001072, 1950009001073, 1950009001074, 1950009001075, 1950009002000, 1950009002001, 1950009002002, 1950009002003, 1950009002004, 1950009002005, 1950009002006, 1950009002007, 1950009002008, 1950009002009, 1950009002010, 1950009002011, 1950009002012, 1950009002013, 1950009002014, 1950009002015, 1950009002016, 1950009002017, 1950009002018, 1950009002019, 1950009002020, 1950009002021, 1950009002022, 1950009002023, 1950009002024, 1950009002025, 1950009002026, 1950009002027, 1950009002028, 1950009002029, 1950009002030, 1950009002031, 1950009002032, 1950009002033, 1950009002034, 1950009002035, 1950009002036, 1950009002037, 1950009002038, 1950009002039, 1950009002040, 1950009002041, 1950009002042, 1950009002043, 1950009002044, 1950009002045, 1950009002046, 1950009002047, 1950009002048, 1950009002049, 1950009002050, 1950009002051, 1950009002052, 1950009002053, 1950009002054, 1950009003000, 1950009003001, 1950009003002, 1950009003003, 1950009003004, 1950009003006, 1950009003007, 1950009003008, 1950009003009, 1950009003010, 1950009003011, 1950009003013, 1950009003014, 1950009003015, 1950009003016, 1950009003017, 1950009003018, 1950009003019, 1950009003020, 1950009003021, 1950009003022, 1950009003023, 1950009003024, 1950009003025, 1950009003026, 1950009003027, 1950009003028, 1950009003029, 1950009003030, 1950009003031, 1950009003032, 1950009003033, 1950009003034, 1950009003035, 1950009003036, 1950009003037, 1950009003038, 1950009003039, 1950009003040, 1950009003041, 1950010001023, 1950017001000, 1950017001001, 1950017001002, 1950017002021, 1950017002022, 1950017003004, 1950017003005, 1950017003006, 1950017003007, 1950017003008, 1950017003009, 1950017003010, 1950017003035, 1950017003036; VTD: PRCR, VTD: PRGA: Block(s) 1950012002015; VTD: PROL, VTD: PRSA: Block(s) 1950011001000, 1950011001001, 1950011001002, 1950011001003, 1950011001004, 1950011001005, 1950011001006, 1950011001007, 1950011001008, 1950011001009, 1950011001010, 1950011001011, 1950011001012, 1950011001013, 1950011001014, 1950011001015, 1950011001016, 1950011001017, 1950011001018, 1950011001019, 1950011001020, 1950011001021, 1950011001022, 1950011001023, 1950011001024, 1950011001026, 1950011001027, 1950011001029, 1950011001031, 1950011001032, 1950011001033, 1950011001034, 1950011001035, 1950011001036, 1950011001037, 1950011001038, 1950011001039, 1950011001040, 1950011001041, 1950011001042, 1950011001043, 1950011001044, 1950011001045, 1950011001046, 1950011001047, 1950011001048, 1950011001049, 1950011001050, 1950011002001, 1950011002002, 1950011002003, 1950011002004, 1950011002005, 1950011002006, 1950011002007, 1950011002008, 1950011002009, 1950011002010, 1950011002011, 1950011002012, 1950011002013, 1950011002014, 1950011002015, 1950011002016, 1950011002017, 1950011002018, 1950011002019, 1950011002020, 1950011002021, 1950011002022, 1950011002023, 1950011002024, 1950011002025, 1950011002026, 1950011002027, 1950011002028, 1950011002029,

1950011002030, 1950011002031, 1950011002032, 1950011002033, 1950011002034, 1950011002035; VTD: PRSP, VTD: PRST: Block(s) 1950008022062, 1950008022064, 1950008022065, 1950008023036, 1950008023037, 1950008023038, 1950009003005, 1950010001000, 1950010001001, 1950010001002, 1950010001003, 1950010001004, 1950010001005, 1950010001006, 1950010001007, 1950010001008, 1950010001009, 1950010001010, 1950010001011, 1950010001012, 1950010001013, 1950010001014, 1950010001015, 1950010001016, 1950010001017, 1950010001018, 1950010001019, 1950010001020, 1950010001021, 1950010001022, 1950010001024, 1950010001025, 1950010001026, 1950010001027, 1950010001028, 1950010001029, 1950010001030, 1950010001031, 1950010001032, 1950010001033, 1950010001034, 1950010001035, 1950010001036, 1950010001037, 1950010001038, 1950010001039, 1950010001040, 1950010001041, 1950010001042, 1950010001043, 1950010001044, 1950010001045, 1950010001046, 1950010001047, 1950010001048, 1950010001049, 1950010001050, 1950010001051, 1950010001052, 1950010001053, 1950010001054, 1950010001055, 1950010001056, 1950010001057, 1950010001058, 1950010001059, 1950010001060, 1950010001061, 1950010001062, 1950010001063, 1950010001064, 1950010001065, 1950010001066, 1950010001067, 1950010001068, 1950010001069, 1950010001070, 1950010001071, 1950010001072, 1950010001073, 1950010001074, 1950010001075, 1950010001076, 1950010001077, 1950010001078; VTD: PRTA, VTD: PRTO: Block(s) 1950013003000, 1950013003001, 1950013003002, 1950013003003, 1950013003004, 1950013003005, 1950013003006, 1950013003007, 1950013003008, 1950013003009, 1950013003010, 1950013003011, 1950013003012, 1950013003013, 1950013003014, 1950013003015, 1950013003016, 1950013003017, 1950013003018, 1950013003019, 1950013003020, 1950013004000, 1950013004001, 1950013004002, 1950013004003, 1950013004004, 1950013004005, 1950013004006, 1950013004007, 1950013004008, 1950013004009, 1950013004010, 1950013004011, 1950013004012, 1950013004013, 1950013004014, 1950013004015, 1950013004016, 1950013004017, 1950013004018, 1950013004019, 1950013004020, 1950013004021, 1950013004022, 1950013004023, 1950013004024, 1950013004025, 1950013004026, 1950013004027, 1950013004028, 1950013004029, 1950013004030, 1950013004031, 1950013004032, 1950013004033, 1950013004034, 1950013004035, 1950013004036, 1950013004037, 1950013004038, 1950013004039, 1950013004040, 1950013004041, 1950013004042, 1950013004043, 1950013004044, 1950013004045, 1950013004046, 1950013004047, 1950013004048, 1950013004049, 1950013004050, 1950013004051, 1950013004052, 1950013004053, 1950013004054, 1950013004055; VTD: PRWB: 1950002001047, 1950002001048, 1950002001049, 1950002001050, 1950002001051, 1950002001061; VTD: PRWC: 1950004002000, 1950004002001, 1950004002010, 1950004002011, 1950004002012, 1950004003000, 1950004003001, 1950004003002, 1950004003003, 1950004003004, 1950004003005, 1950004003006, 1950004003007, 1950004003008, 1950004003009, 1950004003010, 1950004003011, 1950004003012, 1950004003013, 1950004003014, 1950004003015, 1950004003016, 1950004003017, 1950004003018, 1950004003019, 1950004003020, 1950004003021, 1950004003022, 1950004003023, 1950004003024, 1950004003025; VTD: PRWD, VTD: PRWE: Block(s) 1950001001000, 1950001001001, 1950001001002, 1950001001003, 1950001001010, 1950001001011, 1950001001013, 1950001001014, 1950001001015, 1950001002000, 1950001002001, 1950001002002, 1950001002011, 1950001002012, 1950001002013, 1950006002000, 1950006002001, 1950006002004, 1950006002005, 1950006002006, 1950006002007, 1950006002008, 1950006002009, 1950006002010, 1950006002011, 1950006002012, 1950006002013, 1950006002014, 1950006002015, 1950006002016, 1950006003000, 1950006003001, 1950006003002, 1950006003003, 1950006003004, 1950006003005, 1950006003006, 1950006003007, 1950006003008, 1950006003009, 1950006003010, 1950006003011,

1950006003012, 1950006003013, 1950006003014, 1950006003015, 1950006003016, 1950006003017, 1950006003018, 1950006003019, 1950006003020, 1950006005019, 1950006005020, 1950006005021, 1950006005022, 1950006005023, 1950006005075, 1950013003021, 1950013003022; VTD: PRWI, VTD: PRWJ, VTD: PRWK, VTD: PRWL, VTD: PRWM, VTD: PRWP. It has one judge.

(6) Superior Court District 10A consists of Wake County Precincts: VTD: 01-01, VTD: 01-02, VTD: 01-06, VTD: 01-07, VTD: 01-14, VTD: 01-16, VTD: 01-23, VTD: 01-29, VTD: 01-31, VTD: 01-32, VTD: 01-33, VTD: 01-41, VTD: 01-48, VTD: 01-49, VTD: 04-01, VTD: 04-02, VTD: 04-03, VTD: 04-04, VTD: 04-06, VTD: 04-07, VTD: 04-10, VTD: 04-11, VTD: 04-12, VTD: 04-13, VTD: 04-14, VTD: 04-15, VTD: 04-16, VTD: 04-19, VTD: 04-20, VTD: 04-21, VTD: 11-02, VTD: 18-01, VTD: 18-04, VTD: 18-06, VTD: 18-08. It has one judge.

(7) Superior Court District 10B consists of Wake County Precincts: VTD: 01-12, VTD: 01-13, VTD: 01-18, VTD: 01-19, VTD: 01-20, VTD: 01-21, VTD: 01-22, VTD: 01-25, VTD: 01-26, VTD: 01-27, VTD: 01-34, VTD: 01-35, VTD: 01-38, VTD: 01-40, VTD: 01-46, VTD: 01-50, VTD: 13-01: Block(s) 1830527043000, 1830527043023, 1830527043024, 1830540081000, 1830540081001, 1830540081002, 1830540081003, 1830540081004, 1830540081005, 1830540081006, 1830540081007, 1830540081008, 1830540081009, 1830540081010, 1830540081011, 1830540081012, 1830540081013, 1830540081014, 1830540081015, 1830540082000, 1830540082001, 1830540082002, 1830540082003, 1830540082004, 1830540082005, 1830540082006, 1830540082007, 1830540082008, 1830540082009, 1830540082010, 1830540082011, 1830540082012, 1830540082013, 1830540082014, 1830540082015, 1830540082016, 1830540083000, 1830540083001, 1830540083002, 1830540083003, 1830540083004, 1830540083005, 1830540083006, 1830540083007, 1830540083008, 1830540083009, 1830540084000, 1830540084001, 1830540084002, 1830540181012, 1830540181013, 1830540181014, 1830540181015, 1830540181016, 1830540181017, 1830540181018, 1830540181027, 1830540181033, 1830540181034, 1830541041022, 1830541041023, 1830541041024, 1830541041025, 1830541041026, 1830541041028, 1830541041030, 1830541041031, 1830541041032, 1830541041033, 1830541041039, 1830541041040, 1830541041041, 1830541041042, 1830541041043, 1830541041044, 1830541041045, 1830541041046, 1830541041047, 1830541041048, 1830541041049, 1830541041050, 1830541042000, 1830541042002, 1830541042010, 1830541042023, 1830541042024, 1830541042025, 1830541042026, 1830541042027, 1830541042029, 1830541042030, 1830541043014, 1830541043015, 1830541043016, 1830541043017, 1830541043018, 1830541043019, 1830541043045; VTD: 13-05, VTD: 13-07, VTD: 16-02, VTD: 16-03, VTD: 16-06, VTD: 16-08, VTD: 17-06, VTD: 17-07, VTD: 17-08, VTD: 17-09, VTD: 17-10, VTD: 17-11. It has one judge.

(8) Superior Court District 10C consists of Wake County Precincts: VTD: 02-01, VTD: 02-02, VTD: 02-03, VTD: 02-04, VTD: 02-05, VTD: 02-06, VTD: 07-02, VTD: 07-06, VTD: 07-07, VTD: 07-11, VTD: 07-12, VTD: 08-02, VTD: 08-03, VTD: 08-04, VTD: 08-05, VTD: 08-06, VTD: 08-07, VTD: 08-08, VTD: 08-09, VTD: 08-10, VTD: 08-11, VTD: 13-10, VTD: 13-11, VTD: 14-01, VTD: 14-02, VTD: 19-03, VTD: 19-04, VTD: 19-05, VTD: 19-06, VTD: 19-07, VTD: 19-09, VTD: 19-10, VTD: 19-11, VTD: 19-12. It has one judge.

(9) Superior Court District 10D consists of Wake County Precincts: VTD: 01-03, VTD: 01-04, VTD: 01-05, VTD: 01-09, VTD: 01-10, VTD: 01-11, VTD: 01-15, VTD: 01-17, VTD: 01-30, VTD: 01-36, VTD: 01-37, VTD: 01-39, VTD: 01-43, VTD: 01-45, VTD: 01-51, VTD: 04-05, VTD: 04-08, VTD: 04-09, VTD: 04-17, VTD: 04-18, VTD: 05-01, VTD: 05-03, VTD: 05-04, VTD: 05-05, VTD: 05-06,

VTD: 07-01, VTD: 07-03, VTD: 07-04, VTD: 07-05, VTD: 07-09, VTD: 07-10, VTD: 07-13, VTD: 11-01, VTD: 20-02, VTD: 20-04, VTD: 20-10. It has one judge.

(10) Superior Court District 10E consists of Wake County Precincts: VTD: 01-28, VTD: 01-42, VTD: 01-44, VTD: 01-47, VTD: 09-01, VTD: 09-02, VTD: 09-03, VTD: 10-01, VTD: 10-02, VTD: 10-03, VTD: 10-04, VTD: 13-01: Block(s) 1830541041000, 1830541041001, 1830541041002, 1830541041003, 1830541041004, 1830541041005, 1830541041006, 1830541041007, 1830541041008, 1830541041009, 1830541041010, 1830541041011, 1830541041012, 1830541041013, 1830541041014, 1830541041015, 1830541041016, 1830541041017, 1830541041018, 1830541041019, 1830541041020, 1830541041021, 1830541042028; VTD: 13-02, VTD: 13-06, VTD: 13-08, VTD: 13-09, VTD: 15-01, VTD: 15-03, VTD: 15-04, VTD: 16-01, VTD: 16-04, VTD: 16-05, VTD: 16-07, VTD: 16-09, VTD: 17-01, VTD: 17-02, VTD: 17-03, VTD: 17-04, VTD: 17-05, VTD: 19-16, VTD: 19-17. It has one judge.

(11) Superior Court District 10F consists of Wake County Precincts: VTD: 03-00, VTD: 06-01, VTD: 06-04, VTD: 06-05, VTD: 06-06, VTD: 06-07, VTD: 12-01, VTD: 12-02, VTD: 12-04, VTD: 12-05, VTD: 12-06, VTD: 12-07, VTD: 12-08, VTD: 12-09, VTD: 15-02, VTD: 18-02, VTD: 18-03, VTD: 18-05, VTD: 18-07, VTD: 20-01, VTD: 20-03, VTD: 20-05, VTD: 20-06, VTD: 20-08, VTD: 20-09, VTD: 20-11, VTD: 20-12. It has one judge.

(12) District 12A: Cumberland County: VTD: AH49, VTD: CC18: Block(s) 0510007011012, 0510007011013, 0510007011014, 0510007011015, 0510007011016, 0510007011021, 0510007011034, 0510007011035, 0510007013011, 0510007013012, 0510007013013, 0510007013014, 0510007013015, 0510007013016, 0510007013017, 0510007013018, 0510007013019, 0510007013020, 0510007013021, 0510007013022, 0510007013023, 0510007013024, 0510007013025, 0510007013026, 0510007013027, 0510007013028, 0510007013029, 0510007013030, 0510007013031, 0510007013032, 0510007022007, 0510007022008; VTD: CC24: 0510020011058, 0510020021002, 0510033022004; VTD: CC25, VTD: CC27, VTD: CC29, VTD: CC31, VTD: CC32, VTD: CC33, VTD: CC34, VTD: CU02, VTD: G10: Block(s) 0510016011001, 0510016011002, 0510016011004, 0510016011005, 0510016011006, 0510016011007, 0510016011009, 0510016011010, 0510016011011, 0510016011012, 0510016011013, 0510016011014, 0510016011015, 0510016011016, 0510016011017, 0510016011018, 0510016011019, 0510016011020, 0510016011021, 0510016011022, 0510016011023, 0510016011024, 0510016011025, 0510016011026, 0510016011027, 0510016011032, 0510016011041, 0510016012041, 0510031021000, 0510031021001, 0510031021002, 0510031021003, 0510031021004, 0510031021005, 0510031021006, 0510031021007, 0510031021008, 0510031021009, 0510031021010, 0510031021011, 0510031021012, 0510031021013, 0510031021014, 0510031021015, 0510031021016, 0510031021017, 0510031021018, 0510031021019, 0510031021020, 0510031021021, 0510031021022, 0510031021023, 0510031021024, 0510031021025, 0510031021026, 0510031021027, 0510031021028, 0510031021029, 0510031021030, 0510031021031, 0510031021032, 0510031021033, 0510031021034, 0510031021035, 0510031021036, 0510031021037, 0510031021038, 0510031021039, 0510031021040, 0510031021041, 0510031021042, 0510031021043, 0510031021044, 0510031021045, 0510031021046, 0510031021047, 0510031021048, 0510031021049, 0510031021050, 0510031021051, 0510031021052, 0510031021053, 0510031021054, 0510031021055, 0510031021056, 0510031021057, 0510031021058, 0510031021059, 0510031021060, 0510031021061, 0510031021062, 0510031031001, 0510031031002, 0510031031003, 0510031031004, 0510031031005, 0510031031006, 0510031031007, 0510031031008, 0510031031009, 0510031031010, 0510031031016, 0510031032004, 0510031032005, 0510031032006, 0510031032007, 0510031032008, 0510031032009, 0510031032010, 0510031032011,

0510031032012, 0510031032013, 0510031032014, 0510031032015, 0510031032017, 0510031032018, 0510031032019, 0510031032020, 0510031032021, 0510031032023, 0510031032024, 0510031032026, 0510031032027, 0510031032028, 0510031032029, 0510031032034, 0510031032036, 0510031032041, 0510031032042, 0510031032043, 0510031032044, 0510031032046, 0510031032047, 0510031032048, 0510031032049, 0510031032052, 0510031032053, 0510031032054, 0510031033000, 0510031033001, 0510031033009, 0510031033010, 0510031033011, 0510031033013, 0510031033015, 0510031033016, 0510031033030, 0510031033036, 0510032012000, 0510032012001, 0510032012002, 0510032012003, 0510032012004, 0510032012005, 0510032012006, 0510032012007, 0510032012008, 0510032012009, 0510032012010, 0510032012011, 0510032012012, 0510032012013, 0510032012014, 0510032012015, 0510032012016, 0510032012017, 0510032012018, 0510032012019, 0510032012020, 0510032012021, 0510032012022, 0510032012023, 0510032012024, 0510032012025, 0510032012026, 0510032012027, 0510032012028, 0510032012029, 0510032013000, 0510032013001, 0510032013002, 0510032013003, 0510032013004, 0510032013005, 0510032013006, 0510032013007, 0510032013008, 0510032013009, 0510032013010, 0510032013011, 0510032013012, 0510032013013, 0510032013014, 0510032013015, 0510032013016, 0510032013017, 0510032013018, 0510032013019, 0510032013020, 0510032013021, 0510032013022, 0510032013023, 0510032013024, 0510032013025, 0510032013026, 0510032013027, 0510032013028, 0510032013029, 0510032013030, 0510032013031, 0510032013032, 0510032013033, 0510032013034, 0510032013035, 0510032013036, 0510032013037, 0510032013038, 0510032013039, 0510032013040, 0510032013041, 0510032013042, 0510032013043, 0510032013044, 0510032013045, 0510032013046, 0510032014026, 0510032014027, 0510032014028, 0510032014029, 0510032014030, 0510032014031, 0510032014032, 0510032014033, 0510032014034, 0510032014040, 0510032014041, 0510032014042, 0510032014045, 0510032014046, 0510032014047, 0510032014048, 0510032014049, 0510032014050, 0510032014051, 0510032014057; VTD: G5, VTD: G8: Block(s) 0510016011003, 0510016011008, 0510017001035, 0510017003011, 0510017003013, 0510017003014, 0510017004022, 0510017004023, 0510017004024, 0510017004025, 0510017004026, 0510017004027, 0510017004028, 0510017004029, 0510017004030, 0510017004031, 0510017004032, 0510017004033, 0510017004034, 0510017004035, 0510017004036, 0510017004037, 0510017004038, 0510017004039, 0510017004040, 0510017004041, 0510017004042, 0510017004043, 0510017004046, 0510017004047, 0510017004048, 0510019011000, 0510019011001, 0510019011002, 0510019011003, 0510019011004, 0510019011005, 0510019011008, 0510019011009, 0510019011010, 0510019011011, 0510019011012, 0510019011013, 0510019011014, 0510019011015, 0510019011016, 0510019011017, 0510019011018, 0510019011020, 0510019011021, 0510019011022, 0510019011023, 0510019011024, 0510019011025, 0510019011026, 0510019011028, 0510019011029, 0510019011030, 0510019011031, 0510019011032, 0510019011033, 0510019011034, 0510019011035, 0510019011036, 0510019011037, 0510019011038, 0510019011039, 0510019011041, 0510019011042, 0510019022014, 0510019022015, 0510019022018, 0510019022022, 0510019022023, 0510019022024, 0510019022025, 0510019022026, 0510019022027, 0510019022028, 0510019022029, 0510019022030, 0510019022031, 0510019022032, 0510019022033, 0510019022034, 0510019022035, 0510019022036, 0510019022037, 0510019022038, 0510019022039, 0510019022040, 0510019022041, 0510019022044, 0510019022045, 0510019022046, 0510019031003, 0510019031004, 0510019031005, 0510019031006, 0510019031007, 0510019031008, 0510019031009, 0510019031010, 0510019031011, 0510019031012, 0510019031015, 0510019031016, 0510019031017, 0510019031018, 0510032014000, 0510032014001, 0510032014002, 0510032014003, 0510032014004, 0510032014005, 0510032014006, 0510032014007, 0510032014008, 0510032014009,

0510032014010, 0510032014011, 0510032014012, 0510032014013, 0510032014014,
0510032014015, 0510032014016, 0510032014017, 0510032014018, 0510032014019,
0510032014020, 0510032014021, 0510032014022, 0510032014023, 0510032014024,
0510032014025, 0510032014035, 0510032014036, 0510032014037, 0510032014038,
0510032014039, 0510032014043, 0510032014044, 0510032014055, 0510032014056,
0510032033016, 0510032033017, 0510032033019, 0510032033020, 0510032033021,
0510032033022, 0510032033023, 0510032044002, 0510032044003, 0510032044004,
0510032044005, 0510032044006, 0510032044007, 0510032044008, 0510032044009,
0510032044010, 0510032044011, 0510032044012, 0510032044013, 0510032044014,
0510032044015, 0510032044016, 0510032044017, 0510032045003, 0510032045004,
0510032045005, 0510032045006, 0510032045007, 0510032045008, 0510032045009,
0510032045011, 0510032045013, 0510032045014, 0510032045015, 0510032045016,
0510032045017, 0510032045018, 0510032045019, 0510032045020, 0510032045021,
0510032045022, 0510032045023, 0510032045024, 0510032045025, 0510032045026,
0510032045027; VTD: MB62: 0510033104011, 0510033111015; VTD: MR02. It has one judge.

(13)   District 12B: Cumberland County: VTD: CC01, VTD: CC03, VTD: CC05, VTD: CC13:
Block(s) 0510008001000, 0510008001002, 0510008001003, 0510008001004, 0510008001018,
0510008001019, 0510010001001, 0510010001002, 0510010001003, 0510010001004,
0510010001005, 0510010001006, 0510010001007, 0510010002000, 0510010002001,
0510010002002, 0510010002003, 0510010002010, 0510010002014, 0510010002015,
0510010002016, 0510010002017, 0510010002018, 0510010002019, 0510010002020,
0510010002021, 0510010002022, 0510010002023, 0510010002024, 0510010002025,
0510010002026, 0510010002027, 0510010002028, 0510010002029, 0510010002030,
0510010002031, 0510010002032, 0510010002033, 0510010002034, 0510011003017,
0510011003018, 0510011003019, 0510011003020, 0510011003021, 0510011003022,
0510011003023, 0510011003024, 0510011003025, 0510011003026; VTD: CC15: 0510006003000,
0510006003001, 0510006003002, 0510006003003, 0510006003004, 0510006003005,
0510006003006, 0510006003007, 0510006003008, 0510006003013, 0510006005000,
0510006005001, 0510006005002, 0510006005003, 0510006005004, 0510006005005,
0510006005006, 0510006005007, 0510006005008, 0510006005009, 0510006005010,
0510006005011, 0510006005012, 0510006005013, 0510006005014, 0510006005015,
0510006005016, 0510006005018, 0510006005019, 0510006005020, 0510006005021,
0510006005022, 0510006005023, 0510038003033, 0510038003034, 0510038003060,
0510038003061; VTD: CC16, VTD: CC17, VTD: CC19, VTD: CL57, VTD: G11: Block(s)
0510025041000, 0510033132008; 0510034011000, 0510034011001, 0510034011002,
0510034011003, 0510034011004, 0510034011005, 0510034011006, 0510034011007,
0510034011008, 0510034011009, 0510034011010, 0510034011011, 0510034011012,
0510034011013, 0510034011014, 0510034011015, 0510034011016, 0510034011017,
0510034011018, 0510034011019, 0510034011020, 0510034011021, 0510034011022,
0510034011023, 0510034011024, 0510034011025, 0510034011026, 0510034011027,
0510034011028, 0510034011029, 0510034011030, 0510034011031, 0510034011032,
0510034011033, 0510034011034, 0510034011035, 0510034011036, 0510034011037,
0510034011038, 0510034011039, 0510034011040, 0510034011041, 0510034011042,
0510034011043, 0510034012000, 0510034012001, 0510034012002, 0510034012003,
0510034012004, 0510034012005, 0510034012006, 0510034012007, 0510034012008,
0510034012009, 0510034012010, 0510034012011, 0510034012012, 0510034012013,
0510034012014, 0510034012015, 0510034012016, 0510034012017, 0510034012018,
0510034012019, 0510034012020, 0510034012021, 0510034012022, 0510034012023,
0510034012024, 0510034012025, 0510034012026, 0510034012027, 0510034012028,
0510034012029, 0510034012030, 0510034012031, 0510034012032, 0510034012033,

0510034012034, 0510034012035, 0510034012036, 0510034012037, 0510034012038, 0510034012039, 0510034012040, 0510034012041, 0510034012042, 0510034012043, 0510034012044, 0510034012045, 0510034012046, 0510034012047, 0510034012048, 0510034012049, 0510034012050, 0510034012051, 0510034012052, 0510034012053, 0510034012054, 0510034012055, 0510034012056, 0510034012057, 0510034012058, 0510034012059, 0510034012060, 0510034012061, 0510034012062, 0510034012063, 0510034012064, 0510034012065, 0510034012066, 0510034012067, 0510034012068, 0510034012069, 0510034021000, 0510034021001, 0510034021002, 0510034021003, 0510034021004, 0510034021005, 0510034021006, 0510034021007, 0510034021008, 0510034021009, 0510034021010, 0510034021011, 0510034021012, 0510034021013, 0510034021014, 0510034021015, 0510034021016, 0510034021017, 0510034021018, 0510034021019, 0510034021020, 0510034021021, 0510034021022, 0510034021023, 0510034021024, 0510034021025, 0510034021026, 0510034021027, 0510034021028, 0510034021029, 0510034021030, 0510034021031, 0510034022000, 0510034022001, 0510034022002, 0510034022003, 0510034031000, 0510034031001, 0510034031002, 0510034031003, 0510034031004, 0510034031005, 0510034031006, 0510034031007, 0510034031008, 0510034031009, 0510034031010, 0510034031011, 0510034031012, 0510034031013, 0510034032000, 0510034032001, 0510034032002, 0510034032003, 0510034032004, 0510034032005, 0510034032006, 0510034032007, 0510034032008, 0510034032009, 0510034032010, 0510034032011, 0510034032012, 0510034032013, 0510034032014, 0510034032015, 0510034041000, 0510034041001, 0510034041002, 0510034041003, 0510034041004, 0510034041005, 0510034041006, 0510034041007, 0510034041008, 0510034041009, 0510034042000, 0510034042001, 0510034042002, 0510034042003, 0510034042004, 0510034042005, 0510034042006, 0510034042007, 0510034042008, 0510034042009, 0510034042010, 0510034042011, 0510034042012, 0510034042013, 0510034042014, 0510034042015, 0510034042016, 0510034042017, 0510034042018, 0510034042019, 0510034051000, 0510034051001, 0510034051002, 0510034051003, 0510034051004, 0510034051005, 0510034051006, 0510034051007, 0510034051008, 0510034051009, 0510034051010, 0510034051011, 0510034051012, 0510034051013, 0510034051014, 0510034051015, 0510034051016, 0510034051017, 0510034051018, 0510034051019, 0510034051020, 0510034051021, 0510034051022, 0510034051023, 0510034051024, 0510034051025, 0510034051026, 0510034051027, 0510034051028, 0510034051029, 0510034051030, 0510034051031, 0510034051032, 0510034061000, 0510034061001, 0510034061002, 0510034061003, 0510034061004, 0510034061005, 0510034061006, 0510034061007, 0510034061008, 0510034061009, 0510034061010, 0510034061011, 0510034061012, 0510034061013, 0510034061014, 0510034061015, 0510034061016, 0510034061017, 0510034061018, 0510034061019, 0510034061020, 0510034061021, 0510034061022, 0510034061023, 0510034061024, 0510034061025, 0510034061026, 0510034061027, 0510034061028, 0510034061029, 0510034061030, 0510034061031, 0510034061032, 0510034061033, 0510034061034, 0510034061035, 0510034061036, 0510034061037, 0510034061038, 0510034061039, 0510034061040, 0510034061041, 0510034061042, 0510034061043, 0510034061044, 0510034061045, 0510034061046, 0510034061047, 0510034061048, 0510034061049, 0510034061050, 0510034061051, 0510034061052, 0510034061053, 0510034061054, 0510034061055, 0510034061056, 0510034061057, 0510034061058, 0510034061059, 0510034061060, 0510034061061, 0510034061062, 0510034061063, 0510034061064, 0510034061065, 0510034061066, 0510034061067, 0510034061068, 0510034061069, 0510034061070, 0510034061071, 0510034061072, 0510034061073, 0510034061074, 0510034061075, 0510034061076, 0510034061077, 0510034061078, 0510034061079, 0510034061080, 0510034061081, 0510034061082, 0510034061083, 0510034061084, 0510034061085, 0510034061086, 0510034061087, 0510034061088, 0510034061089,

0510034061090, 0510034061091, 0510034061092, 0510034061093, 0510034061094,
0510034061095, 0510034061096, 0510034061097, 0510034061098, 0510034061099,
0510034061100, 0510034061101, 0510034061102, 0510034061103, 0510034061104,
0510034061105, 0510034061106, 0510034061107, 0510034061108, 0510034061109,
0510034071000, 0510034071001, 0510034071002, 0510034071003, 0510034071004,
0510034071005, 0510034071006, 0510034071007, 0510034071008, 0510034071009,
0510034071010, 0510034071011, 0510034071012, 0510034071013, 0510034071014,
0510034071015, 0510034071016, 0510034071017, 0510034071018, 0510034072000,
0510034072001, 0510034072002, 0510034072003, 0510034072004, 0510034072005,
0510034072006, 0510034072007, 0510034072008, 0510034072009, 0510034072010,
0510034072011, 0510034081000, 0510034081001, 0510034081002, 0510034081003,
0510034081004, 0510034081005, 0510034081006, 0510034081007, 0510034081008,
0510034081009, 0510034081010, 0510034081011, 0510034081012, 0510034081013,
0510034081014, 0510034081015, 0510034081016, 0510034081017, 0510034081018,
0510034081019, 0510034081020, 0510034081021, 0510034081022, 0510034081023,
0510034081024, 0510034081025, 0510034081026, 0510034081027, 0510034081028,
0510034081029, 0510034081030, 0510034081031, 0510034081032, 0510034081033,
0510034081034, 0510034081035, 0510034081036, 0510034081037, 0510034081038,
0510034081039, 0510034081040, 0510034081041, 0510034081042, 0510034081043,
0510034081044, 0510034081045, 0510034081046, 0510034082000, 0510034082001,
0510034082002, 0510034082003, 0510034082004, 0510034082005, 0510034082006,
0510034082007, 0510034082008, 0510034082009, 0510034082010, 0510034082011,
0510034082012, 0510034082013, 0510034082014, 0510034082015, 0510034082016,
0510034082017, 0510034082018, 0510034082019, 0510034082020, 0510034082021,
0510034082022, 0510034082023, 0510034082024, 0510034082025, 0510034082026,
0510034082027, 0510034082028, 0510034082029, 0510034082030, 0510034082031,
0510034082032, 0510034082033, 0510034082034, 0510034082035, 0510034082036,
0510034082037, 0510034082038, 0510034082039, 0510034082040, 0510034082041,
0510034082042, 0510034082043, 0510034082044, 0510034082045, 0510034082046,
0510034082047, 0510034082048, 0510034082049, 0510034082050, 0510034082051,
0510034082052, 0510034082053, 0510034082054, 0510034082055, 0510034082056,
0510034082057, 0510034082058, 0510034082059, 0510034082060, 0510034082061,
0510034082062, 0510034082063, 0510034082064, 0510034082065, 0510034082066,
0510034082067, 0510034082068, 0510034082069, 0510034082070, 0510034082071,
0510034082072, 0510034082073, 0510034082074, 0510035001000, 0510035001001,
0510035001002, 0510035001003, 0510035001004, 0510035001005, 0510035001006,
0510035001007, 0510035001008, 0510035001009, 0510035001010, 0510035001011,
0510035001012, 0510035001013, 0510035001014, 0510035001015, 0510035001016,
0510035001017, 0510035001018, 0510035001019, 0510035001020, 0510035001021,
0510035001022, 0510035001023, 0510035001024, 0510035001025, 0510035001026,
0510035001027, 0510035001028, 0510035001029, 0510035001030, 0510035002000,
0510035002001, 0510035002002, 0510035002003, 0510035002004, 0510035002005,
0510035002006, 0510035002007, 0510035002008, 0510035002009, 0510035002010,
0510035002011, 0510035002012, 0510035002013, 0510035002014, 0510035002015,
0510035002016, 0510035002017, 0510035002018, 0510035002019, 0510035002020,
0510035002021, 0510035002022, 0510035002023, 0510035002024, 0510035002025,
0510035002026, 0510035002027, 0510035002028, 0510035002029, 0510035003000,
0510035003001, 0510035003002, 0510035003003, 0510035003004, 0510035003005,
0510035003006, 0510035003007, 0510035003008, 0510035003009, 0510035003010,
0510035003011, 0510035003012, 0510035003013, 0510035003014, 0510035003015,
0510035003016, 0510035003017, 0510035003018, 0510035003019, 0510035003020,

0510035003021, 0510035003022, 0510035003023, 0510035003024, 0510035003025,
0510035003026, 0510035003027, 0510035003028, 0510035003029, 0510035003030,
0510035003031, 0510035003032, 0510035003033, 0510035003034, 0510035003035,
0510035003036, 0510035003037, 0510035004000, 0510035004001, 0510035004002,
0510035004003, 0510035004004, 0510035004005, 0510035004006, 0510035004007,
0510035004008, 0510035004009, 0510035004010, 0510035004011, 0510035004012,
0510035004013, 0510035004014, 0510035004015, 0510035004016, 0510035004017,
0510035004018, 0510035004019, 0510035004020, 0510035004021, 0510035004022,
0510035004023, 0510035004024, 0510035004025, 0510035004026, 0510035004027,
0510035004028, 0510035004029, 0510036001011, 0510036001018, 0510036001020,
0510036001023, 0510036001024, 0510036001025, 0510036001026, 0510036001027,
0510036001028, 0510036001029, 0510036001030, 0510036001031, 0510036001032,
0510036001033, 0510036001034, 0510036001035, 0510036001036, 0510036001037,
0510036001038, 0510036001043, 0510036001044, 0510036001045, 0510036001046,
0510036001047, 0510036001048, 0510036001049, 0510036001050, 0510036001051,
0510036001052, 0510036001053, 0510036001054, 0510036001055, 0510036001056,
0510036001057, 0510036001058, 0510036001059, 0510036001060, 0510036002000,
0510036002001, 0510036002002, 0510036002003, 0510036002004, 0510036002005,
0510036002006, 0510036002007, 0510036002008, 0510036002009, 0510036002010,
0510036002011, 0510036002012, 0510036003013, 0510036003034, 0510036003036,
0510036004002, 0510036004003, 0510036004004, 0510036004005, 0510036004006,
0510036004007, 0510036004008, 0510036004009, 0510036004010, 0510036004011,
0510036004012, 0510036004013, 0510036004014, 0510036004015, 0510036004016,
0510036004017, 0510036004018, 0510036004019, 0510036004020, 0510036004021,
0510036004022, 0510036004023, 0510036004024, 0510036004025, 0510036004026,
0510036004027, 0510036004028, 0510036004029, 0510036004030, 0510036004031,
0510036004032, 0510036004033, 0510036004034, 0510036004035, 0510036004036,
0510036004037, 0510036004038, 0510036004039, 0510036004040, 0510036004041,
0510036004042, 0510036004043, 0510036004044, 0510036004045, 0510036004046,
0510036004047, 510036004049, 0510036004050, 0510036004051, 0510036004052,
0510036004053, 0510036004054, 0510036004055, 0510036004056, 0510036004057,
0510036004058, 0510036004059, 0510037001003, 0510037001023, 0510037001024,
0519801001005, 0519801001006, 0519801001009, 0519801001017, 0519801001018,
0519801001019, 0519801001020, 0519801001021, 0519801001022, 0519801001023,
0519801001024, 0519801001025, 0519801001026, 0519801001027, 0519801001028,
0519801001029, 0519801001030, 0519801001031, 0519801001032, 0519801001033,
0519801001034, 0519801001035, 0519801001036, 0519801001037, 0519801001038,
0519801001039, 0519801001040, 0519801001041, 0519801001042, 0519801001043,
0519801001044, 0519801001045, 0519801001046, 0519801001047, 0519801001048,
0519801001049, 0519801001051, 0519801001052, 0519801001053, 0519801001054,
0519801001055, 0519801001056, 0519801001057, 0519801001058, 0519801001059,
0519801001060, 0519801001061, 0519801001062, 0519801001063, 0519801001064,
0519801001065, 0519801001066, 0519801001067, 0519801001068, 0519802001000,
0519802001001, 0519802001002, 0519802001003, 0519802001004, 0519802001005,
0519802001006, 0519802001007, 0519802001008, 0519802001009, 0519802001010,
0519802001011, 0519802001012, 0519802001013, 0519802001014, 0519802001015,
0519802001016, 0519802001017, 0519802001018, 0519802001019, 0519802001020,
0519802001021, 0519802001022, 0519802001023, 0519802001024, 0519802001025,
0519802001026, 0519802001028, 0519802001029, 0519802001030, 0519802001031,
0519802001032, 0519802001033, 0519802001034, 0519802001035, 0519802001036,
0519802001037, 0519802001038, 0519802001039, 0519802001040, 0519802001041,

0519802001042, 0519802001043, 0519802001044, 0519802001045; VTD: G2: 0510012001000, 0510012001001, 0510012001002, 0510012001003, 0510012001004, 0510012001005, 0510012001006, 0510012001007, 0510012001008, 0510012001009, 0510012001010, 0510024022002, 0510024022003, 0510024022005, 0510024022006, 0510024023000, 0510024023001, 0510024023002, 0510024023003, 0510024023004, 0510024023005, 0510024023006, 0510024023007, 0510024023008, 0510024023009, 0510024023011, 0510024023012, 0510024023013, 0510025013009, 0510025013010, 0510025013011, 0510025013012, 0510025013013, 0510025013018, 0510025013019, 0510025013021, 0510025013022, 0510025013024, 0510025013025, 0510025013026, 0510025013027, 0510025013028, 0510025013029, 0510025013030, 0510025013032, 0510025013034, 0510025013035, 0510025013036, 0510025013041, 0510025013042, 0510025013043, 0510025013044, 0510025013045, 0510025013046, 0510025013047, 0510025013048, 0510025013049, 0510025013050, 0510025013051, 0510025013052, 0510025013063, 0510025013064, 0510025013065, 0510025013068, 0510025013071, 0510025013072, 0510025013073, 0510025013074, 0510025013075, 0510025013076; VTD: LR63, VTD: MB62: Block(s) 0510033071009, 0510033071010, 0510033072000, 0510033072001, 0510033072002, 0510033072003, 0510033072004, 0510033072005, 0510033072006, 0510033072007, 0510033072008, 0510033072029, 0510033141000, 0510033141001, 0510033141002, 0510033141003, 0510033141004, 0510033141005, 0510033141006, 0510033141007, 0510033141008, 0510033141009, 0510033141010, 0510033141011, 0510033141012, 0510033141013, 0510033141014, 0510033141015, 0510033141016, 0510033141017, 0510033141018, 0510033141019, 0510033141020, 0510033141021, 0510033141022, 0510033141023, 0510033141024, 0510033141025, 0510033143000, 0510033143001, 0510033143002, 0510033143003, 0510033143009, 0510033143010, 0510033143011, 0510033143012, 0510033143013, 0510033143014. It has one judge.

(14) District 12C: Cumberland County: VTD: AL51, VTD: CC04, VTD: CC06, VTD: CC07, VTD: CC08, VTD: CC10, VTD: CC12, VTD: CC13: Block(s) 0510009004000, 0510009004020; VTD: CC14, VTD: CC15: Block(s) 0510006001000, 0510006001001, 0510006001002, 0510006001003, 0510006001004, 0510006001005, 0510006001006, 0510006001007, 0510006001008, 0510006001009, 0510006001010, 0510006001011, 0510006001012, 0510006001013, 0510006001014, 0510006001015, 0510006001016, 0510006002000, 0510006002001, 0510006002002, 0510006002003, 0510006002004, 0510006002005, 0510006002006, 0510006002007, 0510006002008, 0510006002009, 0510018001000, 0510018001001, 0510018001002, 0510018001003, 0510018001004, 0510018001005, 0510018001006, 0510018001007, 0510018001008, 0510018001009, 0510018002000, 0510018002001, 0510018002002, 0510038003035; VTD: CC18: 0510007022006, 0510007022010, 0510007022011, 0510007022013, 0510007022014, 0510007022015, 0510007022016, 0510007022017, 0510007022018, 0510007022019, 0510007022020, 0510007022021, 0510007022022, 0510007022023, 0510007022024, 0510007022025, 0510007022026, 0510038003030, 0510038003031, 0510038003032, 0510038003055; VTD: CC21, VTD: CC24: Block(s) 0510020011006, 0510020011007, 0510020011008, 0510020011010, 0510020011011, 0510020011012, 0510020011013, 0510020011014, 0510020011015, 0510020011016, 0510020011025, 0510020011026, 0510020011030, 0510020011031, 0510020011032, 0510020011033, 0510020011034, 0510020011035, 0510020011036, 0510020011037, 0510020011038, 0510020011039, 0510020011040, 0510020011041, 0510020011042, 0510020011043, 0510020011044, 0510020011045, 0510020011046, 0510020011047, 0510020011048, 0510020011049, 0510020011050, 0510020011051, 0510020011052, 0510020011053, 0510020011055, 0510020011056, 0510020012000, 0510020012001, 0510020012002, 0510020012003, 0510020012006, 0510020012007, 0510020012008, 0510020012009, 0510020012010, 0510020012011, 0510020012012, 0510020012013,

0510020012014, 0510020012015, 0510020012016, 0510020012017, 0510020012018, 0510020012019, 0510020012021, 0510020012022, 0510020012023, 0510020012024, 0510020021001; VTD: CC26, VTD: EO61-1, VTD: EO61-2, VTD: G1, VTD: G10: Block(s) 0510031031000, 0510031031011, 0510031031012, 0510031031013, 0510031031014, 0510031031015, 0510031031017, 0510031031018, 0510031031019, 0510031031020, 0510031031021, 0510031031022, 0510031032000, 0510031032001, 0510031032002, 0510031032003, 0510031032016, 0510031032022, 0510031032025, 0510031032030, 0510031032031, 0510031032032, 0510031032033, 0510031032035, 0510031032037, 0510031032038, 0510031032039, 0510031032040, 0510031032045, 0510031032050, 0510031032051; VTD: G11: 0510036001000, 0510036001001, 0510036001002, 0510036001003, 0510036001004, 0510036001005, 0510036001006, 0510036001007, 0510036001008, 0510036001009, 0510036001010, 0510036001012, 0510036001013, 0510036001014, 0510036001015, 0510036001016, 0510036001017, 0510036001019, 0510036001021, 0510036001022, 0510036001039, 0510036001040, 0510036001041, 0510036001042, 0510036003000, 0510036003001, 0510036003002, 0510036003003, 0510036003004, 0510036003005, 0510036003006, 0510036003007, 0510036003008, 0510036003009, 0510036003010, 0510036003011, 0510036003012, 0510036003014, 0510036003015, 0510036003016, 0510036003017, 0510036003018, 0510036003019, 0510036003020, 0510036003021, 0510036003022, 0510036003023, 0510036003024, 0510036003025, 0510036003026, 0510036003027, 0510036003028, 0510036003029, 0510036003030, 0510036003031, 0510036003032, 0510036003033, 0510036003035, 0510036003037, 0510036003038, 0510036003039, 0510036003040, 0510036003041, 0510036003042, 0510036003043, 0510036003044, 0510036003045, 0510036003046, 0510036003047, 0510036003048, 0510036003049, 0510036003050, 0510036003051, 0510036004000, 0510036004001, 0510036004048, 0510037001007, 0510037001008, 0510037001009, 0519801001000, 0519801001001, 0519801001002, 0519801001003, 0519801001004, 0519801001007, 0519801001008, 0519801001010, 0519801001011, 0519801001012, 0519801001013, 0519801001014, 0519801001015, 0519801001016; VTD: G2: 0510012004001, 0510012004002, 0510012004003, 0510012004004, 0510012004021, 0510012004022, 0510012004023, 0510012004024, 0510012004025, 0510012004026, 0510012004027, 0510012004028, 0510024011000, 0510024011001, 0510024011002, 0510024011003, 0510024011004, 0510024011005, 0510024011006, 0510024011007, 0510024011008, 0510024011009, 0510024011010, 0510024011011, 0510024011013, 0510024011014, 0510024011015, 0510024011016, 0510024011017, 0510024011018, 0510024011019, 0510024011022, 0510024011024, 0510024011025, 0510024011026, 0510024011027, 0510024011028, 0510024011029, 0510024011030, 0510024011034, 0510024011035, 0510024011036, 0510024011038, 0510024011041, 0510024011042, 0510024011043, 0510024012004, 0510024012007, 0510024012025, 0510024021000, 0510024021005, 0510024022000, 0510024022001, 0510024022004, 0510024022007, 0510025011000, 0510025011001, 0510025011002, 0510025011003, 0510025011004, 0510025011005, 0510025011006, 0510025011007, 0510025011008, 0510025011009, 0510025011010, 0510025011011, 0510025011012, 0510025011013, 0510025011014, 0510025011015, 0510025011016, 0510025011017, 0510025011018, 0510025011019, 0510025011020, 0510025011021, 0510025011022, 0510025011023, 0510025012000, 0510025012001, 0510025012002, 0510025012003, 0510025012004, 0510025012005, 0510025012006, 0510025012007, 0510025012008, 0510025012009, 0510025012010, 0510025012011, 0510025012012, 0510025012013, 0510025012014, 0510025013000, 0510025013001, 0510025013002, 0510025013003, 0510025013004, 0510025013005, 0510025013006, 0510025013007, 0510025013008, 0510025013014, 0510025013015, 0510025013016, 0510025013017, 0510025013020, 0510025013023, 0510025013031, 0510025013033, 0510025013037, 0510025013038, 0510025013039, 0510025013040, 0510025013053,

0510025013054, 0510025013055, 0510025013056, 0510025013057, 0510025013058, 0510025013059, 0510025013060, 0510025013061, 0510025013062, 0510025013066, 0510025013067, 0510025013068, 0510025013069, 0510025013070, 0510025013077, 0510025013078, 0510025013079, 0510025013080, 0510025013081, 0510025021000, 0510025021001, 0510025021002, 0510025021003, 0510025021004, 0510025021005, 0510025021006, 0510025021007, 0510025021008, 0510025021009, 0510025021010, 0510025021011, 0510025021012, 0510025021013, 0510025021014, 0510025021015, 0510025021016, 0510025021017, 0510025021018, 0510025021019, 0510025021020, 0510025021021, 0510025021022, 0510025021023, 0510025021024, 0510025021025, 0510025021026, 0510025021027, 0510025021028, 0510025021029, 0510025021030, 0510025021031, 0510025021032, 0510025021033, 0510025021034, 0510025021035, 0510025021036, 0510025021037, 0510025021038, 0510025021039, 0510025021040, 0510025021041, 0510025021042, 0510025021043, 0510025021044, 0510025021045, 0510025021046, 0510025021047, 0510025021048, 0510025021049, 0510025021050, 0510025021051, 0510025021052, 0510025021053, 0510025021054, 0510025021055, 0510025021056, 0510025021057, 0510025021058, 0510025021059, 0510025021060, 0510025021061, 0510025021062, 0510025021063, 0510025021064, 0510025021065, 0510025021066, 0510025021067, 0510025022000, 0510025022001, 0510025022002, 0510025022003, 0510025022004, 0510025022005, 0510025022006, 0510025022007, 0510025022008, 0510025022009, 0510025022010, 0510025022011, 0510025022012, 0510025022013, 0510025022014, 0510025022015, 0510025022016, 0510025022017, 0510025022018, 0510025022019, 0510025022020, 0510025022021, 0510025022022, 0510025022023, 0510025022024, 0510025022025, 0510025022026, 0510025022027, 0510025022028, 0510025022029, 0510025022030, 0510025022031, 0510025022032, 0510025022033, 0510025022034, 0510025022035, 0510025022036, 0510025022037, 0510025022038, 0510025022039, 0510025022040, 0510025022041, 0510025022042, 0510025022043, 0510025022044, 0510025022045, 0510025022046, 0510025022047, 0510025022048, 0510025022049, 0510025022050, 0510025022051, 0510025022052, 0510025022053, 0510025022054, 0510025022055, 0510025022056, 0510025022057, 0510025022058, 0510025022059, 0510025022060, 0510025022061, 0510025022062, 0510025022063, 0510025022064, 0510025022065, 0510025022066, 0510025022067, 0510025022068, 0510025022069, 0510025022070, 0510025022071, 0510025022072, 0510025022073, 0510025022074, 0510025022075, 0510025022076, 0510025022077, 0510025022078, 0510025022079, 0510025022080, 0510025022081, 0510025022082, 0510025022083, 0510025022084, 0510025023000, 0510025023001, 0510025023002, 0510025023003, 0510025023004, 0510025023005, 0510025023006, 0510025023007, 0510025023008, 0510025023009, 0510025023010, 0510025023011, 0510025023012, 0510025023013, 0510025023014, 0510025023015, 0510025023016, 0510025023017, 0510025023018, 0510025023019, 0510025023020, 0510025023021, 0510025023022, 0510025023023, 0510025023024, 0510025023025, 0510025023026, 0510025023027, 0510025023028, 0510025023029, 0510025023030, 0510025023031, 0510025023032, 0510025023033, 0510025023034, 0510025023035, 0510025023036, 0510025031000, 0510025031001, 0510025031002, 0510025031003, 0510025031004, 0510025031005, 0510025031006, 0510025031007, 0510025031008, 0510025031009, 0510025031010, 0510025031011, 0510025031012, 0510025031013, 0510025031014, 0510025031015, 0510025031016, 0510025031017, 0510025031018, 0510025031019, 0510025031020, 0510025031021, 0510025031022, 0510025031023, 0510025031024, 0510025031025, 0510025032000, 0510025032001, 0510025032002, 0510025032003, 0510025032004, 0510025032005, 0510025032006, 0510025032007, 0510025032008, 0510025032009, 0510025033000, 0510025033001, 0510025033002, 0510025033003, 0510025033004, 0510025033005, 0510025033006, 0510025033007, 0510025033008, 0510025033009, 0510025033010,

0510025033011, 0510025033012, 0510025033013, 0510025033014, 0510025033015, 0510025033016, 0510025033017, 0510025033018, 0510025033019, 0510025033020, 0510025033021, 0510025033022, 0510025033023, 0510025033024, 0510025033025, 0510025033026, 0510025033027, 0510025033028, 0510025033029, 0510025033030, 0510025033031, 0510025033032, 0510025033033, 0510025033034, 0510025033035, 0510025041001, 0510025041002, 0510025041003, 0510025041004, 0510025041005, 0510025041006, 0510025041007, 0510025041008, 0510025041009, 0510025041010, 0510025041011, 0510025041012, 0510025041013, 0510025041014, 0510025041015, 0510025041016, 0510025041017, 0510025041018, 0510025041019, 0510025041020, 0510025041021, 0510025041022, 0510025041023, 0510025041024, 0510025041025, 0510025041026, 0510025041027, 0510025041028, 0510025041029, 0510025041030, 0510025042000, 0510025042001, 0510025042002, 0510025042003, 0510025042004, 0510025042005, 0510025042006, 0510025042007, 0510025042008, 0510025042009, 0510025042010, 0510025042011, 0510025042012, 0510025042013, 0510025042014, 0510025042015, 0510025042016, 0510025042017, 0510025042018, 0510025042019, 0510025042020, 0510025042021, 0510025042022, 0510025042023, 0510025042024, 0510025042025, 0510025042026, 0510025042027, 0510025042028, 0510025042029, 0510025042030, 0510025042031, 0510025042032, 0510025042033, 0510025042034, 0510025042035, 0510025042036, 0510025042037, 0510025042038, 0510025042039, 0510025042040, 0510025042041, 0510025042042, 0510025042043, 0510025042044, 0510025042045, 0510025042046, 0510025042047, 0510025043000, 0510025043001, 0510025043002, 0510025043003, 0510025043004, 0510025043005, 0510025043006, 0510025043007, 0510025043008, 0510025043009, 0510025043010, 0510025043011, 0510025043012, 0510025043013, 0510025043014, 0510025043015, 0510025043016, 0510025043017, 0510025043018, 0510025043019, 0510025043020, 0510025043021, 0510025043022, 0510025043023, 0510025043024, 0510025043025, 0510025043026, 0510025043027, 0510025043028, 0510025043029, 0510025043030, 0510025043031, 0510025043032, 0510025043033, 0510025043034, 0510025043035, 0510025043036, 0510025043037, 0510025043038, 0510026002016, 0510037001001, 0510037001002, 0510037001004, 0510037001005, 0510037001006, 0510037001010, 0510037001011, 0510037001012, 0510037001013, 0510037001014, 0510037001015, 0510037001016, 0510037001017, 0510037001018, 0510037001019, 0510037001020, 0510037001021, 0510037001022, 0510037001025, 0510037001026, 0510037003088, 0510037003089, 0510037003090, 0510037003098, 0510037003099, 0510037003100, 0510037003101, 0510037003103, 0510037003104, 0510037003105, 0510037003106, 0510037003107, 0510037003110, 0510037003111, 0510037003112, 0510037003113, 0510037003114, 0519802001027; VTD: G3, VTD: G4, VTD: G6, VTD: G7, VTD: G8: Block(s) 0510016011000, 0510016011028, 0510016011029, 0510016011030, 0510016011031, 0510016011033, 0510016011034, 0510016011035, 0510016011036, 0510016011037, 0510016011038, 0510016011039, 0510016011040, 0510016011042, 0510016012003, 0510016012004, 0510016012005, 0510016012006, 0510016012007, 0510016012008, 0510016012009, 0510016012012, 0510016012013, 0510016012014, 0510016012016, 0510016012017, 0510016012018, 0510016012019, 0510016012020, 0510016012021, 0510016012022, 0510016012023, 0510016012024, 0510016012025, 0510016012026, 0510016012027, 0510016012028, 0510016012029, 0510016012030, 0510016012032, 0510016012033, 0510016012034, 0510016012035, 0510016012036, 0510016012037, 0510016012038, 0510016012039, 0510016012040, 0510016012042, 0510016012043, 0510016012044, 0510016012045, 0510016012046, 0510016012047, 0510016012048, 0510016012049, 0510016012050, 0510016012051, 0510016012052, 0510016012053, 0510016032017, 0510016032018, 0510016032019, 0510016032020, 0510016032022, 0510016032023, 0510016032028, 0510016032029, 0510016032030, 0510016032031, 0510016032032,

0510016032044, 0510019011006, 0510019011007, 0510019011019, 0510019011027,
0510019011040, 0510019031013, 0510019031014, 0510031033002, 0510031033003,
0510031033004, 0510031033005, 0510031033006, 0510031041002, 0510031041003,
0510031041004, 0510031041005, 0510031041006, 0510031041007, 0510031041008,
0510031041009, 0510031041010, 0510031041011, 0510031041012, 0510031041013,
0510031041014, 0510031041015, 0510031042011, 0510032014052, 0510032014053,
0510032014054; VTD: G9, VTD: Ll65, VTD: SH77. It has two judges.

(15) District 14A: Durham County: VTD: 09, VTD: 12, VTD: 13, VTD: 14, VTD: 15, VTD: 18, VTD: 31: Block(s) 0630010013033, 0630018024009; VTD: 34, VTD: 35: Block(s) 0630020211023, 0630020212002, 0630020212003, 0630020212004, 0630020212005, 0630020212006, 0630020212007, 0630020212008, 0630020212009, 0630020212010, 0630020212013, 0630020212015, 0630020212016, 0630020212018, 0630020212020, 0630020212021, 0630020272052; VTD: 40, VTD: 41, VTD: 42, VTD: 48, VTD: 53-1, VTD: 54, VTD: 55. It has one judge.

(16) District 14B: Durham County: VTD: 01, VTD: 02, VTD: 03, VTD: 04, VTD: 05, VTD: 06, VTD: 07, VTD: 08, VTD: 10, VTD: 16, VTD: 17, VTD: 19, VTD: 20, VTD: 21, VTD: 22, VTD: 23, VTD: 24, VTD: 25, VTD: 26, VTD: 27, VTD: 28, VTD: 29, VTD: 30-1, VTD: 30-2, VTD: 31: Block(s) 0630010013034, 0630010013038, 0630010013039, 0630010013040, 0630010013043, 0630018071037, 0630018071038, 0630018091000, 0630018091001, 0630018091002, 0630018091003, 0630018091004, 0630018091005, 0630018091006, 0630018091007, 0630018091008, 0630018091009, 0630018091010, 0630018091011, 0630018091012, 0630018091013, 0630018091014, 0630018091015, 0630018091016, 0630018091017, 0630018091018, 0630018091019, 0630018091020, 0630018091021, 0630018091022, 0630018091023, 0630018091024, 0630018091025, 0630018091026, 0630018091027, 0630018091028, 0630018091029, 0630018091030, 0630018091031, 0630018091032, 0630018091033, 0630018091034, 0630018091035, 0630018091036, 0630018091037, 0630018091038, 0630018091041, 0630018091042, 0630018091043, 0630018091044, 0630018091045, 0630018091046, 0630018091062, 0630018091063, 0630018091064, 0630018091065, 0630018091066, 0630018091067, 0630018091071, 0630018091072, 0630018091073, 0630018091074, 0630018091077, 0630018091079, 0630018091080, 0630018092000, 0630018092001, 0630018092002, 0630018092003, 0630018092004, 0630018092005, 0630018092006, 0630018092007, 0630018092008, 0630018092009, 0630018092010, 0630018092011, 0630018092012, 0630018092013, 0630018092014, 0630018092015, 0630018092016, 0630018092017, 0630018092018, 0630018092019, 0630018092020, 0630018092021, 0630018092022, 0630018092023, 0630018092024, 0630018092027, 0630018092028, 0630018092029, 0630018092030, 0630018092031, 0630018092032, 0630018092033, 0630020271000, 0630020271001, 0630020271002, 0630020271003, 0630020271004, 0630020271005, 0630020271006, 0630020271007, 0630020271008, 0630020271009, 0630020271010, 0630020271011, 0630020271012, 0630020271013, 0630020271014, 0630020271015, 0630020271016, 0630020271017, 0630020271018, 0630020271019, 0630020271020, 0630020271021, 0630020271022, 0630020271023, 0630020271024, 0630020271025, 0630020271054, 0630020271055, 0630020271063, 0630020271064, 0630020271065, 0630020271067, 0630020271070, 0630020271071, 0639801001012, 0639801001013; VTD: 32, VTD: 33, VTD: 35: Block(s) 0630020131000, 0630020131001, 0630020131002, 0630020131003, 0630020131004, 0630020131005, 0630020131006, 0630020131007, 0630020131008, 0630020131009, 0630020131010, 0630020131011, 0630020131012, 0630020131013, 0630020131014, 0630020132000, 0630020132001, 0630020132002, 0630020132003, 0630020132004, 0630020132005, 0630020132006, 0630020132007, 0630020132008, 0630020132009,

0630020132010, 0630020132011, 0630020132012, 0630020132013, 0630020132014, 0630020132015, 0630020133000, 0630020133001, 0630020133002, 0630020133003, 0630020133004, 0630020133005, 0630020133006, 0630020133007, 0630020133008, 0630020133009, 0630020133010, 0630020133011, 0630020133012, 0630020133013, 0630020133014, 0630020133015, 0630020133016, 0630020133017, 0630020133018, 0630020133019, 0630020202000, 0630020202001, 0630020202002, 0630020202003, 0630020202004, 0630020202005, 0630020202006, 0630020202007, 0630020202008, 0630020202009, 0630020202010, 0630020202011, 0630020202012, 0630020202013, 0630020202014, 0630020202015, 0630020202016, 0630020202017, 0630020202018, 0630020202019, 0630020202020, 0630020202021, 0630020202022, 0630020202023, 0630020202024, 0630020202025, 0630020202026, 0630020202027, 0630020202028, 0630020202029, 0630020202030, 0630020202031, 0630020202032, 0630020202033, 0630020202034, 0630020202035, 0630020202036, 0630020202037, 0630020202038, 0630020202039, 0630020202040, 0630020202041, 0630020202042, 0630020202043, 0630020202044, 0630020202045, 0630020202046, 0630020202047, 0630020202048, 0630020202049, 0630020202050, 0630020202051, 0630020202052, 0630020202053, 0630020202054, 0630020202055, 0630020202056, 0630020202057, 0630020202058, 0630020211021, 0630020211022, 0630020211024, 0630020211049, 0630020211050, 0630020212011, 0630020212014, 0630020212017, 0630020212019, 0630020272070, 0630020272071, 0630020272072, 0630020272073, 0630020272074, 0630020272075; VTD: 36, VTD: 37, VTD: 38, VTD: 39, VTD: 43, VTD: 44, VTD: 45, VTD: 46, VTD: 47, VTD: 50, VTD: 51, VTD: 52, VTD: 53-2. It has three judges.

(17)   District 18A: Guilford County: VTD: FEN1, VTD: FEN2, VTD: G04, VTD: G05, VTD: G06, VTD: G46, VTD: G52, VTD: G67, VTD: G68, VTD: G69, VTD: G70, VTD: G71, VTD: G72, VTD: G73, VTD: G74, VTD: G75, VTD: NCLAY1, VTD: NCLAY2, VTD: PG1, VTD: PG2, VTD: SCLAY. It has one judge.

(18)   District 18B: Guilford County: VTD: H01, VTD: H02, VTD: H03, VTD: H04, VTD: H05, VTD: H06, VTD: H07, VTD: H08, VTD: H09, VTD: H10, VTD: H11, VTD: H12, VTD: H13, VTD: H14, VTD: H15, VTD: H16, VTD: H17, VTD: H18, VTD: H19A, VTD: H19B, VTD: H20A, VTD: H20B, VTD: H21, VTD: H22, VTD: H23, VTD: H24, VTD: H25, VTD: H26, VTD: H27, VTD: HP, VTD: JAM1, VTD: JAM5, VTD: NDRI, VTD: SDRI. It has one judge.

(19)   District 18C: Guilford County: VTD: CG1, VTD: CG2, VTD: CG3A, VTD: CG3B, VTD: FR1, VTD: FR2, VTD: FR3, VTD: FR4, VTD: FR5, VTD: G17, VTD: G30, VTD: G31, VTD: G32, VTD: G33, VTD: G34, VTD: G36, VTD: G37, VTD: G38, VTD: G39, VTD: G40A1, VTD: G40A2, VTD: G40B, VTD: G41, VTD: G42, VTD: G43, VTD: G64, VTD: G65, VTD: G66, VTD: JAM2, VTD: JAM3, VTD: JAM4, VTD: MON3, VTD: NCGR1, VTD: NCGR2, VTD: OR1, VTD: OR2, VTD: SF1, VTD: SF2, VTD: SF3, VTD: SF4, VTD: STOK. It has one judge.

(20)   District 18D: Guilford County: VTD: G01, VTD: G11, VTD: G12, VTD: G13, VTD: G14, VTD: G15, VTD: G16, VTD: G19, VTD: G35, VTD: G44, VTD: G45, VTD: G47, VTD: G48, VTD: G49, VTD: G50, VTD: G51, VTD: G53, VTD: G54, VTD: G55, VTD: G56, VTD: G57, VTD: G58, VTD: G59, VTD: G60, VTD: G61, VTD: G62, VTD: G63, VTD: SUM1, VTD: SUM2, VTD: SUM3, VTD: SUM4. It has one judge.

(21)   District 18E: Guilford County: VTD: G02, VTD: G03, VTD: G07, VTD: G08, VTD: G09, VTD: G10, VTD: G18, VTD: G20, VTD: G21, VTD: G22, VTD: G23, VTD: G24, VTD: G25, VTD: G26, VTD: G27, VTD: G28, VTD: G29, VTD: GIB, VTD: GR, VTD: JEF1, VTD: JEF2, VTD: JEF3, VTD:

JEF4, VTD: MON1, VTD: MON2, VTD: NMAD, VTD: NWASH, VTD: RC1, VTD: RC2, VTD: SMAD, VTD: SWASH. It has one judge.

(22) District 21A: Forsyth County: VTD: 051, VTD: 052, VTD: 053, VTD: 054, VTD: 055, VTD: 071, VTD: 072, VTD: 073, VTD: 074, VTD: 075, VTD: 091, VTD: 092, VTD: 122, VTD: 123, VTD: 131, VTD: 132, VTD: 133, VTD: 701, VTD: 702, VTD: 703, VTD: 704, VTD: 705, VTD: 706, VTD: 707, VTD: 708, VTD: 709, VTD: 806, VTD: 807, VTD: 808. It has one judge.

(23) District 21B: Forsyth County: VTD: 042, VTD: 043, VTD: 501, VTD: 502, VTD: 503, VTD: 504, VTD: 505, VTD: 506, VTD: 507, VTD: 601, VTD: 602, VTD: 603, VTD: 604, VTD: 605, VTD: 606, VTD: 607, VTD: 901, VTD: 902, VTD: 903, VTD: 904, VTD: 905, VTD: 907. It has one judge.

(24) District 21C: Forsyth County: VTD: 011, VTD: 012, VTD: 013, VTD: 014, VTD: 015, VTD: 021, VTD: 031, VTD: 032, VTD: 033, VTD: 034, VTD: 061, VTD: 062, VTD: 063, VTD: 064, VTD: 065, VTD: 066, VTD: 067, VTD: 068, VTD: 101, VTD: 111, VTD: 112, VTD: 801, VTD: 802, VTD: 803, VTD: 804, VTD: 805, VTD: 809, VTD: 906, VTD: 908, VTD: 909. It has one judge.

(25) District 21D: Forsyth County: VTD: 081, VTD: 082, VTD: 083, VTD: 201, VTD: 203, VTD: 204, VTD: 205, VTD: 206, VTD: 207, VTD: 301, VTD: 302, VTD: 303, VTD: 304, VTD: 305, VTD: 306, VTD: 401, VTD: 402, VTD: 403, VTD: 404, VTD: 405. It has one judge.

(26) District 26A: Mecklenburg County: VTD: 011, VTD: 012, VTD: 013, VTD: 014, VTD: 015, VTD: 016, VTD: 022, VTD: 023, VTD: 024, VTD: 025, VTD: 026, VTD: 027, VTD: 031, VTD: 033, VTD: 039: Block(s) 1190039021000, 1190039021001, 1190039021002, 1190039021003, 1190039021004, 1190039021005, 1190039021006, 1190039021007, 1190039021008, 1190039021009, 1190039021010, 1190039021011, 1190039021012, 1190039021013, 1190039021014, 1190039021015, 1190039021016, 1190039021017, 1190039021018, 1190039021019, 1190039021020, 1190039021021, 1190039022008, 1190039022014, 1190039022015, 1190039022016, 1190039024000, 1190039024001, 1190039024002, 1190039024003, 1190039024004, 1190039024005, 1190039024006, 1190039024007, 1190039024008, 1190039024009, 1190039024013, 1190039024014, 1190039024015, 1190039024016, 1190039024017, 1190039024018, 1190039024019, 1190039031002, 1190039031003, 1190039031004, 1190039031009, 1190039031010, 1190039032000, 1190039032001, 1190039032002, 1190039032003, 1190039032004, 1190039032005, 1190039032006, 1190039032007, 1190039032008, 1190039032009, 1190039032010, 1190039032011, 1190039032012, 1190039032013, 1190039032014, 1190039032015, 1190039032016, 1190039032017, 1190039032018, 1190039032019, 1199801001000, 1199801001001, 1199801001002, 1199801001003, 1199801001004, 1199801001005, 1199801001006, 1199801001007, 1199801001008, 1199801001009, 1199801001010, 1199801001011, 1199801001012, 1199801001013, 1199801001014, 1199801001015, 1199801001016, 1199801001017, 1199801001018, 1199801001019, 1199801001020, 1199801001021, 1199801001035, 1199801001036, 1199801001042, 1199801001043, 1199801001044, 1199801001045, 1199801001046; VTD: 041, VTD: 042, VTD: 046, VTD: 052, VTD: 054, VTD: 055, VTD: 056, VTD: 058, VTD: 060, VTD: 077: Block(s) 1190038072004, 1190038072005, 1190038072007, 1190038072008, 1190038072009, 1190038072010, 1190038072011, 1190038072012, 1190038072013, 1190038072014, 1190038072015, 1190038072016, 1190038072017, 1190038082014, 1190058241000, 1190058241001, 1190058241002, 1190058241003, 1190058241004, 1190058241005, 1190058241006, 1190058241007, 1190058241008, 1190058241009, 1190058241010, 1190058241011, 1190058241012, 1190058241013, 1190058241014, 1190058241015, 1190058241016, 1190058241017, 1190058241018, 1190058241019, 1190058241020, 1190058241021,

1190058241022, 1190058241026, 1190058241046, 1190058241047, 1190058241048, 1190058241049, 1190059162000, 1190059162001, 1190059162002, 1190059162003, 1190059162004, 1190059162005, 1190059162006, 1190059162007, 1190059162008, 1190059162009, 1190059162010, 1190059162011, 1190059162012, 1190059162013, 1190059162014, 1190059162015, 1190059162016, 1190059162017, 1190059162018, 1190059162019, 1190059162020, 1190059162021, 1190059162022, 1190059162023; VTD: 078.1: 1190038022014, 1190038022022, 1190038022023, 1190038022024, 1190038022025, 1190038051005, 1190038051006, 1190038051007, 1190038051012, 1190038051013, 1190038051014, 1190038051018, 1190038051019, 1190038051020, 1190038051027, 1190038051028, 1190038051029, 1190038051030, 1190038051036, 1190038051037, 1190038051038, 1190038064000, 1190038064001, 1190038064002, 1190038064003, 1190038064004, 1190038064005, 1190038064006, 1190038064007, 1190038064008, 1190038064009, 1190038064010, 1190038064011, 1190038064012, 1190038064013, 1190038064014, 1190038064015, 1190038064016, 1190038064017, 1190038064018, 1190038064019, 1190038064020, 1190038064021, 1190038064022, 1190038064023, 1190038064024, 1190038064025, 1190038064026, 1190038064027, 1190038064028, 1190038064029, 1190038064030, 1190038064031, 1190038064032, 1190038064033, 1190038064034; VTD: 082, VTD: 097: Block(s) 1190058241050, 1190058241051; 1190058271000, 1190058271001, 1190058271002, 1190058271003, 1190058271004, 1190058271005, 1190058271006, 1190058271007, 1190058271008, 1190058271009, 1190058271010; VTD: 098, VTD: 104: Block(s) 1190015101000, 1190015101001, 1190015101002, 1190015101003, 1190015101004, 1190015101005, 1190015101006, 1190015101007, 1190015101008, 1190015101009, 1190015101010, 1190015101011, 1190015101012, 1190015101013, 1190015101014, 1190015101015, 1190015101016, 1190015101018, 1190015101019, 1190015101020, 1190015101021, 1190015101022, 1190015102000, 1190015102001, 1190015102002, 1190015102003, 1190015102004, 1190015102005, 1190015102006, 1190015102007, 1190015102008, 1190015102009, 1190015102010; VTD: 109: 1190025002002; VTD: 120, VTD: 126: Block(s) 1190055245029, 1190055246000, 1190055246001, 1190055246002, 1190055246003, 1190055246020, 1190055246021, 1190055246022, 1190055246023, 1190055246026, 1190055246027; VTD: 132, VTD: 147: Block(s) 1190038061000, 1190038061007, 1190038061008, 1190038061009, 1190038061010, 1190038061011, 1190038061012, 1190038061013, 1190038061014, 1190038061015, 1190038061016, 1190038061017, 1190038061018, 1190038061019, 1190038061020, 1190038061021, 1190038061022, 1190038061023, 1190038062000, 1190038062001, 1190038062002, 1190038062003, 1190038062004, 1190038062005, 1190038062006, 1190038062007, 1190038062008, 1190038062009, 1190038062010, 1190038062011, 1190038062012, 1190038062013, 1190038062014, 1190038062015, 1190038062016, 1190038062017, 1190038062018, 1190038062019, 1190038062020, 1190038062021, 1190038062022, 1190038063000, 1190038063001, 1190038063002, 1190038063003, 1190038063004, 1190038063005, 1190038063006, 1190038063007, 1190038063008, 1190038063009, 1190038063010, 1190038063011; VTD: 200: 1199801001024, 1199801001033; VTD: 210, VTD: 213: Block(s) 1190054031007, 1190054031013, 1190054031014, 1190054031015, 1190054031016, 1190054031017, 1190054031018, 1190054031019, 1190054031020, 1190054031021, 1190054031022, 1190054031024, 1190054031025, 1190054031026, 1190054031027, 1190054031028, 1190054031029, 1190054031030, 1190054031031, 1190054031032, 1190054031033, 1190054031034, 1190054031035, 1190054031036, 1190054032006, 1190054041018. It has two judges.

(27) District 26B: Mecklenburg County: VTD: 001, VTD: 002, VTD: 003, VTD: 004, VTD: 005, VTD: 006, VTD: 007, VTD: 008, VTD: 009, VTD: 010, VTD: 017, VTD: 018, VTD: 020, VTD: 021, VTD: 028, VTD: 029, VTD: 030, VTD: 032, VTD: 034, VTD: 035, VTD: 036, VTD: 037, VTD: 038,

VTD: 043, VTD: 044, VTD: 045, VTD: 047, VTD: 051, VTD: 061, VTD: 062, VTD: 063, VTD: 065, VTD: 066, VTD: 067, VTD: 068, VTD: 069, VTD: 070: Block(s) 1190030072011, 1190030072012, 1190030072020; VTD: 071, VTD: 074, VTD: 083, VTD: 084, VTD: 086, VTD: 087: Block(s) 1190058292006, 1190058292007, 1190058292008; VTD: 093, VTD: 094, VTD: 095, VTD: 100: Block(s) 1190030171000, 1190030171001, 1190030171002, 1190030171003, 1190030181000, 1190030181001, 1190030181002, 1190030181003, 1190030181004, 1190030181005, 1190030181006, 1190030181008, 1190030181009, 1190030181010, 1190030181011, 1190030181013, 1190030181014, 1190030181015, 1190030181018, 1190030181019; VTD: 101, VTD: 103: Block(s) 1190030151005, 1190030151010, 1190030152000, 1190030152001, 1190030152002, 1190030152003, 1190030152004, 1190030152005, 1190030152006, 1190030152007, 1190030152008, 1190030152009, 1190030152010, 1190030152011, 1190030152012, 1190030153000, 1190030153001, 1190030153002, 1190030153004, 1190030153005, 1190030153006, 1190030153007, 1190030153008, 1190030153010, 1190030153011; VTD: 104: 1190015071000, 1190015071005, 1190015072000, 1190015072001, 1190015072002, 1190015072003, 1190015072004, 1190015073000, 1190015073001, 1190015073002, 1190015073003, 1190015073004, 1190015073005, 1190015073013, 1190015073014; VTD: 105, VTD: 106, VTD: 107.1, VTD: 108, VTD: 109: Block(s) 1190011001009, 1190011001010, 1190011001011, 1190011001012, 1190011001013, 1190011001014, 1190011001020, 1190011001021, 1190011001022, 1190011001024, 1190011002000, 1190011002001, 1190011002002, 1190011002003, 1190011002004, 1190011002005, 1190011002006, 1190011002007, 1190011002008, 1190011002009, 1190011002010, 1190011002011, 1190011002012, 1190011002013, 1190011002014, 1190011002017, 1190011002018, 1190011002019, 1190011002020, 1190011002021, 1190011002022, 1190011002023, 1190011002024, 1190011002025, 1190011002028, 1190025001000, 1190025001001, 1190025001002, 1190025001003, 1190025001004, 1190025001005, 1190025001006, 1190025001007, 1190025001008, 1190025001009, 1190025001010, 1190025001011, 1190025001012, 1190025002000, 1190025002001, 1190025002013, 1190025002014, 1190025002015, 1190025002016, 1190025002017, 1190025002018, 1190025002023, 1190025002024, 1190025002025, 1190025002026, 1190025002033, 1190025002034, 1190025002035, 1190025002036, 1190025002037, 1190025002038, 1190025002039, 1190025002040, 1190025002044, 1190025002045; VTD: 115, VTD: 116, VTD: 123, VTD: 124, VTD: 125, VTD: 126: Block(s) 1190055241001, 1190055241002, 1190055241003, 1190055241004, 1190055241005, 1190055241006, 1190055241007, 1190055243001, 1190055243002, 1190055243004, 1190055243006, 1190055243012, 1190055244000, 1190055244001, 1190055244002, 1190055244003, 1190055244004, 1190055244006, 1190055244007, 1190055245000, 1190055245001, 1190055245002, 1190055245003, 1190055245004, 1190055245005, 1190055245006, 1190055245007, 1190055245008, 1190055245009, 1190055245010, 1190055245011, 1190055245012, 1190055245013, 1190055245014, 1190055245015, 1190055245016, 1190055245017, 1190055245018, 1190055245019, 1190055245020, 1190055245021, 1190055245023, 1190055245024, 1190055245025, 1190055245026, 1190055245027, 1190055245028, 1190055245030, 1190055245031, 1190055245032, 1190055245033, 1190055245034, 1190055245035, 1190055245036; VTD: 128, VTD: 130, VTD: 141, VTD: 145, VTD: 146, VTD: 149, VTD: 151, VTD: 203, VTD: 204.1, VTD: 205, VTD: 212, VTD: 214, VTD: 217: Block(s) 1190030153003, 1190030153009; VTD: 237, VTD: 238.1, VTD: 239. It has three judges.

(28) District 26C: Mecklenburg County: VTD: 019, VTD: 039: Block(s) 1190039024010, 1190039031000, 1190039031001, 1190039031005, 1190039031006, 1190039031007, 1190039031008, 1190039031011, 1190039031012, 1190039031013, 1190039031014, 1190039031015, 1190039031016, 1190039031017; VTD: 040, VTD: 048, VTD: 049, VTD: 050, VTD: 053, VTD: 057, VTD: 059, VTD: 064, VTD: 070: Block(s) 1190029041000, 1190029041001,

149

1190029041002, 1190029041003, 1190029041004, 1190029041005, 1190029041006, 1190029041007, 1190029041008, 1190029041009, 1190029041010, 1190029041011, 1190029044002, 1190030072000, 1190030072001, 1190030072002, 1190030072003, 1190030072013, 1190030072014, 1190030072015; VTD: 072, VTD: 073, VTD: 075, VTD: 076, VTD: 077: Block(s) 1190058241024, 1190058241025; VTD: 078.1: 1190038051000, 1190038051001, 1190038051002, 1190038051003, 1190038051004, 1190038051008, 1190038051009, 1190038051010, 1190038051011, 1190038051015, 1190038051016, 1190038051017, 1190038051021, 1190038051022, 1190038051023, 1190038051024, 1190038051025, 1190038051026, 1190039024011, 1190039024012; VTD: 079, VTD: 080, VTD: 081, VTD: 085, VTD: 087: Block(s) 1190058261012, 1190058261014, 1190058261015, 1190058261016, 1190058261017, 1190058261018, 1190058261019, 1190058261020, 1190058262000, 1190058262001, 1190058262002, 1190058262003, 1190058262004, 1190058262005, 1190058262006, 1190058262007, 1190058262008, 1190058262009, 1190058262010, 1190058262011, 1190058262012, 1190058262013, 1190058262014, 1190058262015, 1190058262016, 1190058262017, 1190058262018, 1190058262019, 1190058262020, 1190058262021, 1190058262022, 1190058262024, 1190058262025, 1190058301000, 1190058301001, 1190058301002, 1190058301003, 1190058301004, 1190058301005, 1190058301006, 1190058301007, 1190058301008, 1190058301009, 1190058302014, 1190058302015, 1190058302016, 1190058371021, 1190058371022; VTD: 088, VTD: 089, VTD: 090, VTD: 091, VTD: 092, VTD: 096, VTD: 097: Block(s) 1190058241052, 1190058291008; VTD: 099, VTD: 100: Block(s) 1190030171004, 1190030171005, 1190030171006, 1190030171007, 1190030171008, 1190030171009, 1190030171010, 1190030172000, 1190030172013, 1190030172014, 1190030181007, 1190030181012, 1190030181016, 1190030181017, 1190030181020, 1190030181021, 1190030181022; VTD: 102, VTD: 103: Block(s) 1190030151000, 1190030151001, 1190030151002, 1190030151003, 1190030151004, 1190030151006, 1190030151007, 1190030151008, 1190030151009, 1190030151011, 1190030151012; VTD: 110, VTD: 111, VTD: 112, VTD: 113, VTD: 114, VTD: 117, VTD: 118, VTD: 119, VTD: 121, VTD: 122, VTD: 127, VTD: 129, VTD: 131, VTD: 133, VTD: 134, VTD: 135, VTD: 136, VTD: 137, VTD: 138, VTD: 139.1, VTD: 140, VTD: 142, VTD: 143, VTD: 144, VTD: 147: Block(s) 1190038051031, 1190038051032, 1190038051033, 1190038051034, 1190038051035, 1190038061001, 1190038061002, 1190038061003, 1190038061004, 1190038061005, 1190038061006; VTD: 148, VTD: 150, VTD: 200: Block(s) 1190059061032, 1190059061033, 1190059061034, 1190059061035, 1190059061036, 1190059061037, 1190059061038, 1190059061039, 1190059061040, 1190059061041, 1190059061042, 1190059061043, 1190059061044, 1190059061045, 1190059061046, 1190059061047, 1190059061048, 1190059061049, 1190059061050, 1190059061052, 1190059061053, 1190059061054, 1190059061055, 1190059061056, 1190059061057, 1190059061058, 1190059061059, 1190059061060, 1190059061061, 1190059061062, 1190059061063, 1190059061064, 1190059061065, 1190059061066, 1190059061067, 1190059061068, 1190059061069, 1190059061070, 1190059061071, 1190059061072, 1190059061073, 1190059061074, 1190059061075, 1190059061076, 1190059061077, 1190059061078, 1190059061079, 1190059061080, 1190059061081, 1190059061082, 1190059061083, 1190059061084, 1190059061085, 1190059061086, 1190059061087, 1190059061088, 1190059061089, 1190059061090, 1190059062014, 1190059062024, 1190059062025, 1190059062026, 1190059062027, 1190059062028, 1190059062029, 1190059062030, 1190059062037, 1190059062038, 1190059062039, 1190059063000, 1190059063001, 1190059063002, 1190059063003, 1190059063004, 1190059063005, 1190059063006, 1190059063007, 1190059063008, 1190059063009, 1190059063010, 1190059063011, 1190059063012, 1190059063013, 1190059063014, 1190059063015, 1190059063016, 1190059063017, 1190059063018, 1190059063019, 1190059063020, 1190059063021, 1190059063022, 1190059063023, 1190059063024, 1190059063025, 1190059063026,

1190059063027, 1190059063028, 1190059063029, 1190059063030, 1190059063031, 1190059063032, 1190059064000, 1190059064001, 1190059064002, 1190059064003, 1190059064004, 1190059064005, 1190059064006, 1190059064007, 1190059064008, 1190059064009, 1190059064010, 1190059064011, 1190059064012, 1190059064013, 1190059064014, 1190059064015, 1190059064016, 1190059064017, 1190059064018, 1190059064019, 1190059064020, 1190059064021, 1190059064022, 1190059064023, 1190059064024, 1190059064025, 1190059064026, 1190059064027, 1190059064028, 1190059064029, 1190059064030, 1190059064031, 1190059064032, 1190059064033, 1190059064034, 1190059064035, 1190059064036, 1199801001022, 1199801001023, 1199801001025, 1199801001026, 1199801001027, 1199801001028, 1199801001029, 1199801001030, 1199801001031, 1199801001032, 1199801001034, 1199801001037, 1199801001038, 1199801001039, 1199801001040, 1199801001041; VTD: 201, VTD: 202, VTD: 206, VTD: 207, VTD: 208, VTD: 209, VTD: 211, VTD: 213: Block(s) 1190054011000, 1190054011001, 1190054011002, 1190054011003, 1190054011004, 1190054011005, 1190054011006, 1190054011007, 1190054011008, 1190054011009, 1190054011010, 1190054011011, 1190054011012, 1190054011013, 1190054011014, 1190054011015, 1190054011016, 1190054011017, 1190054011018, 1190054011019, 1190054011020, 1190054011021, 1190054011022, 1190054011023, 1190054011024, 1190054011025, 1190054011026, 1190054011027, 1190054011028, 1190054011029, 1190054011030, 1190054011031, 1190054011035, 1190054011036, 1190054011037, 1190054031001, 1190054031002, 1190054031003, 1190054031004, 1190054031005, 1190054031006, 1190054031008, 1190054031009, 1190054031010, 1190054031011, 1190054031012, 1190054031023, 1190054032000, 1190054032001, 1190054032002, 1190054032003, 1190054032004, 1190054032005, 1190054032007, 1190054032009; VTD: 215, VTD: 216, VTD: 217: Block(s) 1190058121002, 1190058121003, 1190058121005, 1190058121006, 1190058121007, 1190058121008, 1190058121009, 1190058121010, 1190058121011, 1190058121012, 1190058121016, 1190058121017, 1190058121018, 1190058121019, 1190058122008, 1190058122009, 1190058122010, 1190058122011, 1190058122012, 1190058122013, 1190058122014, 1190058122018, 1190058122019, 1190058122020, 1190058122021, 1190058122022, 1190058122023, 1190058122024, 1190058122025, 1190058122026, 1190058122027, 1190058122028, 1190058122029, 1190058122030, 1190058122031, 1190058122032, 1190058122033, 1190058122034, 1190058122035, 1190058122036, 1190058122037, 1190058122038, 1190058122039, 1190058122040, 1190058122041, 1190058122042, 1190058122043, 1190058333000, 1190058333001, 1190058333002; VTD: 218, VTD: 219, VTD: 220, VTD: 221, VTD: 222, VTD: 223.1, VTD: 224, VTD: 225, VTD: 226, VTD: 227, VTD: 228, VTD: 229, VTD: 230, VTD: 231, VTD: 232, VTD: 233, VTD: 234, VTD: 235, VTD: 236, VTD: 240, VTD: 241, VTD: 242, VTD: 243. It has two judges.

(c) In subsection (b) above, the names and boundaries of voting tabulation districts, tracts, block groups, and blocks specified in this section are as shown on the 2010 Census Redistricting TIGER/Line Shapefiles.

(c1) If any voting tabulation district boundary is changed, that change shall not change the boundary of a judicial district, which shall remain the same as it is depicted by the 2010 Census Redistricting TIGER/Line Shapefiles.

(c2) The Legislative Services Officer shall certify a true copy of the block assignment file associated with any mapping software used to generate the language in subsection (b) of this section. The certified true copy of the block assignment file shall be delivered by the Legislative Services Officer to the Principal Clerk of the Senate and the Principal Clerk of the House of Representatives. If any area within North Carolina is not assigned to a specific district by subsection (b) of this section, the certified true copy of the block assignment file delivered to the Principal Clerk of the Senate and the Principal Clerk of the House of Representatives shall control.

(d) The several judges, their terms of office, and their assignments to districts are as follows:

(1) In the first superior court district, J. Herbert Small and Thomas S. Watts serve terms expiring December 31, 1994.

(2) In the second superior court district, William C. Griffin serves a term expiring December 31, 1994.

(3) In the third-A superior court district, David E. Reid serves a term expiring on December 31, 1992.

(4) In the third-B superior court district, Herbert O. Phillips, III, serves a term expiring on December 31, 1994.

(5) In the fourth-A superior court district, Henry L. Stevens, III, serves a term expiring December 31, 1994.

(6) In the fourth-B superior court district, James R. Strickland serves a term expiring December 31, 1992.

(7) In the fifth superior court district, no election shall be held in 1992 for the full term of the seat now occupied by Bradford Tillery, and the holder of that seat shall serve until a successor is elected in 1994 and qualifies. The succeeding term begins January 1, 1995. In the fifth superior court district, Napoleon B. Barefoot serves a term expiring December 31, 1994.

(8) In the sixth-A superior court district, Richard B. Allsbrook serves a term expiring December 31, 1990.

(9) In the sixth-B superior court district, a judge shall be elected in 1988 to serve an eight-year term beginning January 1, 1989.

(10)   In the seventh-A superior court district, Charles B. Winberry, serves a term expiring December 31, 1994.

(11)   In the seventh-B superior court district, a judge shall be elected in 1988 to serve an eight-year term beginning January 1, 1989.

(12)   In the seventh-C superior court district, Franklin R. Brown serves a term expiring December 31, 1990.

(13)   In the eighth-A superior court district, James D. Llewellyn serves a term expiring December 31, 1994.

(14)   In the eighth-B superior court district, Paul M. Wright serves a term expiring December 31, 1992.

(15)   In the ninth superior court district, Robert H. Hobgood and Henry W. Hight, Jr., serve terms expiring December 31, 1994.

(16)   In the tenth-A superior court district, a judge shall be elected in 1988 to serve an eight-year term beginning January 1, 1989.

(17)   In the tenth-B superior court district, Robert L. Farmer serves a term expiring December 31, 1992. In the tenth-B superior court district, no election shall be held in 1990 for the full term of the seat now occupied by Henry V. Barnette, Jr., and the holder of that seat shall serve until a successor is elected in 1992 and qualifies. The succeeding term begins January 1, 1993.

(18)   In the tenth-C superior court district, Edwin S. Preston, serves a term expiring December 31, 1990. In the tenth-D superior court district, Donald Stephens serves a term expiring December 31, 1988.

(19)   In the eleventh superior court district, Wiley F. Bowen serves a term expiring December 31, 1990.

(20)   In the twelfth-A superior court district, D.B. Herring, Jr., serves a term expiring December 31, 1990.

(21)   In the twelfth-B superior court district, a judge shall be elected in 1988 to serve an eight-year term beginning January 1, 1989.

(22) In the twelfth-C superior court district, no election shall be held in 1992 for the full term of the seat now occupied by Coy E. Brewer, Jr., and the holder of that seat shall serve until a successor is elected in 1994 and qualifies. The succeeding term begins January 1, 1995. In the twelfth-C superior court district, E. Lynn Johnson serves a term expiring December 31, 1994.

(23) In the thirteenth superior court district, Giles R. Clark serves a term expiring December 31, 1994.

(24) In the fourteenth-A superior court district, a judge shall be elected in 1988 to serve an eight-year term beginning January 1, 1989.

(25) In the fourteenth-B superior court district, no election shall be held in 1992 for the full term of the seat now occupied by Anthony M. Brannon, and the holder of that seat shall serve until a successor is elected in 1994 and qualifies. The succeeding term begins July 1, 1995.

(26) In the fourteenth-B superior court district, no election shall be held in 1990 for the full term of the seat now occupied by Thomas H. Lee, and the holder of that seat shall serve until a successor is elected in 1994 and qualifies. The succeeding term begins January 1, 1995. In the fourteenth-B superior court district, J. Milton Read, Jr., serves a term expiring December 31, 1994.

(27) In the fifteenth-A superior court district, J.B. Allen, Jr., serves a term expiring December 31, 1994.

(28) In the fifteenth-B superior court district, F. Gordon Battle serves a term expiring December 31, 1994.

(29) In the sixteenth-A superior court district, B. Craig Ellis serves a term expiring December 31, 1994.

(30) In the sixteenth-B superior court district, a judge shall be elected in 1988 to serve an eight-year term beginning January 1, 1989. In the sixteenth-B judicial [superior court] district, a judge shall be appointed by the Governor to serve until the results of the 1990 general election are certified. A person shall be elected in the 1990 general election to serve the remainder of the term expiring December 31, 1996.

(31) In the seventeenth-A superior court district, Melzer A. Morgan, Jr., serves a term expiring December 31, 1990.

(32) In the seventeenth-B superior court district, James M. Long serves a term expiring December 31, 1994.

(33) In the eighteenth-A superior court district, a judge shall be elected in 1988 to serve an eight-year term beginning January 1, 1989.

(34) In the eighteenth-B superior court district, Edward K. Washington's term expired December 31, 1986, but he is holding over because of a court order enjoining an election from being held in 1986. A successor shall be elected in 1988 to serve an eight-year term beginning January 1, 1989.

(35) In the eighteenth-C superior court district, W. Douglas Albright serves a term expiring December 31, 1990.

(36) In the eighteenth-D superior court district, Thomas W. Ross's term expired December 31, 1986, but he is holding over because of a court order enjoining an election from being held in 1986. A successor shall be elected in 1988 to serve an eight-year term beginning January 1, 1989.

(37) In the eighteenth-E superior court district, Joseph John's term expired December 31, 1986, but he is holding over because of a court order enjoining an election from being held in 1986. A successor shall be elected in 1988 to serve an eight-year term beginning January 1, 1989.

(38) In the nineteenth-A superior court district, James C. Davis serves a term expiring December 31, 1992.

(39) In the nineteenth-B1 superior court district, Russell G. Walker, Jr., serves a term expiring December 31, 1990. No election shall be held in 1998 for the full term of the seat now occupied by Russell G. Walker, Jr., and the holder of that seat shall serve until a successor is elected in 2000 and qualifies. The succeeding term shall begin January 1, 2001. The superior court judgeship held on June 12, 1996, in Superior Court District 20A by a resident of Moore County (James M. Webb) is allocated to Superior Court District 19B2. The term of that judge expires December 31, 2000. The judge's successor shall be elected in the 2000 general election.

(40) In the nineteenth-C superior court district, Thomas W. Seay, Jr., serves a term expiring December 31, 1990.

(41) In the twentieth-A superior court district, F. Fetzer Mills serves a term expiring December 31, 1992.

(42) In the twentieth-B superior court district, William H. Helms serves a term expiring December 31, 1990.

(43) In the twenty-first-A superior court district, William Z. Wood serves a term expiring December 31, 1990.

(44) In the twenty-first-B superior court district, Judson D. DeRamus, Jr., serves a term expiring December 31, 1988.

(45) In the twenty-first-C superior court district, William H. Freeman serves a term expiring December 31, 1990.

(46) In the twenty-first-D superior court district, a judge shall be elected in 1988 to serve an eight-year term beginning January 1, 1989.

(47) In the twenty-second superior court district, no election shall be held in 1992 for the full term of the seat now occupied by Preston Cornelius, and the holder of that seat shall serve until a successor is elected in 1994 and qualifies. The succeeding term shall begin January 1, 1995. In the twenty-second superior court district, Robert A. Collier serves a term expiring December 31, 1994.

(48) In the twenty-third superior court district, Julius A. Rousseau, Jr., serves a term expiring December 31, 1990.

(49) In the twenty-fourth superior court district, Charles C. Lamm, Jr., serves a term expiring December 31, 1994.

(50) In the twenty-fifth-A superior court district, Claude S. Sitton serves a term expiring December 31, 1994.

(51) In the twenty-fifth-B superior court district, Forrest A. Ferrell serves a term expiring December 31, 1990.

(52) In the twenty-sixth-A superior court district, no election shall be held in 1994 for the full term of the seat now occupied by W. Terry Sherrill, and the holder of that seat shall serve until a successor is elected in 1996 and qualifies. The succeeding term shall begin January 1, 1997. In the twenty-sixth-A superior

court district, a judge shall be elected in 1988 to serve an eight-year term beginning January 1, 1989.

(53)   In the twenty-sixth-B superior court district, Frank W. Snepp, Jr., and Kenneth A. Griffin serve terms expiring December 31, 1990.

(54)   In the twenty-sixth-C superior court district, no election shall be held in 1992 for the full term of the seat now occupied by Chase Boone Saunders, and the holder of that seat shall serve until a successor is elected in 1994 and qualifies. The succeeding term shall begin January 1, 1995. In the twenty-sixth-C superior court district, Robert M. Burroughs serves a term expiring December 31, 1994.

(55)   In the twenty-seventh-A superior court district, no election shall be held in 1988 for the full term of the seat now occupied by Robert E. Gaines, and the holder of that seat shall serve until a successor is elected in 1990 and qualifies. The succeeding term begins January 1, 1991. In the twenty-seventh-A superior court district, Robert W. Kirby serves a term expiring December 31, 1990.

(56)   In the twenty-seventh-B superior court district, John M. Gardner serves a term expiring December 31, 1994.

(57)   In the twenty-eighth superior court district, Robert D. Lewis and C. Walter Allen serve terms expiring December 31, 1990.

(58)   In the twenty-ninth superior court district, Hollis M. Owens, Jr., serves a term expiring December 31, 1990.

(59)   In the thirtieth-A superior court district, James U. Downs serves a term expiring December 31, 1990.

(60)   In the thirtieth-B superior court district, Janet M. Hyatt serves a term expiring December 31, 1994. (1969, c. 1171, ss. 1-3; c. 1190, s. 4; 1971, c. 377, s. 5; c. 997; 1973, c. 47, s. 2; c. 646; c. 855, s. 1; 1975, c. 529; c. 956, ss. 1, 2; 1975, 2nd Sess., c. 983, s. 114; 1977, c. 1119, ss. 1, 3, 4; c. 1130, ss. 1, 2; 1977, 2nd Sess., c. 1238, s. 1; c. 1243, s. 4; 1979, c. 838, s. 119; c. 1072, s. 1; 1979, 2nd Sess., c. 1221, s. 1; 1981, c. 964, ss. 1, 2; 1981 (Reg. Sess., 1982), c. 1282, s. 71.2; 1983 (Reg. Sess., 1984), c. 1109, ss. 4, 4.1; 1985, c. 698, s. 11(a); 1987, c. 509, s. 1; c. 549, s. 6.6; c. 738, s. 124; 1987 (Reg. Sess., 1988), c. 1037, s. 1; c. 1056, ss. 14, 15; 1989, c. 795, s. 22(a); 1991, c. 746, s. 1; 1993, c. 321, ss. 200.4(a), 200.5(a), (d); 1995, c. 51, s. 1; c. 509, s. 3; 1995 (Reg.

Sess., 1996), c. 589, s. 1(a), (c); 1998-212, s. 16.16A(a); 1998-217, s. 67.3(c); 1999-237, ss. 17.12(b), 17.19(a)-(d), 17.20(a)-(c); 1999-396, s. 1; 2000-67, s. 15.6(a); 2000-140, s. 36; 2001-333, ss. 1, 2; 2001-424, s. 22.4(b); 2001-507, ss. 3, 4; 2003-284, ss. 13.14(a), 13.14(b); 2004-124, s. 14.6(b); 2004-127, s. 2(a); 2005-276, ss. 14.2(a), 14.2(e1); 2006-96, s. 2; 2007-323, s. 14.25(a); 2011-203, ss. 1-3; 2011-417, s. 1; 2012-182, s. 2(a), (b); 2013-360, s. 18B.22(a).)

§ 7A-41.1. District and set of districts defined; senior resident superior court judges and their authority.

(a) In this section and in any other law which refers to this section:

(1) "District" means any superior court district established by G.S. 7A-41 which consists exclusively of one or more entire counties;

(2) "Set of districts" means any set of two or more superior court districts established under G.S. 7A-41, none of which consists exclusively of one or more entire counties, but both or all of which include territory from the same county or counties and together comprise all of the territory of that county or those counties;

(3) "Regular resident superior court judge of the district or set of districts" means a regular superior court judge who is a resident judge of any of the superior court districts established under G.S. 7A-41 which comprise or are included in a district or set of districts as defined herein.

(b) There shall be one and only one senior resident superior court judge for each district or set of districts as defined in subsection (a) of this section, who shall be:

(1) Where there is only one regular resident superior court judge for the district, that judge; and

(2) Where there are two or more regular resident superior court judges for the district or set of districts, the judge who, from among all the regular resident superior court judges of the district or set of districts, has the most continuous service as a regular resident superior court judge; provided if two or more judges are of equal seniority, the oldest of those judges shall be the senior regular resident superior court judge.

(3) Where there is a set of districts, the Chief Justice of the Supreme Court shall designate one of the judges as senior resident superior court judge to serve in that capacity at the pleasure of the Chief Justice, if that set of districts are wholly contained in one county that is specified in law as the sole proper venue for certain actions.

(c) Senior resident superior court judges and regular resident superior court judges possess equal judicial jurisdiction, power, authority and status, but all duties placed by the Constitution or statutes on the resident judge of a superior court district, including the appointment to and removal from office, which are not related to a case, controversy or judicial proceeding and which do not involve the exercise of judicial power, shall be discharged, throughout a district as defined in subsection (a) of this section or throughout all of the districts comprising a set of districts so defined, for each county in that district or set of districts, by the senior resident superior court judge for that district or set of districts. That senior resident superior court judge alone among the superior court judges of that district or set of districts shall receive the salary and benefits of a senior resident superior court judge.

(d) A senior resident superior court judge for a district or set of districts as defined in subsection (a) of this section with two or more regular resident superior court judges, by notice in writing to the Administrative Officer of the Courts, may decline to exercise the authority vested in him by this section, in which event such authority shall be exercised by the regular resident superior court judge who, among the other regular resident superior court judges of the district or set of districts, is next senior in point of service or age, respectively.

(e) In the event a senior resident superior court judge for a district or set of districts with one or more regular resident superior court judges is unable, due to mental or physical incapacity, to exercise the authority vested in him by the statute, and the Chief Justice, in his discretion, has determined that such incapacity exists, the Chief Justice shall appoint an acting senior regular resident superior court judge from the other regular resident judges of the district or set of districts, to exercise, temporarily, the authority of the senior regular resident judge. Such appointee shall serve at the pleasure of the Chief Justice and until his temporary appointment is vacated by appropriate order. (1987 (Reg. Sess., 1988), c. 1037, s. 2; 2010-105, s. 1; 2012-194, s. 63.5.)

§ 7A-41.2. Nomination and election of regular superior court judges.

Candidates for the office of regular superior court judge shall be both nominated and elected by the qualified voters of the superior court district for which the election is sought. (1996, 2nd Ex. Sess., c. 9, s. 1.)

§ 7A-42. Sessions of superior court in cities other than county seats.

(a) Sessions of the superior court shall be held in each city in the State which is not a county seat and which has a population of 35,000 or more, according to the 1960 federal census.

(a1) In addition to the sessions of superior court authorized by subsection (a) of this section, sessions of superior court in the following counties may be held in the additional seats of court listed by order of the Senior Resident Superior Court Judge after consultation with the Chief District Court Judge:

County	Additional Seats of Court
Davidson	Thomasville
Iredell	Mooresville

The courtrooms and related judicial facilities for these sessions of superior court may be provided by the municipality, and in such cases the facilities fee collected for the State by the clerk of superior court shall be remitted to the municipality to assist in meeting the expense of providing those facilities.

(b) For the purpose of segregating the cases to be tried in any city referred to in subsection (a), and to designate the place of trial, the clerk of superior court in any county having one or more such cities shall set up a criminal docket and a civil docket, which dockets shall indicate the cases and proceedings to be tried in each such city in his county. Such dockets shall bear the name of the city in which such sessions of court are to be held, followed by the word "Division." Summons in actions to be tried in any such city shall clearly designate the place of trial.

(c) For the purpose of determining the proper place of trial of any action or proceeding, whether civil or criminal, the county in which any city described in subsection (a) is located shall be divided into divisions, and the territory embraced in the division in which each such city is located shall consist of the township in which such city lies and all contiguous townships within such county, such division of the superior court to be known by the name of such city followed by the word "Division." All other townships of any such county shall constitute a division of the superior court to be known by the name of the county seat followed by the word "Division." All laws, rules, and regulations now or hereafter in force and effect in determining the proper venue as between the superior courts of the several counties of the State shall apply for the purpose of determining the proper place of trial as between such divisions within such county and as between each of such divisions and any other county of the superior court in North Carolina.

(d) The clerk of superior court of any county with an additional seat of superior court may, but shall not be required to, hear matters in any place other than at his office at the county seat.

(e) The grand jury for the several divisions of court of any county in which a city described in subsection (a) is located shall be drawn from the whole county, and may hold hearings and meetings at either the county seat or elsewhere within the county as it may elect, or as it may be directed by the judge holding any session of superior court within such county; provided, however, that in arranging the sessions of the court for the trial of criminal cases for any county in which any such city is located a session of one week or more shall be held at the county seat preceding any session of one week or more to be held in any such city, so as to facilitate the work of the grand jury, and so as to confine its meetings to the county seat as fully as may be practicable. All petit jurors for all sessions of court in the several divisions of such county shall be drawn, as now or hereafter provided by law, from the whole of the county in which any such city is located for all sessions of courts in the several divisions of such county.

(f) Special sessions of court for the trial of either civil or criminal cases in any city described in subsection (a) may be arranged as by law now or hereafter provided for special sessions of the superior court.

(g) All court records of all such divisions of the superior court of any such county shall be kept in the office of the clerk of the superior court at the county seat, but they may be temporarily removed under the direction and supervision of the clerk to any such division or divisions. No judgment or order rendered at any session held in any such city shall become a lien upon or otherwise affect the title to any real estate within such county until it has been docketed in the office of the clerk of the superior court at the county seat as now or may hereafter be provided by law; provided, that nothing herein shall affect the provisions of G.S. 1-233 and the equities therein provided for shall be preserved as to all judgments and orders rendered at any session of the superior court in any such city.

(h)   It shall be the duty of the board of county commissioners of the county in which any such city is located to provide a suitable place for holding such sessions of court, and to provide for the payment of the extra expense, if any, of the sheriff and his deputies in attending the sessions of court of any such division, and the expense of keeping, housing and feeding prisoners while awaiting trial.

(i)   Notwithstanding the provisions of this section, when exigent circumstances exist, sessions of superior court may be conducted at a location outside a county seat by order of the Senior Resident Superior Court Judge of a county, with the prior approval of the location and the facilities by the Administrative Office of the Courts and after consultation with the Clerk of Superior Court and county officials of the county. An order entered under this subsection shall be filed in the office of the Clerk of Superior Court in the county and posted at the courthouse within the county seat and notice shall be posted in other conspicuous locations. The order shall be limited to such session or sessions as are approved by the Chief Justice of the Supreme Court of North Carolina. (1943, c. 121; 1969, c. 1190, s. 48; 1987 (Reg. Sess., 1988), c. 1037, s. 2.1; 1997-304, s. 4.)

§ 7A-43. Reserved for future codification purposes.

§§ 7A-43.1 through 7A-43.3. Repealed by Session Laws 1967, c. 1049, s. 6.

§ 7A-44. Salary and expenses of superior court judge.

(a)   A judge of the superior court, regular or special, shall receive the annual salary set forth in the Current Operations Appropriations Act, and in addition shall be paid the same travel allowance as State employees generally by G.S. 138-6(a), provided that no travel allowance be paid for travel within his county of residence. The Administrative Officer of the Courts may also reimburse superior court judges, in addition to the above funds for travel, for travel and subsistence expenses incurred for professional education.

(b)   In lieu of merit and other increment raises paid to regular State employees, a judge of the superior court, regular or special, shall receive as longevity pay an annual amount equal to four and eight-tenths percent (4.8%) of the annual salary set forth in the Current Operations Appropriations Act payable monthly after five years of service, nine and six-tenths percent (9.6%) after 10 years of service, fourteen and four-tenths percent (14.4%) after 15 years of service, nineteen and two-tenths percent (19.2%) after 20 years of service, and twenty-four percent (24%) after 25 years of service. "Service" means service as a justice or judge of the General Court of Justice or as a member of the Utilities Commission or as director or assistant director of the Administrative Office of the Courts. Service shall also mean service as a district attorney or as a clerk of superior court. (Code, ss. 918, 3734; 1891, c. 193; 1901, c. 167; 1905, c. 208; Rev., s. 2765; 1907, c. 988; 1909, c. 85; 1911, c. 82; 1919, c. 51; C.S., s. 3884; 1921, c. 25, s. 3; 1925, c. 227; 1927, c. 69, s. 2; 1949, c. 157, s. 1; 1953, c. 1080, s. 1; 1957, c. 1416; 1961, c. 957, s. 2; 1963, c. 839, s. 2; 1965, c. 921, s. 2; 1967, c. 691, s. 40; 1969, c. 1190, s. 36; 1973, c. 1474; 1975, 2nd Sess., c. 983, s. 13; 1977, c. 802, s. 41.1; 1979, 2nd Sess., c. 1137, s. 28; 1981, c. 964, s. 18; 1983, c. 761, s. 244; 1983 (Reg. Sess., 1984), c. 1034, s. 165; c. 1109, ss. 2.2, 11, 13.1; 1985, c. 698, s. 10(a); 1987 (Reg. Sess., 1988), c. 1086, s. 30(b); c. 1100, s. 15(c); 2007-323, s. 28.18A(c); 2009-451, s. 15.10; 2009-575, s. 13.)

§ 7A-44.1. Secretarial and clerical help.

(a)   Each senior resident superior court judge may appoint a judicial secretary to serve at his pleasure and under his direction the secretarial and clerical needs of the superior court judges of the district or set of districts as defined by G.S. 7A-41.1(a) for which he is the senior resident superior court judge. The appointment may be full-or part-time and the compensation and allowances of such secretary shall be fixed by the senior regular resident superior court judge, within limits determined by the Administrative Office of the Courts, and paid by the State.

(b)   Each senior resident superior court judge may apply to the Director of the Administrative Office of the Courts to enter into contracts with local governments for the provision by the State of services of judicial secretaries pursuant to G.S. 153A-212.1 or G.S. 160A-289.1.

(c)   The Director of the Administrative Office of the Courts may provide assistance requested pursuant to subsection (b) of this section only upon a showing by the senior resident superior court judge, supported by facts, that the overwhelming public interest warrants the use of additional resources for the speedy disposition of cases involving drug offenses, domestic violence, or other offenses involving a threat to public safety.

(d) The terms of any contract entered into with local governments pursuant to subsection (b) of this section shall be fixed by the Director of the Administrative Office of the Courts in each case. Nothing in this section shall be construed to obligate the General Assembly to make any appropriation to implement the provisions of this section or to obligate the Administrative Office of the Courts to provide the administrative costs of establishing or maintaining the positions or services provided for under this section. Further, nothing in this section shall be construed to obligate the Administrative Office of the Courts to maintain positions or services initially provided for under this section. (1975, c. 956, s. 3; 1987 (Reg. Sess., 1988), c. 1037, s. 3; 2000-67, s. 15.4(a).)

§ 7A-45: Repealed by Session Laws 1987, c. 509, s. 7, effective January 1, 1989.

§ 7A-45.1. Special judges.

(a) Effective November 1, 1993, the Governor may appoint two special superior court judges to serve terms expiring September 30, 2000. Effective October 1, 2000, one of those positions is abolished. Successors to the special superior court judge appointed pursuant to this subsection shall be appointed to a five-year term. A special judge takes the same oath of office and is subject to the same requirements and disabilities as are or may be prescribed by law for regular judges of the superior court, save the requirement of residence in a particular district.

(a1) Effective October 1, 1995, the Governor may appoint two special superior court judges to serve terms expiring September 30, 2000. Successors to the special superior court judges appointed pursuant to this subsection shall be appointed to five-year terms. A special judge takes the same oath of office and is subject to the same requirements and disabilities as are or may be prescribed by law for regular judges of the superior court, save the requirement of residence in a particular district.

(a2) Effective December 15, 1996, the Governor may appoint four special superior court judges to serve terms expiring five years from the date that each judge takes office. Successors to the special superior court judges appointed pursuant to this subsection shall be appointed to five-year terms. A special judge takes the same oath of office and is subject to the same requirements and disabilities as are or may be prescribed by law for regular judges of the superior court, save the requirement of residence in a particular district.

(a3)   Effective December 15, 1998, the Governor may appoint a special superior court judge to serve a term expiring five years from the date that judge takes office. Successors to the special superior court judge appointed pursuant to this subsection shall be appointed to five-year terms. A special judge takes the same oath of office and is subject to the same requirements and disabilities as are or may be prescribed by law for regular judges of the superior court, save the requirement of residence in a particular district.

(a4)   Effective October 1, 1999, the Governor may appoint four special superior court judges to serve terms expiring five years from the date that each judge takes office. Successors to the special superior court judges appointed pursuant to this subsection shall be appointed to five-year terms. A special judge takes the same oath of office and is subject to the same requirements and disabilities as are or may be prescribed by law for regular judges of the superior court, save the requirement of residence in a particular district.

(a5)   Effective October 1, 2001, the Governor may appoint a special superior court judge to serve a term expiring five years from the date that judge takes office. Successors to the special superior court judge appointed pursuant to this subsection shall be appointed to five-year terms. A special judge takes the same oath of office and is subject to the same requirements and disabilities as are or may be prescribed by law for regular judges of the superior court, save the requirement of residence in a particular district.

(a6)   Effective December 1, 2004, the Governor may appoint a special superior court judge to serve a term expiring five years from the date that each judge takes office. Successors to the special superior court judge appointed pursuant to this subsection shall be appointed to five-year terms. A special judge takes the same oath of office and is subject to the same requirements and disabilities as are or may be prescribed by law for regular judges of the superior court, save the requirement of residence in a particular district.

(a7)   Effective January 1, 2008, the Governor may appoint two special superior court judges to serve terms expiring five years from the date that each judge takes office. Successors to the special superior court judges appointed pursuant to this subsection shall be appointed to five-year terms. A special judge takes the same oath of office and is subject to the same requirements and disabilities as are or may be prescribed by law for regular judges of the superior court, save the requirement of residence in a particular district.

(b) A special judge is subject to removal from office for the same causes and in the same manner as a regular judge of the superior court, and a vacancy occurring in the office of special judge is filled by the Governor by appointment for the unexpired term.

(c) A special judge, in any court in which he is duly appointed to hold, has the same power and authority in all matters that a regular judge holding the same court would have. A special judge, duly assigned to hold the court of a particular county, has during the session of court in that county, in open court and in chambers, the same power and authority of a regular judge in all matters arising in the district or set of districts as defined in G.S. 7A-41.1(a) in which that county is located, that could properly be heard or determined by a regular judge holding the same session of court.

(d) A special judge is authorized to settle cases on appeal and to make all proper orders in regard thereto after the time for which he was commissioned has expired. (1987, c. 738, s. 123(a); 1987 (Reg. Sess., 1988), c. 1037, s. 5; 1993, c. 321, s. 200.5(g); 1995, c. 507, s. 21.1(f); 1996, 2nd Ex. Sess., c. 18, s. 22.6(a); 1998-212, s. 16.22(a), (b); 1999-237, s. 17.12(a); 2000-67, s. 15.8(a); 2001-424, s. 22.4(a); 2004-124, s. 14.6(a); 2007-323, s. 14.24.)

§ 7A-45.2. Emergency special judges of the superior court; qualifications, appointment, removal, and authority.

(a) Any justice or judge of the appellate division of the General Court of Justice who:

(1) Retires under the provisions of the Consolidated Judicial Retirement Act, Article 4 of Chapter 135 of the General Statutes, or who is eligible to receive a retirement allowance under that act;

(2) Has not reached the mandatory retirement age specified in G.S. 7A-4.20;

(3) Has served at least five years as a superior court judge or five years as a justice or judge of the appellate division of the General Court of Justice, or any

combination thereof, whether or not eligible to serve as an emergency justice or judge of the appellate division of the General Court of Justice; and

(4)   Whose judicial service ended within the preceding 10 years;

may apply to the Governor for appointment as an emergency special superior court judge in the same manner as is provided for application as an emergency superior court judge in G.S. 7A-53. If the Governor is satisfied that the applicant meets the requirements of this section and is physically and mentally able to perform the duties of a superior court judge, the Governor shall issue a commission appointing the applicant as an emergency special superior court judge until the applicant reaches the mandatory retirement age for superior court judges specified in G.S. 7A-4.20.

(b)   Any emergency special superior court judge appointed as provided in this section shall:

(1)   Have the same powers and duties, when duly assigned to hold court, as provided for an emergency superior court judge by G.S. 7A-48;

(2)   Be subject to assignment in the same manner as provided for an emergency superior court judge by G.S. 7A-46;

(3)   Receive the same compensation, expenses, and allowances, when assigned to hold court, as an emergency superior court judge as provided by G.S. 7A-52(b);

(4)   Be subject to the provisions and requirements of the Canons of Judicial Conduct; and

(5)   Not engage in the practice of law during any period for which the emergency special superior court judgeship is commissioned. However, this subdivision shall not be construed to prohibit an emergency special superior court judge appointed pursuant to this section from serving as a referee, arbitrator, or mediator, during service as an emergency special superior court judge when the service does not conflict with or interfere with the emergency special superior court judge's judicial service in emergency status.

(c)   Upon reaching mandatory retirement age for superior court judges as set forth in G.S. 7A-4.20, any emergency special superior court judge appointed pursuant to this section, whose commission has expired, may be recalled as a recalled emergency special superior court judge to preside over any regular or special session of the superior court under the following circumstances:

(1)   The judge shall consent to the recall;

(2)   The Chief Justice may order the recall;

(3)   Prior to ordering recall, the Chief Justice shall be satisfied that the recalled judge is capable of efficiently and promptly discharging the duties of the office to which recalled;

(4)   Jurisdiction of a recalled emergency special superior court judge is as set forth in G.S. 7A-48;

(5)   Orders of recall and assignment shall be in writing and entered upon the minutes of the court to which assigned; and

(6)   Compensation, expenses, and allowances of recalled emergency special superior court judges are the same as for recalled emergency superior court judges under G.S. 7A-52(b).

(d)   Any former justice or judge of the appellate division of the General Court of Justice who otherwise meets the requirements of subsection (a) of this section to be appointed an emergency special superior court judge but has already reached the mandatory retirement age for superior court judges set forth in G.S. 7A-4.20 on retirement may, in lieu of serving as an emergency judge of the court from which he retired, apply to the Governor to be appointed as an emergency special superior court judge as provided in this section. If the Governor issues a commission to the applicant, the retired justice or judge is subject to recall as an emergency special superior court judge as provided in subsection (c) of this section.

(e)   No justice or judge appointed as an emergency special superior court judge or subject to recall as provided in this section shall, during the period so appointed or subject to recall, contemporaneously serve as an emergency justice or judge of the appellate division of the General Court of Justice. (1993, c. 321, s. 199.)

§ 7A-45.3. Superior court judges designated for complex business cases.

The Chief Justice may exercise the authority under rules of practice prescribed pursuant to G.S. 7A-34 to designate one or more of the special superior court judges authorized by G.S. 7A-45.1 to hear and decide complex business cases as prescribed by the rules of practice. Any judge so designated shall be known as a Business Court Judge and shall preside in the Business Court. If there is more than one business court judge, the Chief Justice may designate one of them as the Senior Business Court Judge. If there is no designation by the Chief Justice, the judge with the longest term of service on the court shall serve as Senior Business Court Judge until the Chief Justice makes an appointment to the position. (2005-425, s. 1.1.)

§ 7A-45.4. Designation of mandatory complex business cases.

(a) A mandatory complex business case is an action that involves a material issue related to:

(1) The law governing corporations, except charitable and religious organizations qualified under G.S. 55A-1-40(4) on the grounds of religious purpose, partnerships, limited liability companies, and limited liability partnerships, including issues concerning governance, involuntary dissolution of a corporation, mergers and acquisitions, breach of duty of directors, election or removal of directors, enforcement or interpretation of shareholder agreements, and derivative actions.

(2) Securities law, including proxy disputes and tender offer disputes.

(3) Antitrust law, except claims based solely on unfair competition under G.S. 75-1.1.

(4) State trademark or unfair competition law, except claims based solely on unfair competition under G.S. 75-1.1.

(5) Intellectual property law, including software licensing disputes.

(6) The Internet, electronic commerce, and biotechnology.

(7) Tax law, when the dispute has been the subject of a contested tax case for which judicial review is requested under G.S. 105-241.16 or the dispute is a civil action under G.S. 105-241.17.

(b) Any party may designate a civil action or a petition for judicial review under G.S. 105-241.16 as a mandatory complex business case by filing a Notice of Designation in the Superior Court in which the action has been filed and simultaneously serving the notice on each opposing party or counsel and on the Special Superior Court Judge for Complex Business Cases who is then the senior Business Court Judge. A copy of the notice shall also be sent contemporaneously by e-mail or facsimile transmission to the Chief Justice of the Supreme Court for approval of the designation of the action as a mandatory complex business case and assignment to a specific Business Court Judge.

(c) The Notice of Designation shall, in good faith and based on information reasonably available, succinctly state the basis of the designation and include a certificate by or on behalf of the designating party that the civil action meets the criteria for designation as a mandatory complex business case pursuant to subsection (a) of this section.

(d) The Notice of Designation shall be filed:

(1) By the plaintiff, the third-party plaintiff, or the petitioner for judicial review contemporaneously with the filing of the complaint, third-party complaint, or the petition for judicial review in the action.

(2) By any intervenor when the intervenor files a motion for permission to intervene in the action.

(3) By any defendant or any other party within 30 days of receipt of service of the pleading seeking relief from the defendant or party.

(e) Within 30 days after service of the Notice of Designation, any other party may, in good faith, file and serve an opposition to the designation of the action as a mandatory business case. Based on the opposition or ex mero motu, the Business Court Judge may determine that the action should not be designated as a mandatory complex business case. If a party disagrees with the decision, the party may appeal to the Chief Justice of the Supreme Court.

(f) Once a designation is filed under subsection (d) of this section, and after preliminary approval by the Chief Justice, a case shall be designated and administered a complex business case. All proceedings in the action shall be before the Business Court Judge to whom it has been assigned unless and until an order has been entered under subsection (e) of this section ordering that the case not be designated a mandatory complex business case or the Chief

Justice revokes approval. If complex business case status is revoked or denied, the action shall be treated as any other civil action, unless it is designated as an exceptional civil case or a discretionary complex business case pursuant to Rule 2.1 of the General Rules of Practice for the Superior and District Courts. (2005-425, s. 2; 2007-491, s. 4.)

§ 7A-46. Special sessions.

Whenever it appears to the Chief Justice of the Supreme Court that there is need for a special session of superior court in any county, he may order a special session in that county, and order any regular, special, or emergency judge to hold such session. The Chief Justice shall notify the clerk of the superior court of the county, who shall initiate action under Chapter 9 of the General Statutes to provide a jury for the special session, if a jury is required.

Special sessions have all the jurisdiction and powers that regular sessions have. (R.C., c. 31, s. 22; 1868-9, c. 273; 1876-7, c. 44; Code, ss. 914, 915, 916; Rev., ss. 1512, 1513, 1516; C.S., ss. 1450, 1452, 1455; Ex. Sess. 1924, c. 100; 1951, c. 491, ss. 1, 3; 1959, c. 360; 1969, c. 1190, s. 46.)

§ 7A-47. Powers of regular judges holding courts by assignment or exchange.

A regular superior court judge, duly assigned to hold the courts of a county, or holding such courts by exchange, shall have the same powers in the district or set of districts as defined in G.S. 7A-41.1(a) in which that county is located, in open court and in chambers as the resident judge or any judge regularly assigned to hold the courts of the district or set of districts as defined in G.S. 7A-41.1(a) has, and his jurisdiction in chambers shall extend until the session is adjourned or the session expires by operation of law, whichever is later. (1951, c. 740; 1969, c. 1190, s. 42; 1987 (Reg. Sess., 1988), c. 1037, s. 6.)

§ 7A-47.1. Jurisdiction in vacation or in session.

In any case in which the superior court in vacation has jurisdiction, and all the parties unite in the proceedings, they may apply for relief to the superior court in vacation, or during a session of court, at their election. Any regular resident superior court judge of the district or set of districts as defined in G.S. 7A-41.1(a) and any special superior court judge residing in the district or set of districts and the judge regularly presiding over the courts of the district or set of districts have concurrent jurisdiction throughout the district or set of districts in all matters and proceedings in which the superior court has jurisdiction out of session; provided, that in all matters and proceedings not requiring a jury or in which a jury is waived, any regular resident superior court judge of the district or set of districts and any special superior court judge residing in the district or set of districts shall have concurrent jurisdiction throughout the district or set of districts with the judge holding the courts of the district or set of districts and any such regular or special superior court judge, in the exercise of such concurrent jurisdiction, may hear and pass upon such matters and proceedings in vacation, out of session or during a session of court. (1871-2, c. 3; Code, c. 10, s. 230; Rev., s. 1501; C.S., s. 1438; 1939, c. 69; 1945, c. 142; 1951, c. 78, s. 2; 1969, c. 1190, s. 47; 1987 (Reg. Sess., 1988), c. 1037, s. 7.)

§ 7A-47.2. Repealed by Session Laws 1987 (Reg. Sess., 1988), c. 1037,s. 8.

§ 7A-47.3. Rotation and assignment; sessions.

(a) To effect the intent of Article IV, Section 11 of the North Carolina Constitution, each regular resident superior court judge may, upon each rotation, be assigned to hold the courts either of one of the districts or of one of the sets of districts, as defined in G.S. 7A-41.1(a), in that judge's judicial division.

(b) All sessions of superior court shall be for an entire county, whether that county comprises or is located in a district or in a set of districts as defined in G.S. 7A-41.1(a), and at each session all matters and proceedings arising anywhere in the county shall be heard. (1987, c. 509, s. 3, (Reg. Sess., 1988), c. 1037, s. 9.)

§ 7A-48. Jurisdiction of emergency judges.

Emergency superior court judges have the same power and authority in all matters whatsoever, in the courts which they are assigned to hold, that regular judges holding the same courts would have. An emergency judge duly assigned to hold the courts of a county or district or set of districts as defined in G.S. 7A-41.1(a) has the same powers in that county and district or set of districts in open court and in chambers as a resident judge of the district or set of districts or any judge regularly assigned to hold the courts of the district or set of districts would have, but his jurisdiction in chambers extends only until the session is adjourned or the session expires by operation of law, whichever is later. (Ex. Sess. 1921, c. 94, s. 1; C.S., s. 1435(b); 1925, c. 8; 1941, c. 52, s. 2; 1951, c. 88; 1969, c. 1190, s. 39; 1987 (Reg. Sess., 1988), c. 1037, s. 10.)

§ 7A-49. Orders returnable to another judge; notice.

When any special or emergency judge makes any matter returnable before him, and thereafter he is called upon by the Chief Justice to hold court elsewhere, he shall order the matter heard before some other judge, setting forth in the order the time and place where it is to be heard, and he shall send copies of the order to the attorneys representing the parties in such matter. (Ex. Sess. 1921, c. 94, s. 2; C.S., s. 1435(c); 1951, c. 491, s. 1; 1969, c. 1190, s. 40.)

§ 7A-49.1. Disposition of motions when judge disqualified.

Whenever a judge before whom a motion is made, either in open court or in chambers, disqualifies himself from determining it, he may in his discretion refer the motion for disposition to a regular resident superior court judge of, or any judge regularly holding the courts of, the district or set of districts as defined in G.S. 7A-41.1(a) in which the county in which the cause arose is located, or of any adjoining district or set of districts, who shall have full power and authority to hear and determine the motion in the same manner as if he were the presiding judge of a session of superior court for that county. (1939, c. 48; 1961, c. 50; 1969, c. 1190, s. 43; 1987 (Reg. Sess., 1988), c. 1037, s. 11.)

§ 7A-49.2. Civil business at criminal sessions; criminal business at civil sessions.

(a)   At criminal sessions of court, motions in civil actions may be heard upon due notice, and trials in civil actions may be heard by consent of parties. Motions for confirmation or rejection of referees' reports may also be heard upon 10 days' notice and judgment may be entered on such reports. The court may also enter consent orders and consent judgments, and try uncontested civil actions.

(b)   For sessions of court designated for the trial of civil cases only, no grand juries shall be drawn and no criminal process shall be made returnable to any civil session. (1901, c. 28; Rev., ss. 1507, 1508; 1913, c. 196; Ex. Sess. 1913, c. 23; 1915, cc. 68, 240; 1917, c. 13; C.S., ss. 1444, 1445; 1931, c. 394; 1947, c. 25; 1969, c. 1190, s. 44; 1973, c. 503, s. 1.)

§ 7A-49.3. Repealed by Session Laws 1999-428, s. 2.

§ 7A-49.4. Superior court criminal case docketing.

(a)   Criminal Docketing. - Criminal cases in superior court shall be calendared by the district attorney at administrative settings according to a criminal case docketing plan developed by the district attorney for each superior court district in consultation with the superior court judges residing in that district and after opportunity for comment by members of the local bar. Each criminal case docketing plan shall, at a minimum, comply with the provisions of this section, but may contain additional provisions not inconsistent with this section.

(b)   Administrative Settings. - An administrative setting shall be calendared for each felony within 60 days of indictment or service of notice of indictment if required by law, or at the next regularly scheduled session of superior court if later than 60 days from indictment or service if required. At an administrative setting:

(1)   The court shall determine the status of the defendant's representation by counsel;

(2)   After hearing from the parties, the court shall set deadlines for the delivery of discovery, arraignment if necessary, and filing of motions;

(3)   If the district attorney has made a determination regarding a plea arrangement, the district attorney shall inform the defendant as to whether a plea arrangement will be offered and the terms of any proposed plea arrangement, and the court may conduct a plea conference if supported by the interest of justice;

(4)   The court may hear pending pretrial motions, set such motions for hearing on a date certain, or defer ruling on motions until the trial of the case; and

(5) The court may schedule more than one administrative setting if requested by the parties or if it is found to be necessary to promote the fair administration of justice in a timely manner.

Whenever practical, administrative settings shall be held by a superior court judge residing within the district, but may otherwise be held by any superior court judge.

If the parties have not otherwise agreed upon a trial date, then upon the conclusion of the final administrative setting, the district attorney shall announce a proposed trial date. The court shall set that date as the tentative trial date unless, after providing the parties an opportunity to be heard, the court determines that the interests of justice require the setting of a different date. In that event, the district attorney shall set another tentative trial date during the final administrative setting. The trial shall occur no sooner than 30 days after the final administrative setting, except by agreement of the State and the defendant.

Nothing in this section precludes the disposition of a criminal case by plea, deferred prosecution, or dismissal prior to an administrative setting.

(c) Definite Trial Date. - When a case has not otherwise been scheduled for trial within 120 days of indictment or of service of notice of indictment if required by law, then upon motion by the defendant at any time thereafter, the senior resident superior court judge, or a superior court judge designated by the senior resident superior court judge, may hold a hearing for the purpose of establishing a trial date for the defendant.

(d) Venue for Administrative Settings. - Venue for administrative settings may be in any county within the district when necessary to comply with the terms of the criminal case docketing plan. The presence of the defendant is only required for administrative settings held in the county where the case originated.

(e) Setting and Publishing of Trial Calendar. - No less than 10 working days before cases are calendared for trial, the district attorney shall publish the trial calendar. The trial calendar shall schedule the cases in the order in which the district attorney anticipates they will be called for trial and should not contain cases that the district attorney does not reasonably expect to be called for trial. In counties in which multiple sessions of court are being held, the district attorney may publish a trial calendar for each session of court.

(f) Order of Trial. - The district attorney, after calling the calendar and determining cases for pleas and other disposition, shall announce to the court the order in which the district attorney intends to call for trial the cases remaining on the calendar. Deviations from the announced order require approval by the presiding judge if the defendant whose case is called for trial objects; but the defendant may not object if all the cases scheduled to be heard before the defendant's case have been disposed of or delayed with the approval of the presiding judge or by consent of the State and the defendant. A case may be continued from the trial calendar only by consent of the State and the defendant or upon order of the presiding judge or resident superior court judge for good cause shown. The district attorney, after consultation with the parties, shall schedule a new trial date for cases not reached during that session of court.

(g) Nothing in this section shall be construed to deprive any victim of the rights granted under Article I, Section 37 of the North Carolina Constitution and Article 46 of Chapter 15A of the General Statutes.

(h) Nothing in this section shall be construed to affect the authority of the court in the call of cases calendared for trial. (1999-428, s. 1.)

§ 7A-49.5. Statewide electronic filing in courts.

(a) The General Assembly finds that the electronic filing of pleadings and other documents required to be filed with the courts may be a more economical, efficient, and satisfactory procedure to handle the volumes of paperwork routinely filed with, handled by, and disseminated by the courts of this State, and therefore authorizes the use of electronic filing in the courts of this State.

(b) The Supreme Court may adopt rules governing this process and associated costs and may supervise its implementation and operation through the Administrative Office of the Courts. The rules adopted under this section shall address the waiver of electronic fees for indigents.

(c) The Administrative Office of the Courts may contract with a vendor to provide electronic filing in the courts.

(d) Any funds received by the Administrative Office of the Courts from the vendor selected pursuant to subsection (c) of this section, other than applicable statutory court costs, as a result of electronic filing, shall be deposited in the

Court Information Technology Fund in accordance with G.S. 7A-343.2. (2006-187, s. 2(c); 2007-323, s. 14.17(c); 2012-142, s. 16.5(f).)

Article 8.

Retirement of Judges of the Superior Court; Retirement Compensation for Superior Court Judges; Recall to Emergency Service of Judges of the District and Superior Court; Disability Retirement for Judges of the Superior Court.

§ 7A-50. Emergency judge defined.

As used in this Article "emergency judge" means any judge of the superior court who has retired subject to recall to active service for temporary duty. (1967, c. 108, s. 2.)

§ 7A-51. Age and service requirements for retirement of judges of the superior court and of the Administrative Officer of the Courts.

(a) Any judge of the superior court, or Administrative Officer of the Courts, who has attained the age of sixty-five years, and who has served for a total of fifteen years, whether consecutive or not, as a judge of the superior court, or as Administrative Officer of the Courts, or as judge of the superior court and as Administrative Officer of the Courts combined, may retire and receive for life compensation equal to two thirds of the total annual compensation, including longevity and additional payment for service as senior resident superior court judge, but excluding any payments in the nature of reimbursement for expenses or subsistence allowances, from time to time received by the occupant of the office from which he retired.

(b) Any judge of the superior court, or Administrative Officer of the Courts, who has served for twelve years, whether consecutive or not, as a judge of the superior court, or as Administrative Officer of the Courts, or as judge of the superior court and as Administrative Officer of the Courts combined may, at age sixty-eight, retire and receive for life compensation equal to two thirds of the total annual compensation, including longevity and additional payment for service as senior resident superior court judge, but excluding any payments in the nature of reimbursement for expenses or subsistence allowances, from time to time received by the occupant of the office from which he retired.

(c) Any person who has served for a total of twenty-four years, whether continuously or not, as a judge of the superior court, or as Administrative Officer of the Courts, or as judge of the superior court and as Administrative Officer of the Courts combined, may retire, regardless of age, and receive for life compensation equal to two thirds of the total annual compensation, including longevity and additional payment for service as senior resident superior court judge, but excluding any payments in the nature of reimbursement for expenses or subsistence allowances, from time to time received by the occupant of the office from which he retired. In determining whether a person meets the requirements of this subsection, time served as district attorney of the superior court prior to January 1, 1971, may be included, so long as the person has served at least eight years as a judge of the superior court, or as Administrative Officer of the Courts, or as judge of the superior court and Administrative Officer of the Courts combined.

(d) Repealed by Session Laws 1971, c. 508, s. 3.

(e) For purposes of this section, the "occupant or occupants of the office from which" the retired judge retired will be deemed to be a superior court judge holding the same office and with the same service as the retired judge had immediately prior to retirement. (1967, c. 108, s. 2; 1971, c. 508, s. 3; 1973, c. 47, s. 2; 1983 (Reg. Sess., 1984), c. 1109, ss. 13.10-13.13.)

§ 7A-52. Retired district and superior court judges may become emergency judges subject to recall to active service; compensation for emergency judges on recall.

(a) Judges of the district court and judges of the superior court who have not reached the mandatory retirement age specified in G.S. 7A-4.20, but who have retired under the provisions of G.S. 7A-51, or under the Uniform Judicial Retirement Act after having completed five years of creditable service, may apply as provided in G.S. 7A-53 to become emergency judges of the court from which they retired. The Chief Justice of the Supreme Court may order any emergency judge of the district or superior court who, in his opinion, is competent to perform the duties of a judge of the court from which such judge retired, to hold regular or special sessions of such court, as needed. Order of assignment shall be in writing and entered upon the minutes of the court to which such emergency judge is assigned.

(b) In addition to the compensation or retirement allowance the judge would otherwise be entitled to receive by law, each emergency judge of the district or superior court who is assigned to temporary active service by the Chief Justice shall be paid by the State the judge's actual expenses, plus four hundred dollars ($400.00) for each day of active service rendered upon recall. No recalled retired trial judge shall receive from the State total annual compensation for judicial services in excess of that received by an active judge of the bench to which the judge is recalled. (1967, c. 108, s. 2; 1973, c. 640, s. 4; 1977, c. 736, s. 3; 1979, c. 878, s. 2; 1981, c. 455, s. 6; c. 859, s. 47; 1981 (Reg. Sess., 1982), c. 1253, s. 3; 1983, c. 784; 1985, c. 698, s. 9(b); 1987, c. 738, s. 132; 1987 (Reg. Sess., 1988), c. 1086, s. 31(b); 1989, c. 116; 1993, c. 321, s. 200.3; 1998-212, s. 16.27(a); 2007-323, s. 14.26; 2007-345, s. 9.)

§ 7A-53. Application to the Governor; commission as emergency judge.

No retired judge of the district or superior court may become an emergency judge except upon his written application to the Governor certifying his desire and ability to serve as an emergency judge. If the Governor is satisfied that the applicant qualifies under G.S. 7A-52(a) to become an emergency judge and that he is physically and mentally able to perform the official duties of an emergency judge, he shall issue to such applicant a commission as an emergency judge of the court from which he retired. The commission shall be effective upon the date of its issue and shall terminate when the judge to whom it is issued reaches the maximum age for judicial service under G.S. 7A-4.20(a). (1967, c. 108, s. 2; 1977, c. 736, s. 4; 1979, c. 878, s. 3.)

§ 7A-53.1. Jurisdiction of emergency district court judges.

Emergency district court judges have the same power and authority in all matters whatsoever, in the courts which they are assigned to hold, that regular district court judges holding the same courts would have. An emergency district court judge duly assigned to hold district court in a particular county or district has the same powers in the county or district in open court and in chambers as a resident district court judge or any district court judge regularly assigned to hold district court in that district, but his jurisdiction in chambers extends only until the session is adjourned or the session expires by operation of law, whichever is later. (1981, c. 455, s. 5.)

§ 7A-54. Article applicable to judges retired under prior law.

All judges of the superior court who have heretofore retired and who are receiving retirement compensation under the provisions of any judicial retirement law previously enacted shall be entitled to the benefits of this article. All such judges shall be subject to assignment as emergency judges by the Chief Justice of the Supreme Court, except judges retired for total disability. (1967, c. 108, s. 2.)

§ 7A-55. Retirement on account of total and permanent disability.

Every judge of the superior court or Administrative Officer of the Courts who has served for eight years or more on the superior court, or as Administrative Officer of the Courts, or on the superior court and as Administrative Officer of the Courts combined, and who while in active service becomes totally and permanently disabled so as to be unable to perform efficiently the duties of his office, and who retires by reason of such disability, shall receive for life compensation equal to two thirds of the annual salary from time to time received by the occupant of the office from which he retired. In determining whether a person meets the requirements for retirement under this section, time served as district solicitor of the superior court prior to January 1, 1971, may be included. Whenever any judge claims retirement benefits under this section on account of total and permanent disability, the Governor and Council of State, acting together, shall, after notice and an opportunity to be heard is given the applicant, by a majority vote of said body, make findings of fact from the evidence offered. Such findings of fact shall be reduced to writing and entered upon the minutes of the Council of State. The findings so made shall be conclusive as to such matters and determine the right of the applicant to retirement benefits under this section. Judges retired under the provisions of this section are not subject to recall as emergency judges. (1967, c. 108, s. 2.)

§ 7A-56. Applicability of §§ 7A-51 and 7A-55.

The provisions of G.S. 7A-51 and 7A-55 shall apply only to judges (and any Administrative Officer of the Courts) who entered office prior to January 1, 1974. The extent of such application is specified in Chapter 135, Article 4 (Uniform Judicial Retirement Act). (1973, c. 640, s. 6; 1975, c. 19, s. 2.)

§ 7A-57. Recall of active and emergency trial judges who have reached mandatory retirement age.

Superior and district court judges retired because they have reached the mandatory retirement age, and emergency superior and district court judges whose commissions have expired because they have reached the mandatory retirement age, may be recalled to preside over regular or special sessions of the court from which retired under the following circumstances:

(1) The judge must consent to the recall.

(2) The Chief Justice is authorized to order the recall.

(3) Prior to ordering recall, the Chief Justice shall satisfy himself that the recalled judge is capable of efficiently and promptly discharging the duties of the office to which recalled.

(4) Jurisdiction of a recalled retired superior court judge is as set forth in G.S. 7A-48, and jurisdiction of a recalled retired district court judge is as set forth in G.S. 7A-53.1.

(5) Orders of recall and assignment shall be in writing and entered upon the minutes of the court to which assigned.

(6) Compensation of recalled retired trial judges is the same as for recalled emergency trial judges under G.S. 7A-52(b). (1981, ch. 455, s. 4.)

§ 7A-58. Reserved for future codification purposes.

§ 7A-59. Reserved for future codification purposes.

Article 9.

District Attorneys and Prosecutorial Districts.

§ 7A-60. District attorneys and prosecutorial districts.

(a) The State shall be divided into prosecutorial districts, as shown in subsection (a1) of this section. There shall be a district attorney for each prosecutorial district, as provided in subsections (b) and (c) of this section who shall be a resident of the prosecutorial district for which elected. A vacancy in the office of district attorney shall be filled as provided in Article IV, Sec. 19 of the Constitution.

(a1) (Effective until January 1, 2015) (See Editor's note for staffing changes) The counties of the State are organized into prosecutorial districts, and each district has the counties and the number of full-time assistant district attorneys set forth in the following table:

No. of Full-Time

Prosecutorial District	Counties	Asst. District Attorneys
1	Camden, Chowan, Currituck, Dare, Gates, Pasquotank, Perquimans	11
2	Beaufort, Hyde, Martin, Tyrrell, Washington	8
3A	Pitt	11
3B	Carteret, Craven, Pamlico	12
4	Duplin, Jones, Onslow, Sampson	18
5	New Hanover, Pender	18
6A	Halifax	5
6B	Bertie, Hertford, Northampton	5
7	Edgecombe, Nash, Wilson	18
8	Greene, Lenoir, Wayne	14
9	Franklin, Granville, Vance, Warren	10
9A	Person, Caswell	6
10	Wake	41
11A	Harnett, Lee	9

11B	Johnston	10
12	Cumberland	23
13	Bladen, Brunswick, Columbus	13
14	Durham	18
15A	Alamance	11
15B	Orange, Chatham	10
16A	Scotland, Hoke	7
16B	Robeson	12
17A	Rockingham	7
17B	Stokes, Surry	8
18	Guilford	32
19A	Cabarrus	9
19B	Montgomery, Randolph	9
19C	Rowan	8
19D	Moore	5
20A	Anson, Richmond, Stanly	11
20B	Union	10
21	Forsyth	25
22A	Alexander, Iredell	11
22B	Davidson, Davie	11
23	Alleghany, Ashe, Wilkes, Yadkin	8
24	Avery, Madison, Mitchell, Watauga, Yancey	7
25	Burke, Caldwell, Catawba	18

26	Mecklenburg	58
27A	Gaston	14
27B	Cleveland, Lincoln	11
28	Buncombe	14
29A	McDowell, Rutherford	7
29B	Henderson, Polk, Transylvania	8
30	Cherokee, Clay, Graham, Haywood, Jackson, Macon, Swain.	10

(a1) (Effective January 1, 2015) The counties of the State are organized into prosecutorial districts, and each district has the counties and the number of full-time assistant district attorneys set forth in the following table:

No. of Full-Time Prosecutorial District	Counties	Asst. District Attorneys
1	Camden, Chowan, Currituck, Dare, Gates, Pasquotank, Perquimans	11
2	Beaufort, Hyde, Martin, Tyrrell, Washington	8
3A	Pitt	11
3B	Carteret, Craven, Pamlico	12
4	Duplin, Jones, Onslow, Sampson	18
5	New Hanover, Pender	18
6	Bertie, Halifax, Hertford, Northampton	10
7	Edgecombe, Nash, Wilson	18

8	Greene, Lenoir, Wayne	14
9	Franklin, Granville, Vance, Warren	10
9A	Person, Caswell	6
10	Wake	41
11A	Harnett, Lee	9
11B	Johnston	10
12	Cumberland	23
13	Bladen, Brunswick, Columbus	13
14	Durham	18
15A	Alamance	11
15B	Orange, Chatham	10
16A	Scotland, Hoke	7
16B	Robeson	12
16C	Anson, Richmond	6
17A	Rockingham	7
17B	Stokes, Surry	8
18	Guilford	32
19A	Cabarrus	9
19B	Montgomery, Randolph	9
19C	Rowan	8
19D	Moore	5
20A	Stanly	5
20B	Union	10
21	Forsyth	25

22A	Alexander, Iredell	11
22B	Davidson, Davie	11
23	Alleghany, Ashe, Wilkes, Yadkin	8
24	Avery, Madison, Mitchell, Watauga, Yancey	7
25	Burke, Caldwell, Catawba	18
26	Mecklenburg	58
27A	Gaston	14
27B	Cleveland, Lincoln	11
28	Buncombe	14
29A	McDowell, Rutherford	7
29B	Henderson, Polk, Transylvania	8
30	Cherokee, Clay, Graham, Haywood, Jackson, Macon, Swain.	10

(a2) Upon the convening of each regular session of the General Assembly and its reconvening in the even-numbered year, the Administrative Office of the Courts shall report its recommendations regarding the allocation of assistant district attorneys for the upcoming fiscal biennium and fiscal year to the General Assembly, including any request for additional assistant district attorneys. The report shall include the number of assistant district attorneys that the Administrative Office of the Courts recommends to be allocated to each prosecutorial district and the caseload and criteria on which each recommended allocation is based. Any reports required under this subsection shall be made to the Joint Legislative Commission of Governmental Operations, the House of Representatives and Senate Appropriations Subcommittees on Justice and Public, and the Fiscal Research Division.

(b) Except as provided in subsection (c) of this section, each district attorney for a prosecutorial district as defined in subsection (a1) of this section, other than District 19B, who is in office on December 31, 1988, shall continue in office for that prosecutorial district, for a term expiring December 31, 1990. In the general election of 1990, and every four years thereafter, a district attorney shall be elected for a four-year term for each prosecutorial district other than Districts 16A and 19B, and shall take office on the January 1 following such election. The district attorney for Prosecutorial District 19B, who is elected in the general election of 1988 for a four-year term beginning January 1, 1989, shall serve that term for Prosecutorial District 19B. In the general election of 1992, and every four years thereafter, a district attorney shall be elected for a four-year term for Prosecutorial Districts 16A and 19B and shall take office on the January 1 following such election.

(c) The office and term of the district attorney for Prosecutorial District 12 formerly consisting of Cumberland and Hoke Counties are allocated to Prosecutorial District 12 as defined by subsection (a1) of this section. The office and the term of the district attorney for former Prosecutorial District 16 consisting of Robeson and Scotland Counties are allocated to Prosecutorial District 16B as defined by subsection (a1) of this section. The initial district attorney for Prosecutorial District 16A as defined in subsection (a1) of this section shall be elected in the general election of November 1988, from nominations made in accordance with G.S. 163-114 as if a vacancy had occurred in nomination, and shall serve an initial term expiring December 31, 1992. In all other respects, subsection (b) of this section shall apply to the district attorneys for Prosecutorial Districts 12, 16A, and 16B to the same extent as all other district attorneys. (1967, c. 1049, s. 1; 1975, c. 956, s. 4; 1977, c. 1130, s. 3; 1977, 2nd Sess., c. 1238, s. 2; 1981, c. 964, ss. 2, 3; 1987, c. 509, ss. 4, 5; c. 738, s. 127(a); 1987 (Reg. Sess., 1988), c. 1056, s. 1; c. 1086, s. 111; 1989, c. 770, ss. 1, 56; c. 795, s. 24(a), (e); 1991, c. 742, s. 13; 1991 (Reg. Sess., 1992), c. 900, s. 120(a), (b); 1993, c. 321, ss. 200.4(l), 200.7(a), (b); 1995, c. 507, s. 21.7; 1995 (Reg. Sess., 1996), c. 589, s. 3(a); 1996, 2nd Ex. Sess., c. 18, s. 22(a); 1997-443, s. 18.11(a); 1998-212, s. 16.20(a); 1999-237, s. 17.8(a); 2004-124, s. 14.6(h); 2005-276, s. 14.2(l); 2006-66, ss. 14.3(a), 14.19(a); 2007-323, ss. 14.14(a), (b), 14.25(j); 2008-107, s. 14.6; 2009-451, s. 15.17E(a); 2012-194, s. 1(b); 2013-360, s. 18B.22(k).)

§ 7A-61. Duties of district attorney.

The district attorney shall prepare the trial dockets, prosecute in a timely manner in the name of the State all criminal actions and infractions requiring prosecution in the superior and district courts of his prosecutorial district, advise the officers of justice in his district, and perform such duties related to appeals to the Appellate Division from his district as the Attorney General may require. Effective January 1, 1971, the district attorney shall also represent the State in juvenile cases in which the juvenile is represented by an attorney. Each district attorney shall devote his full time to the duties of his office and shall not engage in the private practice of law. (1967, c. 1049, s. 1; 1969, c. 1190, s. 5; 1971, c. 377, s. 5.1; 1973, c. 47, s. 2; 1985, c. 764, s. 7; 1985 (Reg. Sess., 1986), c. 852, s. 17; 1987 (Reg. Sess., 1988), c. 1037, s. 12; 1999-428, s. 3.)

§ 7A-62. Acting district attorney.

When a district attorney becomes for any reason unable to perform his duties, the Governor shall appoint an acting district attorney to serve during the period of disability. An acting district attorney has all the power, authority and duties of the regular district attorney. He shall take the oath of office prescribed for the regular district attorney, and shall receive the same compensation as the regular district attorney. (1967, c. 1049, s. 1; 1973, c. 47, s. 2.)

§ 7A-63. Assistant district attorneys.

Each district attorney shall be entitled to the number of full-time assistant district attorneys set out in this Subchapter, to be appointed by the district attorney, to serve at his pleasure. A vacancy in the office of assistant district attorney shall be filled in the same manner as the initial appointment. An assistant district attorney shall take the same oath of office as the district attorney, and shall perform such duties as may be assigned by the district attorney. He shall devote his full time to the duties of his office and shall not engage in the private practice of law during his term. (1967, c. 1049, s. 1; 1969, c. 1190, s. 6; 1971, c. 377, s. 6; 1973, c. 47, s. 2.)

§ 7A-64. Temporary assistance for district attorneys.

(a) A district attorney may apply to the Director of the Administrative Office of the Courts to:

(1) Temporarily assign an assistant district attorney from another district, after consultation with the district attorney thereof, to assist in the prosecution of cases in the requesting district;

(2) Authorize the temporary appointment, by the requesting district attorney, of a qualified attorney to assist the requesting district attorney; or

(3) Enter into contracts with local governments for the provision of services by the State pursuant to G.S. 153A-212.1 or G.S. 160A-289.1.

(a1) Repealed by Session Laws 2012-7, s. 9, effective June 7, 2012.

(b) The Director of the Administrative Office of the Courts may provide this assistance only upon a showing by the requesting district attorney or the Chair of the North Carolina Innocence Inquiry Commission, as appropriate, supported by facts, that:

(1) Criminal cases have accumulated on the dockets of the superior or district courts of the district beyond the capacity of the district attorney and the district attorney's full-time assistants to keep the dockets reasonably current;

(2) The overwhelming public interest warrants the use of additional resources for the speedy disposition of cases involving drug offenses, domestic violence, or other offenses involving a threat to public safety; or

(3) There is an allegation of or evidence of prosecutorial misconduct in the case that is the subject of the hearing under G.S. 15A-1469.

(c) The length of service and compensation of any temporary appointee or the terms of any contract entered into with local governments shall be fixed by Director of the Administrative Office of the Courts in each case. Nothing in this section shall be construed to obligate the General Assembly to make any appropriation to implement the provisions of this section or to obligate the Administrative Office of the Courts to provide the administrative costs of establishing or maintaining the positions or services provided for under this section. Further, nothing in this section shall be construed to obligate the Administrative Office of the Courts to maintain positions or services initially provided for under this section. (1967, c. 1049, s. 1; 1973, c. 47, s. 2; 1999-237, s. 17.17(a); 2000-67, s. 15.4(g); 2010-171, s. 2; 2012-7, s. 9.)

§ 7A-65. Compensation and allowances of district attorneys and assistant district attorneys.

(a) The annual salary of:

(1) District attorneys shall be as provided in the Current Operations Appropriations Act.

(2) Full-time assistant district attorneys shall be as provided in the Current Operations Appropriations Act.

When traveling on official business, each district attorney and assistant district attorney is entitled to reimbursement for his or her subsistence expenses to the same extent as State employees generally. When traveling on official business outside his or her county of residence, each district attorney and assistant district attorney is entitled to reimbursement for travel expenses to the same extent as State employees generally. For purposes of this subsection, the term "official business" does not include regular, daily commuting between a person's home and the district attorney's office. Travel distances, for purposes of reimbursement for mileage, shall be determined according to the travel policy of the Administrative Office of the Courts.

(b) Repealed by Session Laws 1985, c. 689, s. 2.

(c) In lieu of merit and other increment raises paid to regular State employees, a district attorney shall receive as longevity pay an amount equal to four and eight-tenths percent (4.8%) of the annual salary set forth in the Current Operations Appropriations Act payable monthly after five years of service, and nine and six-tenths percent (9.6%) after 10 years of service, fourteen and four-tenths percent (14.4%) after 15 years of service, nineteen and two-tenths percent (19.2%) after 20 years of service, and twenty-four percent (24%) after 25 years of service. Service shall mean service in the elective position of a district attorney and shall not include service as a deputy or acting district attorney. Service shall also mean service as a justice or judge of the General Court of Justice, clerk of superior court, assistant district attorney, public defender, appellate defender, or assistant public or appellate defender.

(d) In lieu of merit and other increment raises paid to regular State employees, an assistant district attorney shall receive as longevity pay an amount equal to four and eight-tenths percent (4.8%) of the annual salary set forth in the Current Operations Appropriations Act payable monthly after five years of service, nine and six-tenths percent (9.6%) after 10 years of service, fourteen and four-tenths percent (14.4%) after 15 years of service, nineteen and two-tenths percent (19.2%) after 20 years of service, and twenty-four percent (24%) after 25 years of service. "Service" means service as an assistant district attorney, district attorney, resource prosecutor, public defender, appellate defender, assistant public or appellate defender, justice or judge of the General Court of Justice, or clerk of superior court. For purposes of this subsection, "resource prosecutor" means a former assistant district attorney who has left the employment of the district attorney's office to serve in a specific, time-limited position with the Conference of District Attorneys. (1967, c. 1049, s. 1; 1973, c. 47, s. 2; 1983, c. 761, ss. 246, 248; 1983 (Reg. Sess., 1984), c. 1034, ss. 92, 165; c. 1109, s. 13.1; 1985, c. 689, s. 2; c. 698, s. 10(b); 1985 (Reg. Sess., 1986), c. 1014, s. 224; 1987, c. 738, s. 33(a); 1995, c. 507, s. 7.4A; 1999-237, s. 28.19(a); 2000-67, s. 26.3A(a); 2003-284, ss. 30.19A(a), 30.19A(b); 2005-276, s. 29.23A; 2007-323, ss. 28.15A, 28.18A(d); 2009-451, s. 15.17B(b).)

§ 7A-66. Removal of district attorneys.

The following are grounds for suspension of a district attorney or for his removal from office:

(1)   Mental or physical incapacity interfering with the performance of his duties which is, or is likely to become, permanent;

(2)   Willful misconduct in office;

(3)   Willful and persistent failure to perform his duties;

(4)   Habitual intemperance;

(5)   Conviction of a crime involving moral turpitude;

(6)   Conduct prejudicial to the administration of justice which brings the office into disrepute; or

(7)   Knowingly authorizing or permitting an assistant district attorney to commit any act constituting grounds for removal, as defined in subdivisions (1) through (6) hereof.

A proceeding to suspend or remove a district attorney is commenced by filing with the clerk of superior court of the county where the district attorney resides a sworn affidavit charging the district attorney with one or more grounds for removal. The clerk shall immediately bring the matter to the attention of the senior regular resident superior court judge for the district or set of districts as defined in G.S. 7A-41.1(a) in which the county is located who shall within 30 days either review and act on the charges or refer them for review and action within 30 days to another superior court judge residing in or regularly holding the courts of that district or set of districts. If the superior court judge upon review finds that the charges if true constitute grounds for suspension, and finds probable cause for believing that the charges are true, he may enter an order suspending the district attorney from performing the duties of his office until a final determination of the charges on the merits. During the suspension the salary of the district attorney continues. If the superior court judge finds that the charges if true do not constitute grounds for suspension or finds that no probable cause exists for believing that the charges are true, he shall dismiss the proceeding.

If a hearing, with or without suspension, is ordered, the district attorney should receive immediate written notice of the proceedings and a true copy of the charges, and the matter shall be set for hearing not less than 10 days nor more than 30 days thereafter. The matter shall be set for hearing before the judge who originally examined the charges or before another regular superior court judge resident in or regularly holding the courts of that district or set of districts. The hearing shall be open to the public. All testimony shall be recorded. At the hearing the superior court judge shall hear evidence and make findings of fact and conclusions of law and if he finds that grounds for removal exist, he shall enter an order permanently removing the district attorney from office, and terminating his salary. If he finds that no grounds exist, he shall terminate the suspension, if any.

The district attorney may appeal from an order of removal to the Court of Appeals on the basis of error of law by the superior court judge. Pending decision of the case on appeal, the district attorney shall not perform any of the duties of his office. If, upon final determination, he is ordered reinstated either by the appellate division or by the superior court upon remand his salary shall be restored from the date of the original order of removal. (1967, c. 1049, s. 1; 1973, c. 47, s. 2; c. 148, s. 1; 1977, c. 21, ss. 1, 2; 1987 (Reg. Sess., 1988), c. 1037, s. 13.)

§ 7A-66.1. Office of solicitor may be denominated as office of district attorney; "solicitor" and "district attorney" made interchangeable; interchangeable use authorized in proceedings, documents, and quotations.

(a)   The constitutional office of solicitor may be denominated as the office of "district attorney" for all purposes, and the terms "solicitor" and "district attorney" shall be identical in meaning and interchangeable in use. All terms derived from or related to the term "solicitor" may embody this denomination.

(b)   Repealed by Session Laws 1975, c. 956, s. 5.

(c)   The interchangeable use authorized in this section includes use in all forms of oral, written, visual, and other communication including:

(1)   Oaths of office;

(2)   Other oaths or orations required or permitted in court or official proceedings;

(3)   Ballots;

(4)   Statutes;

(5)   Regulations;

(6)   Ordinances;

(7)   Judgments and other court orders and records;

(8)   Opinions in cases;

(9)   Contracts;

(10)   Bylaws;

(11)   Charters;

(12)   Official commissions, orders of appointment, proclamations, executive orders, and other official papers or pronouncements of the Governor or any executive, legislative, or judicial official of the State or any of its subdivisions;

(13) Official and unofficial letterheads;

(14) Campaign advertisements;

(15) Official and unofficial public notices; and

(16) In all other contexts not enumerated.

The interchangeability authorized in this section extends to the privilege of substituting terminology in matter quoted in oral, written, and other modes of communication without making indication of such change, except where such change may result in a substantive misunderstanding. Reprints or certifications of the text of the Constitution of North Carolina made by the Secretary of State, however, must retain the original terminology and indicate in brackets beside the original terminology the appropriate alternative words. (1973, c. 47, s. 1; 1975, c. 956, s. 5.)

§ 7A-67. Repealed by Session Laws 1971, c. 377, s. 32.

§ 7A-68. Administrative assistants.

(a) Each district attorney shall be entitled to one administrative assistant to be appointed by the district attorney and to serve at his pleasure. The assistant need not be an attorney licensed to practice law in the State of North Carolina.

(b) It shall be the duty of the administrative assistant to assist the district attorney in preparing cases for trial and in expediting the criminal court docket, and to assist in such other duties as may be assigned by the district attorney.

(c) When traveling on official business, each administrative assistant is entitled to reimbursement for his subsistence and travel expenses to the same extent as State employees generally. (1973, c. 807.)

§ 7A-69. Investigatorial assistants.

The district attorney in prosecutorial districts 1, 3B, 4, 5, 7, 8, 11, 12, 13, 14, 15A, 15B, 16A, 18, 19B, 20A, 20B, 21, 22A, 22B, 24, 25, 26, 27A, 27B, 28, 29A, 29B, and 30 is entitled to one investigatorial assistant, and the district attorney in prosecutorial district 10 is entitled to two investigatorial assistants, to be appointed by the district attorney and to serve at his pleasure.

It shall be the duty of the investigatorial assistant to investigate cases preparatory to trial and to perform such other Duties as may be assigned by the district attorney. The investigatorial assistant is entitled to reimbursement for his subsistence and travel expenses to the same extent as State employees generally. (1975, c. 956, s. 6; 1977, c. 969, s. 1; 1981, c. 964, s. 2; 1993, c. 321, s. 200.7(e); 1997-443, s. 18.16; 1998-212, s. 16.21; 1999-237, s. 17.9; 2004-124, s. 14.7(a); 2005-276, s. 14.2(p); 2007-323, s. 14.25(n).)

§ 7A-69.1: Repealed by Session Laws 1985 (Reg. Sess., 1986), c. 998, s. 3.

Article 10.

§§ 7A-70 through 7A-94. Reserved for future codification purposes.

Article 11.

Special Regulations.
§ 7A-95. Reporting of trials.

(a)   Court reporting personnel shall be utilized if available, for the reporting of trials in the superior court. If court reporters are not available in any county, electronic or other mechanical devices shall be provided by the Administrative Office of the Courts upon the request of the senior regular resident superior court judge.

(b)   The Administrative Office of the Courts shall from time to time investigate the state of the art and techniques of recording testimony, and shall provide such electronic or mechanical devices as are found to be most efficient for this purpose.

(c)   If an electronic or other mechanical device is utilized, it shall be the duty of the clerk of the superior court or some person designated by the clerk to operate the device while a trial is in progress, and the clerk shall thereafter preserve the record thus produced, which may be transcribed, as required, by any person designated by the Administrative Office of the Courts. If stenotype, shorthand, or stenomask equipment is used, the original tapes, notes, discs or other records are the property of the State, and the clerk shall keep them in his custody.

(d) Reporting of any trial may be waived by consent of the parties.

(e) Appointment of a reporter or reporters for superior court proceedings in each district or set of districts as defined in G.S. 7A-41.1(a) shall be made by the senior regular resident superior court judge of that district or set of districts. The compensation and allowances of reporters in each such district or set of districts shall be fixed by the senior regular resident superior court judge, within limits determined by the Administrative Officer of the Courts, and paid by the State.

(f) Repealed by Sessions Laws 1971, c. 377, s. 32. (1965, c. 310, s. 1; 1969, c. 1190, s. 7; 1971, c. 377, s. 32; 1987, c. 384, s. 1; 1987 (Reg. Sess., 1988), c. 1037, s. 14.)

§ 7A-96. Court adjourned by sheriff when judge not present.

If the judge of a superior court shall not be present to hold any session of court at the time fixed therefor, he may order the sheriff to adjourn the court to any day certain during the session, and on failure to hear from the judge it shall be the duty of the sheriff to adjourn the court from day to day, unless he shall be sooner informed that the judge for any reason cannot hold the session. (Code, s. 926; 1887, c. 13; 1901, c. 269; Rev., s. 1510; C.S., s. 1448; 1969, c. 1190, s. 49.)

§ 7A-97. Court's control of argument.

In all trials in the superior courts there shall be allowed two addresses to the jury for the State or plaintiff and two for the defendant, except in capital felonies, when there shall be no limit as to number. The judges of the superior court are authorized to limit the time of argument of counsel to the jury on the trial of actions, civil and criminal as follows: to not less than one hour on each side in misdemeanors and appeals from justices of the peace; to not less than two hours on each side in all other civil actions and in felonies less than capital; in capital felonies, the time of argument of counsel may not be limited otherwise than by consent, except that the court may limit the number of those who may address the jury to three counsel on each side. Where any greater number of addresses or any extension of time are desired, motion shall be made, and it shall be in the discretion of the judge to allow the same or not, as the interests of justice may require. In jury trials the whole case as well of law as of fact may be argued to the jury. (1903, c. 433; Rev., s. 216; C.S., s. 203; 1927, c. 52; 1995, c. 431, s. 7.)

§ 7A-98. Reserved for future codification purposes.

§ 7A-99. Reserved for future codification purposes.

Article 12.

Clerk of Superior Court.

§ 7A-100. Election; term of office; oath; vacancy; office and office hours; appointment of acting clerk.

(a)   A clerk of the superior court for each county shall be elected by the qualified voters thereof, to hold office for a term of four years, in the manner prescribed by Chapter 163 of the General Statutes. The clerk, before entering on the duties of his office, shall take the oath of office prescribed by law. If the office of clerk of superior court becomes vacant otherwise than by the expiration of the term, or if the people fail to elect a clerk, the senior regular resident superior court judge for the county shall fill the vacancy by appointment until an election can be regularly held. In cases of death or resignation of the clerk, the senior regular resident superior court judge, pending appointment of a successor clerk, may appoint an acting clerk of superior court for a period of not longer than 30 days.

(b)   The county commissioners shall provide an office for the clerk in the courthouse or other suitable place in the county seat. The clerk shall observe such office hours and holidays as may be directed by the Administrative Officer of the Courts. (Const., art. 4, ss. 16, 17, 29; C.C.P., ss. 139-141; 1871-72, c. 136; Code, ss. 74, 76, 78, 80, 114, 115; 1903, c. 467; Rev., ss. 890-893, 895, 909, 910; C.S., ss. 926, 930, 931, 945, 946; 1935, c. 348; 1939, c. 82; 1941, c. 329; 1949, c. 122, ss. 1, 2; 1971, c. 363, s. 1; 1973, c. 240.)

§ 7A-101. Compensation.

(a) The clerk of superior court is a full-time employee of the State and shall receive an annual salary, payable in equal monthly installments, based on the population of the county as determined in subsection (a1) of this section, according to the following schedule:

Population	Annual Salary
Less than 100,000	$ 83,390
100,000 to 149,999	93,578
150,000 to 249,999	103,766
250,000 and above	113,958

When a county changes from one population group to another, the salary of the clerk shall be changed, on July 1 of the fiscal year for which the change is reported, to the salary appropriate for the new population group, except that the salary of an incumbent clerk shall not be decreased by any change in population group during his continuance in office.

(a1) For purposes of subsection (a) of this section, the population of a county for any fiscal year shall be the population for the beginning of that fiscal year as reported by the Office of State Budget and Management to the Administrative Office of the Courts prior to the beginning of that fiscal year.

(b) The clerk shall receive no fees or commission by virtue of his office. The salary set forth in this section is the clerk's sole official compensation, but if, on June 30, 1975, the salary of a particular clerk, by reason of previous but no longer authorized merit increments, is higher than that set forth in the table, that higher salary shall not be reduced during his continuance in office.

(c) In lieu of merit and other increment raises paid to regular State employees, a clerk of superior court shall receive as longevity pay an amount equal to four and eight-tenths percent (4.8%) of the clerk's annual salary payable monthly after five years of service, nine and six-tenths percent (9.6%) after 10 years of service, fourteen and four-tenths percent (14.4%) after 15 years of service, nineteen and two-tenths percent (19.2%) after 20 years of service, and twenty-four percent (24%) after 25 years of service. Service shall mean service in the elective position of clerk of superior court, as an assistant clerk of court and as a supervisor of clerks of superior court with the Administrative Office of the Courts and shall not include service as a deputy or acting clerk. Service shall also mean service as a justice, judge, or magistrate of the General Court of Justice or as a district attorney. (1965, c. 310, s. 1; 1967, c. 691, s. 5; 1969, c. 1186, s. 3; 1971, c. 877, ss. 1, 2; 1973, c. 571, ss. 1, 2; 1975, c. 956, s. 7; 1975, 2nd Sess., c. 983, s. 11; 1977, c. 802, s. 42; 1977, 2nd Sess., c. 1136, s. 13; 1979, c. 838, s. 85; 1979, 2nd Sess., c. 1137, s. 12; 1981, c. 964, s. 14; c. 1127, s. 12; 1983, c. 761, ss. 200, 247, 249; 1983 (Reg. Sess., 1984), c. 1034, ss. 86, 87; c. 1109, s. 13.1; 1985, c. 479, s. 211; c. 689, s. 3; c. 698, s. 10(c); 1985 (Reg. Sess., 1986), c. 1014, s. 34; 1987, c. 738, s. 20; 1987 (Reg. Sess., 1988), c. 1086, s. 14; c. 1100, ss. 16(a), 17; 1989, c. 752, s. 31; c. 799, s. 27(a); 1991 (Reg. Sess., 1992), c. 900, s. 40; c. 1039, s. 21; 1993, c. 321, s. 57(a); 1993 (Reg. Sess., 1994), c. 769, s. 7.10(a); 1996, 2nd Ex. Sess., c. 18, s. 28.4; 1997-443, s. 33.9; 1998-153, s. 7; 1999-237, s. 28.4; 2000-67, s. 26.4; 2000-140, s. 93.1(b); 2001-424, ss. 12.2(b), 32.5; 2004-124, s. 31.5(b); 2005-276, ss. 29.5, 29.23B; 2006-66, s. 22.5; 2007-323, ss. 28.5, 28.18A(e); 2008-107, s. 26.5; 2012-142, s. 25.1A(e).)

§ 7A-102. Assistant and deputy clerks; appointment; number; salaries; duties.

(a) The numbers and salaries of assistant clerks, deputy clerks, and other employees in the office of each clerk of superior court shall be determined by the Administrative Officer of the Courts after consultation with the clerk concerned. However, no office of clerk of superior court shall have fewer than five total staff positions in addition to the elected clerk of superior court. All personnel in the clerk's office are employees of the State. The clerk appoints the assistants, deputies, and other employees in the clerk's office to serve at his or her pleasure. Assistant and deputy clerks shall take the oath of office prescribed for clerks of superior court, conformed to the office of assistant or deputy clerk, as the case may be. Except as provided by subsection (c2) of this section, the job classifications and related salaries of each employee within the office of each superior court clerk shall be subject to the approval of the Administrative Officer of the Courts after consultation with each clerk concerned and shall be subject to the availability of funds appropriated for that purpose by the General Assembly.

(b) An assistant clerk is authorized to perform all the duties and functions of the office of clerk of superior court, and any act of an assistant clerk is entitled to the same faith and credit as that of the clerk. A deputy clerk is authorized to certify the existence and correctness of any record in the clerk's office, to take the proofs and examinations of the witnesses touching the execution of a will as required by G.S. 31-17, and to perform any other ministerial act which the clerk may be authorized and empowered to do, in his own name and without reciting the name of his principal. The clerk is responsible for the acts of his assistants and deputies. With the consent of the clerk of superior court of each county and the consent of the presiding judge in any proceeding, an assistant or deputy clerk is authorized to perform all the duties and functions of the office of the clerk of superior court in another county in any proceeding in the district or superior court that has been transferred to that county from the county in which the assistant or deputy clerk is employed.

(c)   Notwithstanding the provisions of subsection (a), the Administrative Officer of the Courts shall establish an incremental salary plan for assistant clerks and for deputy clerks based on a series of salary steps corresponding to the steps contained in the Salary Plan for State Employees adopted by the Office of State Human Resources, subject to a minimum and a maximum annual salary as set forth below. On and after July 1, 1985, each assistant clerk and each deputy clerk shall be eligible for an annual step increase in his salary plan based on satisfactory job performance as determined by each clerk. Notwithstanding the foregoing, if an assistant or deputy clerk's years of service in the office of superior court clerk would warrant an annual salary greater than the salary first established under this section, that assistant or deputy clerk shall be eligible on and after July 1, 1984, for an annual step increase in his salary plan. Furthermore, on and after July 1, 1985, that assistant or deputy clerk shall be eligible for an increase of two steps in his salary plan, and shall remain eligible for a two-step increase each year as recommended by each clerk until that assistant or deputy clerk's annual salary corresponds to his number of years of service. Any person covered by this subsection who would not receive a step increase in fiscal year 1995-96 because that person is at the top of the salary range as it existed for fiscal year 1994-95 shall receive a salary increase to the maximum annual salary provided by subsection (c1) of this section.

(c1)   A full-time assistant clerk or a full-time deputy clerk, and up to one full-time deputy clerk serving as head bookkeeper per county, shall be paid an annual salary subject to the following minimum and maximum rates:

Assistant Clerks and Head Bookkeeper   Annual Salary

Minimum $32,609

Maximum   55,424

Deputy Clerks   Annual Salary

Minimum $28,223

Maximum   43,107.

(c2)   The clerk of superior court may appoint assistant clerks, deputy clerks, and a head bookkeeper and set their salaries above the minimum rate established for the positions by subsection (c1) of this section if, in the clerk's discretion, (i) the needs of the clerk's office would be best served by an appointment above the minimum rate, (ii) the appointee's skills and experience support the higher rate, and (iii) the Administrative Office of the Courts certifies that there are sufficient funds available.

(d)   Full-time assistant clerks, licensed to practice law in North Carolina, who are employed in the office of superior court clerk on and after July 1, 1984, and full-time assistant clerks possessing a masters degree in business administration, public administration, accounting, or other similar discipline from an accredited college or university who are employed in the office of superior court clerk on and after July 1, 1997, are authorized an annual salary of not less than three-fourths of the maximum annual salary established for assistant clerks; the clerk of superior court, with the approval of the Administrative Office of the Courts, may establish a higher annual salary but that salary shall not be higher than the maximum annual salary established for assistant clerks. Full-time assistant clerks, holding a law degree from an accredited law school, who are employed in the office of superior court clerk on and after July 1, 1984, are authorized an annual salary of not less than two-thirds of the maximum annual salary established for assistant clerks; the clerk of superior court, with the approval of the Administrative Office of the Courts, may establish a higher annual salary, but the entry-level salary may not be more than three-fourths of the maximum annual salary established for assistant clerks, and in no event may be higher than the maximum annual salary established for assistant clerks. Except as provided by subsection (c2) of this section, the entry-level annual salary for all other assistant and deputy clerks employed on and after July 1, 1984, shall be at the minimum rates as herein established.

(e)   A clerk of superior court may apply to the Director of the Administrative Office of the Courts to enter into contracts with local governments for the provision by the State of services of assistant clerks, deputy clerks, and other employees in the office of each clerk of superior court pursuant to G.S. 153A-212.1 or G.S. 160A-289.1.

(f)   The Director of the Administrative Office of the Courts may provide assistance requested pursuant to subsection (e) of this section only upon a showing by the senior resident superior court judge, supported by facts, that the overwhelming public interest warrants the use of additional resources for the speedy disposition of cases involving drug offenses, domestic violence, or other offenses involving a threat to public safety.

(g)   The terms of any contract entered into with local governments pursuant to subsection (e) of this section shall be fixed by the Director of the Administrative Office of the Courts in each case. Nothing in this section shall be construed to obligate the General Assembly to make any appropriation to implement the provisions of this section or to obligate the Administrative Office of the Courts to provide the administrative costs of establishing or maintaining the positions or services provided for under this section. Further, nothing in this section shall be construed to obligate the Administrative Office of the Courts to maintain positions or services initially provided for under this section. (1777, c. 115, s. 86; P.R.; R.C., c. 19, s. 15; Code, s. 75; 1899, c. 235, ss. 2, 3; Rev., ss. 898-900; 1921, c. 32, ss. 1-3; C.S., ss. 934(a)-934(c), 935-937; 1951, c. 159, ss. 1, 2; 1959, c. 1297; 1963, c. 1187; 1965, c. 264; c. 310, s. 1; 1971, c. 363, s. 2; 1973, c. 678; 1983 (Reg. Sess., 1984), c. 1034, ss. 88, 89; 1985, c. 479, s. 212; c. 757, s. 190; 1985 (Reg. Sess., 1986), c. 1014, s. 35; 1987, c. 738, s. 21(a); 1987 (Reg. Sess., 1988), c. 1086, s. 15; 1989, c. 445; c. 752, s. 32; 1991 (Reg. Sess., 1992), c. 900, ss. 42, 119; 1993, c. 321, ss. 58, 59; 1993 (Reg. Sess., 1994), c. 769, ss. 7.11, 7.12; 1995, c. 507, s. 7.6(a), (b); 1996, 2nd Ex. Sess., c. 18, s. 28.5; 1997-443, ss. 33.12, 33.10(b); 1998-153, s. 8(b); 1999-237, s. 28.5; 2000-67, ss. 15.4(b), 26.5; 2001-424, s. 32.6; 2003-284, s. 30.14B; 2004-124, s. 31.6(b); 2005-276, s. 29.6; 2006-66, s. 22.6; 2007-323, s. 28.6; 2008-107, s. 26.6; 2011-145, s. 15.8; 2012-142, s. 25.1A(f); 2013-382, s. 9.1(c).)

§ 7A-102.1. Transfer of sick leave earned as county or municipal employees by certain employees in offices of clerks of superior court.

(a)   All assistant clerks, deputy clerks and other employees of the clerks of the superior court of this State, secretaries to superior court judges and district attorneys, and court reporters of the superior courts, who have heretofore been, or shall hereafter be, changed in status from county employees to State employees by reason of the enactment of Chapter 7A of the General Statutes, shall be entitled to transfer sick leave accumulated as a county employee pursuant to any county system and standing to the credit of such employee at the time of such change of status to State employee, without any maximum limitation thereof. Such earned sick leave credit shall be certified to the Administrative Office of the Courts by the official or employee responsible for keeping sick leave records for the county, and the Administrative Office of the Courts shall accord such transferred sick leave credit the same status as if it had been earned as a State employee.

(b) All clerks, assistant clerks, deputy clerks and other employees of any court inferior to the superior court which has been or may be abolished by reason of the enactment of Chapter 7A of the General Statutes, who shall thereafter become a State employee by employment in the Judicial Department, shall be entitled to transfer sick leave earned as a municipal or county employee pursuant to any municipal or county system in effect on the date said court was abolished, without any maximum limitation thereof. Such earned sick leave credit shall be certified to the Administrative Office of the Courts by the official or employee responsible for keeping sick leave records for the municipality or county, and the Administrative Office of the Courts shall accord such transferred sick leave credit the same status as if it had been earned as a State employee.

(c) Any employee covered by this section who retires on or after May 22, 1973, shall be given credit for all sick leave accumulated on May 22, 1973. (1967, c. 1187, ss. 1, 2; 1969, c. 1190, s. 8; 1973, c. 47, s. 2; c. 795, ss. 1-3.)

§ 7A-103. Authority of clerk of superior court.

The clerk of superior court is authorized to:

(1) Issue subpoenas to compel the attendance of any witness residing or being in the State, or to compel the production of any document or paper, material to any inquiry in his court.

(2) Administer oaths, and to take acknowledgment and proof of the execution of all instruments or writings.

(3) Issue commissions to take the testimony of any witness within or without the State.

(4)   Issue citations and orders to show cause to parties in all matters cognizable in his court, and to compel the appearance of such parties.

(5)   Enforce all lawful orders and decrees, by execution or otherwise, against those who fail to comply therewith or to execute lawful process. Process may be issued by the clerk, to be executed in any county of the State, and to be returned before him.

(6)   Certify and exemplify, under seal of his court, all documents, papers or records therein, which shall be received in evidence in all the courts of the State.

(7)   Preserve order in this court, punish criminal contempts, and hold persons in civil contempt; subject to the limitations contained in Chapter 5A of the General Statutes of North Carolina.

(8)   Adjourn any proceeding pending before him from time to time.

(9)   Open, vacate, modify, set aside, or enter as of a former time, decrees or orders of his court.

(10)   Enter default or judgment in any action or proceeding pending in his court as authorized by law.

(11)   Award costs and disbursements as prescribed by law, to be paid personally, or out of the estate or fund, in any proceeding before him.

(12)   Compel an accounting by magistrates and compel the return to the clerk of superior court by the person having possession thereof, of all money, records, papers, dockets and books held by such magistrate by virtue or color of his office.

(13)   Grant and revoke letters testamentary, letters of administration, and letters of trusteeship.

(14)   Appoint and remove guardians and trustees, as provided by law.

(15)   Audit the accounts of fiduciaries, as required by law.

(16)   Exercise jurisdiction conferred on him in every other case prescribed by law. (C.C.P., ss. 417, 418, 442; Code, ss. 103, 108; 1901, c. 614, s. 2; Rev., s.

901; 1919, c. 140; C. S., s. 938; 1949, c. 57, s. 1; 1951, c. 28, s. 1; 1961, c. 341, s. 2; 1971, c. 363, s. 3; 1979, 2nd Sess., c. 1080, s. 5.)

§ 7A-104. Disqualification; waiver; removal; when judge acts.

(a) The clerk shall not exercise any judicial powers in relation to any estate, proceeding, or civil action:

(1) If he has, or claims to have, an interest by distribution, by will, or as creditor or otherwise;

(2) If he is so related to any person having or claiming such an interest that he would, by reason of such relationship, be disqualified as a juror, but the disqualification on this ground ceases unless the objection is made at the first hearing of the matter before him;

(3) If clerk or the clerk's spouse is a party or a subscribing witness to any deed of conveyance, testamentary paper or nuncupative will, but this disqualification ceases when such deed, testamentary paper, or will has been finally admitted to probate by another clerk, or before the judge of the superior court;

(4) If clerk or the clerk's spouse is named as executor or trustee in any testamentary or other paper, but this disqualification ceases when the will or other paper is finally admitted to probate by another clerk, or before the judge of the superior court. The clerk may renounce the executorship and endorse the renunciation on the will or on some paper attached thereto, before it is propounded for probate, in which case the renunciation must be recorded with the will if it is admitted to probate.

(a1) The clerk may disqualify himself in a proceeding in circumstances justifying disqualification or recusement by a judge.

(a2) The parties may waive the disqualification specified in this section, and upon the filing of such written waiver, the clerk shall act as in other cases.

(b) When any of the disqualifications specified in this section exist, and there is no waiver thereof, or when there is no renunciation under subdivision (a)(4) of this section, any party in interest may apply to a superior court judge who has jurisdiction pursuant to G.S. 7A-47.1 or G.S. 7A-48 in that county, for an order to remove the proceedings to the clerk of superior court of an adjoining county in the district or set of districts; or he may apply to the judge to make either in vacation or during a session of court all necessary orders and judgments in any proceeding in which the clerk is disqualified, and the judge in such cases is hereby authorized to make any and all necessary orders and judgments as if he had the same original jurisdiction as the clerk over such proceedings.

(c) In any case in which the clerk of the superior court is executor, administrator, collector, or guardian of an estate at the time of his election or appointment to office, in order to enable him to settle such estate, a superior court judge who has jurisdiction pursuant to G.S. 7A-47.1 or G.S. 7A-48 in that county may make such orders as may be necessary in the settlement of the estate; and he may audit the accounts or appoint a commissioner to audit the accounts of such executor or administrator, and report to him for his approval, and when the accounts are so approved, the judge shall order the proper records to be made by the clerk. (C.C.P., ss. 419-421; 1871-72, cc. 196, 197; Code, ss. 104-107; Rev., ss. 902-905; 1913, c. 70, s. 1; C.S., ss. 939-942; 1935, c. 110, s. 1; 1971, c. 363, s. 4; 1977, c. 546; 1987 (Reg. Sess., 1988), c. 1037, s. 15; 1989, c. 493, s. 1.)

§ 7A-105. Suspension, removal, and reinstatement of clerk.

A clerk of superior court may be suspended or removed from office for willful misconduct or mental or physical incapacity, and reinstated, under the same procedures as are applicable to a superior court district attorney, except that the procedure shall be initiated by the filing of a sworn affidavit with the chief district judge of the district in which the clerk resides, and the hearing shall be conducted by the senior regular resident superior court judge serving the county of the clerk's residence. If suspension is ordered, the judge shall appoint some qualified person to act as clerk during the period of the suspension. (1967, c. 691, s. 6; 1971, c. 363, s. 10; 1973, c. 47, s. 2; c. 148, s. 2.)

§ 7A-106. Custody of records and property of office.

(a) It is the duty of the clerk of superior court, upon going out of office for any reason, to deliver to his successor, or such person as the senior regular resident superior court judge may designate, all records, books, papers, moneys, and property belonging to his office, and obtain receipts therefor.

(b) Any clerk going out of office or such other person having custody of the records, books, papers, moneys, and property of the office who fails to transfer and deliver them as directed shall forfeit and pay the State one thousand dollars ($1,000), which shall be sued for by the district attorney. (R.C., c. 19, s. 14; C.C.P., s. 142; Code, ss. 81, 124; Rev., ss. 906, 907; C.S., s. 943; 1971, c. 363, s. 5; 1973, c. 47, s. 2.)

§ 7A-107. Bonds of clerks, assistant and deputy clerks, and employees of office.

The Administrative Officer of the Courts shall require, or purchase, in such amounts as he deems proper, individual or blanket bonds for any and all clerks of superior court, assistant clerks, deputy clerks, and other persons employed in the offices of the various clerks of superior court, or one blanket bond covering all such clerks and other persons, such bond or bonds to be conditioned upon faithful performance of duty, and made payable to the State. The premiums shall be paid by the State. (1965, c. 310, s. 1; 1967, c. 691, s. 7; 1971, c. 363, ss. 10, 11.1; c. 518, s. 2.)

§ 7A-108. Accounting for fees and other receipts; audit.

The Administrative Office of the Courts shall establish procedures for the receipt, deposit, protection, investment, and disbursement of all funds coming into the hands of the clerk of superior court. The fees to be remitted to counties and municipalities shall be paid to them monthly by the clerk of superior court.

The operations of the Administrative Office of the Courts and the Clerks of Superior Court shall be subject to the oversight of the State Auditor pursuant to Article 5A of Chapter 147 of the General Statutes. (1965, c. 310, s. 1; 1969, c. 1190, s. 9; 1971, c. 363, s. 10; 1983, c. 913, s. 5; 2009-516, s. 4.)

§ 7A-109. Record-keeping procedures.

(a) Each clerk shall maintain such records, files, dockets and indexes as are prescribed by rules of the Director of the Administrative Office of the Courts. Except as prohibited by law, these records shall be open to the inspection of the public during regular office hours, and shall include civil actions, special proceedings, estates, criminal actions, juvenile actions, minutes of the court, judgments, liens, lis pendens, and all other records required by law to be maintained. The rules prescribed by the Director shall be designed to accomplish the following purposes:

(1) To provide an accurate record of every determinative legal action, proceeding, or event which may affect the person or property of any individual, firm, corporation, or association;

(2) To provide a record during the pendency of a case that allows for the efficient handling of the matter by the court from its initiation to conclusion and also affords information as to the progress of the case;

(3) To provide security against the loss or destruction of original documents during their useful life and a permanent record for historical uses;

(4) To provide a system of indexing that will afford adequate access to all records maintained by the clerk;

(5) To provide, to the extent possible, for the maintenance of records affecting the same action or proceeding in one rather than several units; and

(6) To provide a reservoir of information useful to those interested in measuring the effectiveness of the laws and the efficiency of the courts in administering them.

(a1) The minutes maintained by the clerk pursuant to this subsection shall record the date and time of each convening of district and superior court, as well as the date and time of each recess or adjournment of district and superior court with no further business before the court.

(b) The rules shall provide for indexing according to the minimum criteria set out below:

(1) Civil actions. - the names of all parties;

(2) Special proceedings. - the names of all parties;

(3) Administration of estates. - the name of the estate and in the case of testacy the name of each devisee;

(4) Criminal actions. - the names of all defendants;

(5) Juvenile actions. - the names of all juveniles;

(6) Judgments, liens, lis pendens, etc. - the names of all parties against whom a lien has been created by the docketing of a judgment, notice of lien, transcript, certificate, or similar document and the names of all parties in those cases in which a notice of lis pendens has been filed with the clerk and abstracted on the judgment docket.

(c) The rules shall require that all documents received for docketing shall be immediately indexed either on a permanent or temporary index. The rules may prescribe any technological process deemed appropriate for the economical and efficient indexing, storage and retrieval of information.

(d) In order to facilitate public access to court records, except where public access is prohibited by law, the Director may enter into one or more nonexclusive contracts under reasonable cost recovery terms with third parties to provide remote electronic access to the records by the public. Costs recovered pursuant to this subsection shall be remitted to the State Treasurer to be held in the Court Information Technology Fund established in G.S. 7A-343.2.

(e) If any contracts entered into under G.S. 7A-109(d) [subsection (d) of this section] are in effect during any calendar year, the Director of the Administrative Office of the Courts shall submit to the Joint Legislative Commission on Governmental Operations not later than February 1 of the following year a report on all those contracts. (Code, ss. 83, 95, 96, 97, 112, 1789; 1887, c. 178, s. 2; 1889, c. 181, s. 4; 1893, c. 52; 1899, c. 1, s. 17; cc. 82, 110; 1901, c. 2, s. 9; c. 89, s. 13; c. 550, s. 3; 1903, c. 51; c. 359, s. 6; 1905, c. 360, s. 2; Rev., s. 915; 1919, c. 78, s. 7; c. 152; c. 197, s. 4; c. 314; C.S., s. 952; 1937, c. 93; 1953, c. 259; c. 973, s. 3; 1959, c. 1073, s. 3; c. 1163, s. 3; 1961, c. 341, ss. 3, 4; c. 960; 1965, c. 489; 1967, c. 691, s. 39; c. 823, s. 2; 1971, c. 192; c. 363, s. 6; 1997-199, ss. 1, 2; 1999-237, s. 17.15(c); 2011-145, s. 15.6(b); 2012-142, s. 16.5(g); 2013-360, s. 18B.8(a).)

§ 7A-109.1. List of prisoners furnished to judges.

(a) The clerk of superior court must furnish to each judge presiding over a criminal court a report listing the name, reason for confinement, period of confinement, and, when appropriate, charge or charges, amount of bail and conditions of release, and next scheduled court appearance of each person listed on the most recent report filed under the provisions of G.S. 153A-229.

(b) The clerk must file the report with superior court judges presiding over mixed or criminal sessions at the beginning of each session and must file the report with district court judges at each session or weekly, whichever is the less frequent. (1973, c. 1286, s. 5; 1975, c. 166, s. 22.)

§ 7A-109.2. (Contingent expiration date - see notes) Records of dispositions in criminal cases.

Each clerk of superior court shall ensure that all records of dispositions in criminal cases, including those records filed electronically, contain all the essential information about the case, including the identity of the presiding judge and the attorneys representing the State and the defendant. (1998-208, s. 2.)

§ 7A-109.2. (Contingent effective date - see notes) Records of dispositions in criminal cases; impaired driving integrated data system.

(a) Each clerk of superior court shall ensure that all records of dispositions in criminal cases, including those records filed electronically, contain all the essential information about the case, including the the name of the presiding judge and the attorneys representing the State and the defendant.

(b) In addition to the information required by subsection (a) of this section for all offenses involving impaired driving as defined by G.S. 20-4.01, all charges of driving while license revoked for an impaired driving license revocation as defined by G.S. 20-28.2, and any other violation of the motor vehicle code involving the operation of a vehicle and the possession, consumption, use, or transportation of alcoholic beverages, the clerk shall include in the electronic records the following information:

(1) The reasons for any pretrial dismissal by the court.

(2) The alcohol concentration reported by the charging officer or chemical analyst, if any.

(3) The reasons for any suppression of evidence. (1998-208, s. 2; 2006-253, s. 20.1.)

§ 7A-109.3. Delivery of commitment order.

(a) Whenever the district court sentences a person to imprisonment and commitment to the custody of the Division of Adult Correction of the Department of Public Safety pursuant to G.S. 15A-1352, the clerk of superior court shall furnish the sheriff with the signed order of commitment within 48 hours of the issuance of the sentence.

(b) Whenever the superior court sentences a person to imprisonment and commitment to the custody of the Division of Adult Correction of the Department of Public Safety pursuant to G.S. 15A-1352, the clerk of superior court shall furnish the sheriff with the signed order of commitment within 72 hours of the issuance of the sentence. (1999-237, s. 18.10(c); 2011-145, s. 19.1(h).)

§ 7A-109.4. Records of offenses involving impaired driving.

The clerk of superior court shall maintain all records relating to an offense involving impaired driving as defined in G.S. 20-4.01(24a) for a minimum of 10 years from the date of conviction. Prior to destroying the record, the clerk shall record the name of the defendant, the judge, the prosecutor, and the attorney or whether there was a waiver of attorney, the alcohol concentration or the fact of refusal, the sentence imposed, and whether the case was appealed to superior court and its disposition. (2006-253, s. 24.)

§ 7A-110. List of attorneys furnished to Secretary of Revenue.

On or before the first of May each year the clerk of superior court shall certify to the Secretary of Revenue the names and addresses of all attorneys-at-law located within the clerk's county who are engaged in the practice of law. (1931, c. 290; 1971, c. 363, s. 7; 1973, c. 476, s. 193.)

§ 7A-111. Receipt and disbursement of insurance and other moneys for minors and incapacitated adults.

(a) When a minor under 18 years of age is named beneficiary in a policy or policies of insurance, and the insured dies prior to the majority of such minor, and the proceeds of each individual policy do not exceed twenty-five thousand dollars ($25,000) such proceeds may be paid to and, if paid, shall be received by the public guardian or clerk of the superior court of the county wherein the beneficiary is domiciled. The receipt of the public guardian or clerk shall be a full and complete discharge of the insurer issuing the policy or policies to the extent of the amount paid to such public guardian or clerk.

Any person having in his possession twenty-five thousand dollars ($25,000) or less for any minor under 18 years of age for whom there is no guardian, may pay such moneys into the office of the public guardian, if any, or the office of the clerk of superior court of the county of the recipient's domicile. The receipt of the public guardian or clerk shall constitute a valid release of the payor's obligation to the extent of the sum delivered to the clerk.

The clerk is authorized under this section to receive, to administer and to disburse the monies held in such sum or sums and at such time or times as in his judgment is in the best interest of the child, except that the clerk must first determine that the parents or other persons responsible for the child's support and maintenance are financially unable to provide the necessities for such child, and also that the child is in need of maintenance and support or other necessities, including, when appropriate, education. The clerk shall require receipts or paid vouchers showing that the monies disbursed under this section were used for the exclusive use and benefit of the child.

(b) When an adult who is mentally incapable on account of sickness, old age, disease or other infirmity to manage his own affairs is named beneficiary in a policy or policies of insurance, and the insured dies during the incapacity of such adult, and the proceeds of each individual policy do not exceed five thousand dollars ($5,000) such proceeds may be paid to and, if paid, shall be received by the public guardian or clerk of the superior court of the county wherein the beneficiary is domiciled. A certificate of mental incapacity, signed by a physician or reputable person who has had an opportunity to observe the mental condition of an adult beneficiary, filed with the clerk, is prima facie evidence of the mental incapacity of such adult, and authorizes the clerk to receive and administer funds under this section. The receipt of the public guardian or clerk shall be a full and complete discharge of the insurer issuing the policy or policies to the extent of the amount paid to such public guardian or clerk.

Any person having in his possession five thousand dollars ($5,000) or less for any incapacitated adult for whom there is no guardian, may pay such monies into the office of the public guardian, if any, or the office of the clerk of superior court of the county of the recipient's domicile. The clerk's receipt shall constitute a valid release of the payor's obligation to the extent of the sum delivered to the clerk.

The clerk is authorized to receive, to administer and, upon a finding of fact that it is in the best interest of the incapacitated adult, to disburse funds directly to a creditor, a relative or to some discreet and solvent neighbor or friend for the purpose of handling the property and affairs of the incapacitated adult. The clerk shall require receipts or paid vouchers showing that the monies disbursed under this section were used for the exclusive use and benefit of the incapacitated adult.

(c) Any monies paid to the clerk of the superior court under subsection (a) of this section shall also include the name, last known address, social security number or taxpayer identification number of the beneficiary or payee, and the name and address of the nearest relative of the beneficiary or payee.

(d) The determination of incapacity authorized in subsection (b) of this section is separate and distinct from the procedure for the determination of incompetency provided in Chapter 35A. (1899, c. 82; Rev., s. 924; 1911, c. 29, s. 1; 1919, c. 91; C.S., s. 962; Ex. Sess., 1924, c. 1, s. 1; 1927, c. 76; 1929, c. 15; 1933, c. 363; 1937, c. 201; 1945, c. 160, ss. 1, 2; 1949, c. 188; 1953, c. 101; 1959, c. 794, ss. 1, 2; 1961, c. 377; 1971, c. 363, s. 8; c. 1231, s. 1; 1983, c. 65, s. 3; 1987, c. 29; c. 550, s. 14.)
§ 7A-112. Investment of funds in clerk's hands.

(a) The clerk of the superior court may in his discretion invest moneys secured by virtue or color of the clerk's office or as receiver in any of the following securities:

(1) Obligations of the United States or obligations fully guaranteed both as to principal and interest by the United States;

(2) Obligations of the State of North Carolina;

(3) Obligations of North Carolina cities or counties approved by the Local Government Commission; and

(4) Shares of any building and loan association organized under the laws of this State, or of any federal savings and loan association having its principal

office in this State, and certificates of deposit for time deposits or savings accounts in any bank or trust company authorized to do business in North Carolina, to the extent in each instance that such shares or deposits are insured by the State or federal government or any agency thereof or by any mutual deposit guaranty association authorized by the Commissioner of Banks of North Carolina to do business in North Carolina pursuant to Article 7A of Chapter 54 of the General Statutes. If the clerk desires to deposit in a bank, saving and loan, or trust company funds entrusted to the clerk by virtue or color of the clerk's office, beyond the extent that such deposits are insured by the State or federal government or an agency thereof or by any mutual deposit guaranty association authorized by the Commissioner of Banks of North Carolina to do business in North Carolina pursuant to Article 7A of Chapter 54 of the General Statutes, the clerk shall require such depository to furnish a corporate surety bond or obligations of the United States or obligations fully guaranteed both as to principal and interest by the United States or obligations of the State of North Carolina, or of counties and municipalities of North Carolina whose obligations have been approved by the Local Government Commission.

(b)   When money in a single account in excess of two thousand dollars ($2,000) is received by the clerk by virtue or color of his office and it can reasonably be expected that the money will remain on deposit with the clerk in excess of six months from date of receipt, the money exceeding two thousand dollars ($2,000) shall be invested by the clerk within 60 days of receipt in investments authorized by this section. The first two thousand dollars ($2,000) of these accounts and money in a single account totaling less than two thousand dollars ($2,000), received by the clerk by virtue or color of his office, shall be invested, or administered, or invested and administered, by the clerk in accordance with regulations promulgated by the Administrative Officer of the Courts. This subsection shall not apply to cash bonds or to money received by the clerk to be disbursed to governmental units.

(c)   The State Auditor is hereby authorized and empowered to inspect the records of the clerk to insure compliance with this section, and he shall report noncompliance with the provisions of this section to the Administrative Officer of the Courts.

(d)   It shall be unlawful for the clerk of the superior court of any county receiving any money by virtue or color of his office to apply or invest any of it except as authorized under this section. Any clerk violating the provisions of this section shall be guilty of a Class 1 misdemeanor. (1931, c. 281, ss. 1-3, 5; 1937, c. 188; 1939, cc. 86, 110; 1943, c. 543; 1971, c. 363, s. 9; c. 956, s. 1; 1973, c.

1446, s. 4; 1975, c. 496, ss. 1, 2; 1989, c. 76, s. 13; 1993, c. 539, s. 4; 1994, Ex. Sess., c. 24, s. 14(c); 1993 (Reg. Sess., 1994), c. 656, s. 1; 2001-193, s. 16.)

§ 7A-112.1. Deposit of money held by clerks.

The clerk of superior court shall deposit any funds that he receives by virtue of his office, except funds invested pursuant to G.S. 7A-112, in an interest-bearing checking account or accounts in a bank, savings and loan, or trust company licensed to do business in North Carolina, at the maximum feasible interest rate available taking into consideration prevailing interest rates and the checking account services provided to the clerk's office by the bank, savings and loan, or trust company. The funds deposited in such checking accounts shall be guaranteed to the same extent and in the same manner as funds invested pursuant to G.S. 7A-112. (1985, c. 475, s. 1.)

§ 7A-113. Bookkeeping and accounting systems equipment.

Notwithstanding the provisions of G.S. 147-64.6(10), proposed changes in the kinds of bookkeeping and accounting systems equipment employed by the clerk of superior court shall be subject to review and approval by the Office of State Budget and Management. The Administrative Officer of the Courts shall, prior to implementing any change in the kinds of equipment, file with the Office of State Budget and Management a request for approval of the change, along with supporting information. If within 30 days of the filing of the request the Office of State Budget and Management has not disapproved the request, the request shall be deemed to be approved. (1983 (Reg. Sess., 1984), c. 1109, s. 9; 2000-140, s. 93.1(a); 2001-424, s. 12.2(b).)

§ 7A-114. Where practical, provision of secure area for domestic violence victims waiting for hearing.

Where practical, upon request of a domestic violence victim, the clerk of Superior Court of any county shall coordinate with the county Sheriff to make available to the victim a secure area, segregated from the general population of the courtroom, to await hearing of their court case. The Clerk shall notify the presiding judge on the date of the hearing that the victim is present in a segregated location. (2007-15, s. 2.)

§§ 7A-115 through 7A-129. Reserved for future codification purposes.

SUBCHAPTER IV. DISTRICT COURT DIVISION

OF THE GENERAL COURT OF JUSTICE.

Article 13.

Creation and Organization of the District Court Division.

§ 7A-130. Creation of district court division and district court districts; seats of court.

The district court division of the General Court of Justice is hereby created. It consists of various district courts organized in territorial districts. The numbers and boundaries of the districts are as provided by G.S. 7A-133. The district court shall sit in the county seat of each county, and at such additional places in each county as the General Assembly may authorize, except that sessions of court are not required at an additional seat of court unless the chief district judge and the Administrative Officer of the Courts concur in a finding that the facilities are adequate. (1965, c. 310, s. 1; 1987, c. 509, s. 14; c. 738, s. 124.)

§ 7A-131. Establishment of district courts.

District courts are established, within districts, in accordance with the following schedule:

(1)   On the first Monday in December, 1966, the first, the twelfth, the fourteenth, the sixteenth, the twenty-fifth, and the thirtieth districts;

(2)   On the first Monday in December, 1968, the second, the third, the fourth, the fifth, the sixth, the seventh, the eighth, the ninth, the tenth, the eleventh, the thirteenth, the fifteenth, the eighteenth, the twentieth, the twenty-first, the twenty-fourth, the twenty-sixth, the twenty-seventh, and the twenty-ninth districts;

(3)   On the first Monday in December, 1970, the seventeenth, the nineteenth, the twenty-second, the twenty-third, and the twenty-eighth districts. (1965, c. 310, s. 1.)

§ 7A-132. Judges, district attorneys, full-time assistant district attorneys and magistrates for district court districts.

Each district court district shall have one or more judges and one district attorney. Each county within each district shall have at least one magistrate.

For each district the General Assembly shall prescribe the numbers of district judges, and the numbers of full-time assistant district attorneys. For each county within each district the General Assembly shall prescribe a minimum number of magistrates. (1965, c. 310, s. 1; 1967, c. 1049, s. 5; 1973, c. 47, s. 2; 2006-187, s. 7(b).)

§ 7A-133. Numbers of judges by districts; numbers of magistrates and additional seats of court, by counties.

(a)   (Effective until January 1, 2015) Each district court district shall have the numbers of judges as set forth in the following table:

District	Judges	County
1	5	Camden
		Chowan
		Currituck
		Dare
		Gates
		Pasquotank
		Perquimans
2	4	Martin
		Beaufort

		Tyrrell
		Hyde
		Washington
3A	5	Pitt
3B	6	Craven
		Pamlico
		Carteret
4	8	Sampson
		Duplin
		Jones
		Onslow
5	9	New Hanover
		Pender
6A	3	Halifax
6B	3	Northampton
		Bertie
		Hertford
7	7	Nash
		Edgecombe
		Wilson
8	6	Wayne

9	4	Greene
		Lenoir
		Granville
		(part of Vance see subsection (b))
		Franklin
9A	2	Person
		Caswell
9B	2	Warren
		(part of Vance see subsection (b))
10	19	Wake
11	11	Harnett
		Johnston
		Lee
12	10	Cumberland
13	6	Bladen
		Brunswick
		Columbus
14	7	Durham

15A	4	Alamance
15B	5	Orange
		Chatham
16A	3	Scotland
		Hoke
16B	5	Robeson
17A	3	Rockingham
17B	4	Stokes
		Surry
18	14	Guilford
19A	4	Cabarrus
19B	7	Montgomery
		Moore
		Randolph
19C	5	Rowan
20A	4	Stanly
		Anson
		Richmond
20B	1	(part of Union see subsection (b))
20C	2	(part of Union

			see subsection (b))
20D	1		Union
21	10		Forsyth
22A	5		Alexander
			Iredell
22B	6		Davidson
			Davie
23	4		Alleghany
			Ashe
			Wilkes
			Yadkin
24	4		Avery
			Madison
			Mitchell
			Watauga
			Yancey
25	9		Burke
			Caldwell
			Catawba
26	21		Mecklenburg
27A	7		Gaston

District	Judges	County
27B	5	Cleveland
		Lincoln
28	7	Buncombe
29A	3	McDowell
		Rutherford
29B	4	Henderson
		Polk
		Transylvania
30	6	Cherokee
		Clay
		Graham
		Haywood
		Jackson
		Macon
		Swain.

(a) (Effective January 1, 2015) Each district court district shall have the numbers of judges as set forth in the following table:

District	Judges	County
1	5	Camden
		Chowan

		Currituck
		Dare
		Gates
		Pasquotank
		Perquimans
2	4	Martin
		Beaufort
		Tyrrell
		Hyde
		Washington
3A	5	Pitt
3B	6	Craven
		Pamlico
		Carteret
4	8	Sampson
		Duplin
		Jones
		Onslow
5	9	New Hanover
		Pender

6	4	Northampton
		Bertie
		Hertford
		Halifax
7	7	Nash
		Edgecombe
		Wilson
8	6	Wayne
		Greene
		Lenoir
9	4	Granville
		(part of Vance see subsection (b))
		Franklin
9A	2	Person
		Caswell
9B	2	Warren
		(part of Vance see subsection (b))
10	19	Wake
11	11	Harnett

		Johnston
		Lee
12	10	Cumberland
13	6	Bladen
		Brunswick
		Columbus
14	7	Durham
15A	4	Alamance
15B	5	Orange
		Chatham
16A	6	Scotland
		Hoke
		Anson
		Richmond
16B	5	Robeson
17A	3	Rockingham
17B	4	Stokes
		Surry
18	14	Guilford
19A	4	Cabarrus

19B	7	Montgomery
		Moore
		Randolph
19C	5	Rowan
20A	2	Stanly
20B	1	(part of Union see subsection (b))
20C	2	(part of Union see subsection (b))
20D	1	Union
21	11	Forsyth
22A	5	Alexander
		Iredell
22B	6	Davidson
		Davie
23	4	Alleghany
		Ashe
		Wilkes
		Yadkin
24	4	Avery
		Madison

		Mitchell
		Watauga
		Yancey
25	9	Burke
		Caldwell
		Catawba
26	21	Mecklenburg
27A	7	Gaston
27B	5	Cleveland
		Lincoln
28	7	Buncombe
29A	3	McDowell
		Rutherford
29B	4	Henderson
		Polk
		Transylvania
30	6	Cherokee
		Clay
		Graham
		Haywood

Jackson

Macon

Swain.

(b) For district court districts of less than a whole county, or with part or all of one county with part of another, the composition of the district is as follows:

(1) District Court District 9 consists of Franklin and Granville Counties and the remainder of Vance County not in District Court District 9B.

(2) District Court District 9B consists of Warren County and East Henderson I, North Henderson I, North Henderson II, Middleburg, Townsville, and Williamsboro Precincts of Vance County.

(3) District Court District 20C consists of the remainder of Union County not in District Court District 20B.

(4) District Court District 20B consists of Precinct 01: Tract 204.01: Block Group 2: Block 2040, Block 2057, Block 2058, Block 2060, Block 2061, Block 2062, Block 2064, Block 2065; Tract 204.02: Block Group 2: Block 2001, Block 2002, Block 2003, Block 2004, Block 2005, Block 2006, Block 2007, Block 2008, Block 2009, Block 2010, Block 2011, Block 2012, Block 2013, Block 2014, Block 2015, Block 2016, Block 2017, Block 2018, Block 2023, Block 2024, Block 2025, Block 2026, Block 2027, Block 2028, Block 2029, Block 2030, Block 2031, Block 2032, Block 2033, Block 2034; Block Group 3: Block 3000, Block 3003, Block 3004, Block 3005, Block 3006, Block 3007, Block 3008, Block 3009, Block 3010, Block 3011, Block 3012, Block 3013, Block 3014, Block 3015, Block 3016, Block 3017, Block 3018, Block 3019, Block 3020, Block 3021, Block 3022, Block 3023, Block 3024, Block 3025, Block 3026, Block 3027, Block 3028, Block 3029, Block 3030, Block 3031, Block 3032, Block 3033, Block 3034, Block 3035, Block 3036, Block 3037, Block 3038, Block 3039, Block 3040, Block 3041, Block 3042, Block 3043, Block 3044, Block 3045, Block 3046, Block 3047; Block Group 4: Block 4035, Block 4054, Block 4055; Precinct 02: Tract 205: Block Group 1: Block 1000, Block 1001, Block 1002, Block 1003, Block 1004, Block 1005, Block 1006, Block 1007, Block 1009, Block 1010, Block 1011, Block 1012, Block 1013, Block 1014, Block 1015, Block 1016, Block 1017, Block 1018, Block 1019, Block 1020, Block 1021, Block 1022, Block 1023, Block 1037, Block 1038; Block Group 2: Block 2081, Block 2082, Block 2092, Block 2099, Block 2100, Block 2101, Block 2102; Tract 206: Block Group 3: Block 3036, Block 3038, Block 3039, Block

3040, Block 3048; Block Group 4: Block 4053; Precinct 03, Precinct 04, Precinct 06: Tract 202.02: Block Group 1: Block 1012, Block 1013, Block 1014, Block 1015, Block 1017, Block 1018, Block 1021, Block 1022, Block 1023; Tract 204.01: Block Group 2: Block 2000, Block 2001, Block 2002, Block 2003, Block 2004, Block 2005, Block 2033, Block 2034, Block 2035, Block 2036, Block 2041, Block 2042, Block 2043, Block 2044, Block 2045, Block 2056, Block 2063, Block 2999; Precinct 08, Precinct 09, Precinct 10, Precinct 13, Precinct 23: Tract 206: Block Group 4: Block 4051; Precinct 25: Tract 206: Block Group 4: Block 4036; Precinct 34, Precinct 36, Precinct 43 of Union County.

Precinct boundaries as used in this section for Vance County are those shown on maps on file with the Legislative Services Office on May 1, 1991, for Union County, are those shown on the Legislative Services Office's redistricting computer database on January 1, 2005; and for other counties are those reported by the United States Bureau of the Census under Public Law 94-171 for the 1990 Census in the IVTD Version of the TIGER files.

(b1)   The qualified voters of District Court District 11 shall elect all eight judges established for the District in subsection (a) of this section, but only persons who reside in Johnston County may be candidates for five of the judgeships, only persons who reside in Harnett County may be candidates for two of the judgeships, and only persons who reside in Lee County may be candidates for the remaining judgeship.

(b2)   The qualified voters of District Court District 13 shall elect all six judges established for the District in subsection (a) of this section, but only persons who reside in Bladen County may be candidates for one of those judgeships, only persons who reside in Columbus County may be candidates for two of those judgeships, and only persons who reside in Brunswick County may be candidates for three of those judgeships. These district court judgeships shall be numbered and assigned for residency purposes as follows:

(1)   Seat number one, established for residents of Brunswick County by this section, shall be the seat currently held by Judge Barefoot.

(2)   Seat number two, established for residents of Brunswick County by this section, shall be the seat currently held by Judge Fairley.

(3)   Seat number three, established for residents of Brunswick County by this section, shall be the seat currently held by Judge Warren.

(4)   Seat number four, established for residents of Columbus County by this section, shall be the seat currently held by Judge Jolly.

(5)   Seat number five, established for residents of Columbus County by this section, shall be the seat currently held by Judge Tyler.

(6)   Seat number six, established for residents of Bladen County by this section, shall be the seat currently held by Judge Ussery.

(b3)   The qualified voters of District Court District 22A shall elect all five judges established for the District in subsection (a) of this section, but only persons who reside in Alexander County may be candidates for two of the judgeships, and only persons who reside in Iredell County may be candidates for three of the judgeships.

(b4)   The qualified voters of District Court District 22B shall elect all six judges established for the District in subsection (a) of this section, but only persons who reside in Davie County may be candidates for two of the judgeships, and only persons who reside in Davidson County may be candidates for four of the judgeships.

(c)   Each county shall have the numbers of magistrates and additional seats of district court, as set forth in the following table:

County	Magistrates Min.	Additional Seats of Court
Camden	3	
Chowan	3	
Currituck	3	
Dare	4	
Gates	2	
Pasquotank	4	
Perquimans	3	

Martin	3	
Beaufort	4	
Tyrrell	3	
Hyde	3.5	
Washington	3	
Pitt	10.5	Farmville
		Ayden
Craven	8	Havelock
Pamlico	3	
Carteret	6	
Sampson	5	
Duplin	4	
Jones	2	
Onslow	11	
New Hanover	11	
Pender	3.8	
Halifax	7	Roanoke Rapids, Scotland Neck
Northampton	3	

Bertie	3	
Hertford	3	
Nash	9	Rocky Mount
Edgecombe	7	Rocky Mount
Wilson	7	
Wayne	9	Mount Olive
Greene	3	
Lenoir	7	La Grange
Granville	5	
Vance	6	
Warren	3	
Franklin	4	
Person	4	
Caswell	3	
Wake	18.5	Apex, Wendell, Fuquay-Varina, Wake Forest
Harnett	8	Dunn
Johnston	10	Benson,

		Clayton,
		Selma
Lee	5	
Cumberland	19	
Bladen	3	
Brunswick	8	
Columbus	5	Tabor City
Durham	13	
Alamance	12	Burlington
Orange	7	Chapel Hill
Chatham	4	Siler City
Scotland	5	
Hoke	3	
Robeson	12	Fairmont, Maxton, Pembroke, Red Springs, Rowland, St. Pauls
Rockingham	7	Reidsville,

County		
		Eden, Madison
Stokes	3	
Surry	6	Mt. Airy
Guilford	24.4	High Point
Cabarrus	9	Kannapolis
Montgomery	3	
Randolph	9	Liberty
Rowan	9	
Stanly	5	
Union	7	
Anson	3	
Richmond	5	Hamlet
Moore	5	Southern Pines
Forsyth	15	Kernersville
Alexander	3	
Davidson	8	Thomasville
Davie	3	
Iredell	9	Mooresville
Alleghany	2	
	234	

Ashe	3	
Wilkes	6	
Yadkin	3	
Avery	3	
Madison	3	
Mitchell	3	
Watauga	4	
Yancey	3	
Burke	5.6	
Caldwell	6	
Catawba	10	Hickory
Mecklenburg	26.50	
Gaston	17	
Cleveland	7	
Lincoln	5	
Buncombe	15	
Henderson	6.5	
McDowell	3	
Polk	3	
Rutherford	6	

Transylvania	3	
Cherokee	3	
Clay	2	
Graham	2	
Haywood	5	Canton
Jackson	3	
Macon	3	
Swain	3	

(1965, c. 310, s. 1; 1967, c. 691, s. 8; 1969, c. 1190, s. 10; c. 1254; 1971, c. 377, s. 7; cc. 727, 840, 841, 842, 843, 865, 866, 898; 1973, cc. 132, 373, 483; c. 838, s. 1; c. 1376; 1975, c. 956, ss. 8, 10; 1977, cc. 121, 122; c. 678, s. 2; c. 947, s. 1; c. 1130, ss. 4, 5; 1977, 2nd Sess., c. 1238, s. 3; c. 1243, ss. 3, 6; 1979, c. 465; c. 838, ss. 117, 118; c. 1072, ss. 2, 3; 1979, 2nd Sess., c. 1221, s. 2; 1981, c. 964, s. 4; 1983, c. 881, s. 5; 1983 (Reg. Sess., 1984), c. 1109, s. 5; 1985, c. 698, ss. 7(a), 12; 1985 (Reg. Sess., 1986), c. 1014, s. 222; 1987, c. 738, ss. 126(a), 130(a); 1987 (Reg. Sess., 1988), c. 1056, s. 4; c. 1075; c. 1100, s. 17.2(a); 1989, c. 795, s. 23(a), (d), (h); 1991, c. 742, ss. 11, 12(a); 1993, c. 321, ss. 200.4(e), 200.6(a), (d); 1993 (Reg. Sess., 1994), c. 769, s. 24.9; 1995, c. 507, s. 21.1(c); 1995 (Reg. Sess., 1996), c. 589, s. 2(a); 1996, 2nd Ex. Sess., c. 18, ss. 22.4, 22.7(a); 1997-443, ss. 18.12(a), 18.13; 1998-212, ss. 16.11, 16.16(a); 1998-217, s. 67.3(a); 1999-237, ss. 17.4, 17.6(a); 2000-67, ss. 15.2, 15.3(a); 2001-400, s. 1; 2001-424, ss. 22.16, 22.17(a); 2003-284, s. 13.8; 2004-124, ss. 14.1(a), 14.6(e); 2005-276, s. 14.2(f), (f1); 2005-345, s. 27(a), (b); 2006-66, ss. 14.4(a), 14.5; 2006-96, s. 1; 2006-187, s. 7(a); 2006-221, s. 14(a); 2006-264, s. 93(a); 2007-323, ss. 14.13(a), (d), 14.25(e), (f); 2007-484, s. 25(a), 36; 2008-107, s. 14.13(a); 2009-341, s. 1; 2012-194, s. 1(c), (d); 2013-360, s. 18B.22(f).)

§ 7A-134. Repealed by Session Laws 1973, c. 1339, s. 2.

§ 7A-135. Transfer of pending cases when present inferior courts replaced by district courts.

On the date that the district court is established in any county, cases pending in the inferior court or courts of that county shall be transferred to the appropriate division of the General Court of Justice, and all records of these courts shall be transferred to the office of clerk of superior court in that county pursuant to rule of Supreme Court. (1965, c. 310, s. 1.)

§ 7A-136. Reserved for future codification purposes.

§ 7A-137. Reserved for future codification purposes.

§ 7A-138. Reserved for future codification purposes.

§ 7A-139. Reserved for future codification purposes.

Article 14.

District Judges.

§ 7A-140. Number; election; term; qualification; oath.

There shall be at least one district judge for each district. Each district judge shall be elected by the qualified voters of the district court district in which he or she is to serve at the time of the election for members of the General Assembly. The number of judges for each district shall be determined by the General Assembly. Each judge shall be a resident of the district for which elected, and shall serve a term of four years, beginning on the first day in January next after election.

Each district judge shall devote his or her full time to the duties of the office. He or she shall not practice law during the term, nor shall he or she during such term be the partner or associate of any person engaged in the practice of law.

Before entering upon his or her duties, each district judge, in addition to other oaths prescribed by law, shall take the oath of office prescribed for a judge of the General Court of Justice. (1965, c. 310, s. 1; 1969, c. 1190, s. 11; 2005-425, s. 3.1.)

§ 7A-141. Designation of chief judge; assignment of judge to another district for temporary or specialized duty.

When more than one judge is authorized in a district, the Chief Justice of the Supreme Court shall designate one of the judges as chief district judge to serve in such capacity at the pleasure of the Chief Justice. In a single judge district, the judge is the chief district judge.

The Chief Justice may transfer a district judge from one district to another for temporary or specialized duty. (1965, c. 310, s. 1.)

§ 7A-142. Vacancies in office.

A vacancy in the office of district judge shall be filled for the unexpired term by appointment of the Governor. The bar of the judicial district, as defined in G.S. 84-19, shall nominate five persons who are residents of the judicial district who are duly authorized to practice law in the district for consideration by the Governor. The nominees shall be selected by vote of only those bar members who reside in the district. In the event fewer than five persons are nominated, upon providing the nominations to the Governor, the bar shall certify that there were insufficient nominations in the district to comply with this section. Prior to filling the vacancy, the Governor shall give due consideration to the nominations provided by the bar of the judicial district. (1965, c. 310, s. 1; 1975, c. 441; 1981, c. 763, ss. 1, 2; 1985 (Reg. Sess., 1986), c. 1006, s. 1; 1987 (Reg. Sess., 1988), c. 1037, s. 16; c. 1056, s. 7; c. 1086, s. 112(b); 1991, c. 742, s. 16; 1999-237, s. 17.10; 2001-403, s. 2(a); 2002-159, s. 58; 2011-28, s. 2; 2013-387, s. 4.)

§ 7A-143. Repealed by Session Laws 1973, c. 148, s. 6.

§ 7A-144. Compensation.

(a) Each judge shall receive the annual salary provided in the Current Operations Appropriations Act, and reimbursement on the same basis as State employees generally, for his or her necessary subsistence expenses and for travel expenses when on official business outside the judge's county of residence. For purposes of this subsection, the term "official business" does not include regular, daily commuting between a judge's home and the court. Travel distances, for purposes of reimbursement for mileage, shall be determined according to the travel policy of the Administrative Office of the Courts.

(b) Notwithstanding merit, longevity and other increment raises paid to regular State employees, a judge of the district court shall receive as longevity pay an annual amount equal to four and eight-tenths percent (4.8%) of the annual salary set forth in the Current Operations Appropriations Act payable monthly after five years of service, nine and six-tenths percent (9.6%) after 10 years of service, fourteen and four-tenths percent (14.4%) after 15 years of service, nineteen and two-tenths percent (19.2%) after 20 years of service, and twenty-four percent (24%) after 25 years of service. "Service" means service as a justice or judge of the General Court of Justice or as a member of the Utilities Commission or as director or assistant director of the Administrative Office of the Courts. Service shall also mean service as a district attorney or as a clerk of superior court. (1965, c. 310, s. 1; 1967, c. 691, s. 10; 1983, c. 761, s. 245; 1983 (Reg. Sess., 1984), c. 1034, s. 165; c. 1109, ss. 11, 13.1; 1985, c. 698, s. 10(a); 1987 (Reg. Sess., 1988), c. 1100, s. 15(d); 1989, c. 770, s. 5; 2007-323, s. 28.18A(f); 2009-451, s. 15.17B(a).)

§ 7A-145. Repealed by Session Laws 1971, c. 377, s. 32.

§ 7A-146. Administrative authority and duties of chief district judge.

The chief district judge, subject to the general supervision of the Chief Justice of the Supreme Court, has administrative supervision and authority over the operation of the district courts and magistrates in his district. These powers and duties include, but are not limited to, the following:

(1) Arranging schedules and assigning district judges for sessions of district courts.

(2) Arranging or supervising the calendaring of noncriminal matters for trial or hearing.

(3) Supervising the clerk of superior court in the discharge of the clerical functions of the district court.

(4) Assigning matters to magistrates, and consistent with the salaries set by the Administrative Officer of the Courts, prescribing times and places at which magistrates shall be available for the performance of their duties; however, the chief district judge may in writing delegate his authority to prescribe times and places at which magistrates in a particular county shall be available for the

performance of their duties to another district court judge or the clerk of the superior court, or the judge may appoint a chief magistrate to fulfill some or all of the duties under subdivision (12) of this section, and the person to whom such authority is delegated shall make monthly reports to the chief district judge of the times and places actually served by each magistrate.

(5)   Making arrangements with proper authorities for the drawing of civil court jury panels and determining which sessions of district court shall be jury sessions.

(6)   Arranging for the reporting of civil cases by court reporters or other authorized means.

(7)   Arranging sessions, to the extent practicable for the trial of specialized cases, including traffic, domestic relations, and other types of cases, and assigning district judges to preside over these sessions so as to permit maximum practicable specialization by individual judges.

(8)   Repealed by Session Laws 1991 (Regular Session, 1992), c. 900, s. 118(b), effective July 15, 1992.

(9)   Assigning magistrates during an emergency to temporary duty outside the county of their residence but within that district pursuant to the policies and procedures prescribed under G.S. 7A-343(11); and, upon the request of a chief district judge of an adjoining district and upon the approval of the Administrative Officer of the Courts, to temporary duty in the district of the requesting chief district judge pursuant to the policies and procedures prescribed under G.S. 7A-343(11).

(10)   Designating another district judge of his district as acting chief district judge, to act during the absence or disability of the chief district judge.

(11)   Designating certain magistrates to appoint counsel pursuant to Article 36 of this Chapter. This designation may only be given to magistrates who are duly licensed attorneys and does not give any magistrate the authority to: (i) appoint counsel for potentially capital offenses, as defined by rules adopted by the Office of Indigent Defense Services; or (ii) accept a waiver of counsel.

(12)   Designating a full-time magistrate in a county to serve as chief magistrate for that county for an indefinite term and at the judge's pleasure. The chief magistrate shall have the derivative administrative authority assigned by

the chief district court judge under subdivision (4) of this section. This subdivision applies only to counties in which the chief district court judge determines that designating a chief magistrate would be in the interest of justice. (1965, c. 310, s. 1; 1971, c. 377, s. 8; 1977, c. 945, s. 1; 1983, c. 586, s. 1; 1983 (Reg. Sess., 1984), c. 1034, s. 85; 1985, c. 425, s. 2; c. 764, s. 8; 1985 (Reg. Sess., 1986), c. 852, s. 17; 1991 (Reg. Sess., 1992), c. 900, s. 118(b); 2009-419, s. 2; 2011-411, s. 2(b); 2013-89, s. 1.)

§ 7A-147. Specialized judgeships.

(a)   Prior to January 1 of each year in which elections for district court judges are to be held, the Administrative Officer of the Courts may, with the approval of the chief district judge, designate one or more judgeships in districts having three or more judgeships, as specialized judgeships, naming in each case the specialty. Designations shall become effective when filed with the State Board of Elections. Nominees for the position or positions of specialist judge shall be made in the ensuing primary and the position or positions shall be filled at the general election thereafter. The State Board of Elections shall prepare primary and general election ballots to effectuate the purposes of this section.

(b)   The designation of a specialized judgeship shall in no way impair the right of the chief district judge to arrange sessions for the trial of specialized cases and to assign any district judge to preside over these sessions. A judge elected to a specialized judgeship has the same powers as a regular district judge.

(c)   The policy of the State is to encourage specialization in juvenile cases by district court judges who are qualified by training and temperament to be effective in relating to youth and in the use of appropriate community resources to meet their needs. The Administrative Office of the Courts is therefore authorized to encourage judges who hear juvenile cases to secure appropriate training whether or not they were elected to a specialized judgeship as provided herein. Such training shall be provided within the funds available to the Administrative Office of the Courts for such training, and judges attending such training shall be reimbursed for travel and subsistence expenses at the same rate as is applicable to other State employees.

The Administrative Office of the Courts shall develop a plan whereby a district court judge may be better qualified to hear juvenile cases by reason of training, experience, and demonstrated ability. Any district court judge who completes the training under this plan shall receive a certificate to this effect from the Administrative Office of the Courts. In districts where there is a district court judge who has completed this training as herein provided, the chief district judge shall give due consideration in the assignment of such cases where practical and feasible. (1965, c. 310, s. 1; 1975, c. 823; 1979, c. 622, s. 1.)

§ 7A-148. Annual conference of chief district judges.

(a) The chief district judges of the various district court districts shall meet at least once a year upon call of the Chief Justice of the Supreme Court to discuss mutual problems affecting the courts and the improvement of court operations, to prepare and adopt uniform schedules of offenses for the types of offenses specified in G.S. 7A-273(2) and G.S. 7A-273(2a) for which magistrates and clerks of court may accept written appearances, waivers of trial or hearing and pleas of guilty or admissions of responsibility, and establish a schedule of penalties or fines therefor, and to take such further action as may be found practicable and desirable to promote the uniform administration of justice.

(b) The chief district judges shall prescribe a multicopy uniform traffic ticket and complaint for exclusive use in each county of the State not later than December 31, 1970. (1965, c. 310, s. 1; 1967, c. 691, s. 11; 1983, c. 586, s. 2; 1985, c. 425, s. 1; c. 764, s. 9; 1985 (Reg. Sess., 1986), c. 852, s. 17; 1991, c. 151, s. 1; c. 609, s. 2; 1991 (Reg. Sess., 1992), c. 900, s. 118(a); 1999-80, s. 2.)

§ 7A-149. Jurisdiction; sessions.

(a) Notwithstanding any other provision of law, a district court judge of a district court district which is in a set of districts as defined by G.S. 7A-200 has jurisdiction in the entire county or counties in which the district is located to the same extent as if the district encompassed the entire county, and has jurisdiction in the entire set of districts to the same extent as if the district encompassed the entire set of districts.

(b) All sessions of district court shall be for an entire county, whether that county comprises or is located in a district or in a set of districts as defined in G.S. 7A-200, and at each session all matters and proceedings arising anywhere in the county may be heard.

(c) All clerks of court for a county have jurisdiction over the entire county, notwithstanding that the county may be part of a set of districts. (1995, c. 507, s. 21.1(b).)

§§ 7A-150 through 7A-159. Reserved for future codification purposes.

Article 15.

District Prosecutors.

§§ 7A-160 through 7A-165: Repealed by Session Laws 1967, c. 1049, s. 6.

§ 7A-166. Reserved for future codification purposes.

§ 7A-167. Reserved for future codification purposes.

§ 7A-168. Reserved for future codification purposes.

§ 7A-169. Reserved for future codification purposes.

Article 16.

Magistrates.

§ 7A-170. (Effective until January 1, 2015) Nature of office and oath.

A magistrate is an officer of the district court. Before entering upon the duties of his office, a magistrate shall take the oath of office prescribed for a magistrate of the General Court of Justice. A magistrate possesses all the powers of his office at all times during his term. (1965, c. 310, s. 1; 1969, c. 1190, s. 13; 1977, c. 945, s. 2.)

§ 7A-170. (Effective January 1, 2015) Nature of office and oath; age limit for service.

(a) A magistrate is an officer of the district court. Before entering upon the duties of his office, a magistrate shall take the oath of office prescribed for a magistrate of the General Court of Justice. A magistrate possesses all the powers of his office at all times during his term.

(b) No magistrate may continue in office beyond the last day of the month in which the magistrate reaches the mandatory retirement age for justices and judges of the General Court of Justice specified in G.S. 7A-4.20. (1965, c. 310, s. 1; 1969, c. 1190, s. 13; 1977, c. 945, s. 2; 2013-277, s. 1.)

§ 7A-171. Numbers; appointment and terms; vacancies.

(a) The General Assembly shall establish a minimum quota of magistrates for each county. In no county shall the minimum quota be less than one. The number of magistrates in a county, above the minimum quota set by the General Assembly, is determined by the Administrative Office of the Courts after consultation with the chief district court judge for the district in which the county is located.

(a1) The initial term of appointment for a magistrate is two years and subsequent terms shall be for a period of four years. The term of office begins on the first day of January of the odd-numbered year after appointment. The service of an individual as a magistrate filling a vacancy as provided in subsection (d) of this section does not constitute an initial term. For purposes of this section, any term of office for a magistrate who has served a two-year term is for four years even if the two-year term of appointment was before the effective date of this section, the term is after a break in service, or the term is for appointment in a different county from the county where the two-year term of office was served.

(b) Not earlier than the Tuesday after the first Monday nor later than the third Monday in December of each even-numbered year, the clerk of the superior court shall submit to the senior regular resident superior court judge of the district or set of districts as defined in G.S. 7A-41.1(a) in which the clerk's county is located the names of two (or more, if requested by the judge) nominees for each magisterial office for the county for which the term of office of the magistrate holding that position shall expire on December 31 of that year. Not later than the fourth Monday in December, the senior regular resident superior court judge shall, from the nominations submitted by the clerk of the superior court, appoint magistrates to fill the positions for each county of the judge's district or set of districts.

(c)   If an additional magisterial office for a county is approved to commence on January 1 of an odd-numbered year, the new position shall be filled as provided in subsection (b) of this section. If the additional position takes effect at any other time, it is to be filled as provided in subsection (d) of this section.

(d)   Within 30 days after a vacancy in the office of magistrate occurs the clerk of superior court shall submit to the senior regular resident superior court judge the names of two (or more, if so requested by the judge) nominees for the office vacated. Within 15 days after receipt of the nominations the senior regular resident superior court judge shall appoint from the nominations received a magistrate who shall take office immediately and shall serve until December 31 of the even-numbered year, and thereafter the position shall be filled as provided in subsection (b) of this section. (1965, c. 310, s. 1; 1967, c. 691, s. 15; 1971, s. 84, s. 1; 1973, c. 503, s. 2; 1977, c. 945, ss. 3, 4; 1987 (Reg. Sess., 1988), c. 1037, s. 17; 2004-128, s. 19; 2006-187, s. 7(c).)

§ 7A-171.1. Duty hours, salary, and travel expenses within county.

(a)   The Administrative Officer of the Courts, after consultation with the chief district judge and pursuant to the following provisions, shall set an annual salary for each magistrate.

(1)   A full-time magistrate shall be paid the annual salary indicated in the table set out in this subdivision. A full-time magistrate is a magistrate who is assigned to work an average of not less than 40 hours a week during the term of office. The Administrative Officer of the Courts shall designate whether a magistrate is full-time. Initial appointment shall be at the entry rate. A magistrate's salary shall increase to the next step every two years on the anniversary of the date the magistrate was originally appointed for increases to Steps 1 through 3, and every four years on the anniversary of the date the magistrate was originally appointed for increases to Steps 4 through 6.

Table of Salaries of Full-Time Magistrates

Step Level	Annual Salary
Entry Rate	$33,025

Step 1	35,951
Step 2	39,135
Step 3	42,640
Step 4	46,551
Step 5	50,959
Step 6	55,901.

(2) A part-time magistrate is a magistrate who is assigned to work an average of less than 40 hours of work a week during the term, except that no magistrate shall be assigned an average of less than 10 hours of work a week during the term. A part-time magistrate is included, in accordance with G.S. 7A-170, under the provisions of G.S. 135-1(10) and G.S. 135-40.2(a). The Administrative Officer of the Courts designates whether a magistrate is a part-time magistrate. A part-time magistrate shall receive an annual salary based on the following formula: The average number of hours a week that a part-time magistrate is assigned work during the term shall be multiplied by the annual salary payable to a full-time magistrate who has the same number of years of service prior to the beginning of that term as does the part-time magistrate and the product of that multiplication shall be divided by the number 40. The quotient shall be the annual salary payable to that part-time magistrate.

(3) Notwithstanding any other provision of this subsection, a magistrate who is licensed to practice law in North Carolina or any other state shall receive the annual salary provided in the Table in subdivision (1) of this subsection for Step 4.

(a1) Notwithstanding subsection (a) of this section, the following salary provisions apply to individuals who were serving as magistrates on June 30, 1994:

(1) The salaries of magistrates who on June 30, 1994, were paid at a salary level of less than five years of service under the table in effect that date shall be as follows:

Less than 1 year of service $26,846

1 or more but less than 3 years of service	28,027
3 or more but less than 5 years of service	30,405

Upon completion of five years of service, those magistrates shall receive the salary set as the Entry Rate in the table in subsection (a).

(2) The salaries of magistrates who on June 30, 1994, were paid at a salary level of five or more years of service shall be based on the rates set out in subsection (a) as follows:

Salary Level on June 30, 1994	Salary Level on July 1, 1994
5 or more but less than 7 years of service	Entry Rate
7 or more but less than 9 years of service	Step 1
9 or more but less than 11 years of service	Step 2
11 or more years of service	Step 3

Thereafter, their salaries shall be set in accordance with the provisions in subsection (a).

(3) The salaries of magistrates who are licensed to practice law in North Carolina shall be adjusted to the annual salary provided in the table in subsection (a) as Step 4, and, thereafter, their salaries shall be set in accordance with the provisions in subsection (a).

(4) The salaries of "part-time magistrates" shall be set under the formula set out in subdivision (2) of subsection (a) but according to the rates set out in this subsection.

(a2) The Administrative Officer of the Courts shall provide magistrates with longevity pay at the same rates as are provided by the State to its employees subject to the North Carolina Human Resources Act.

(b) Notwithstanding G.S. 138-6, a magistrate may not be reimbursed by the State for travel expenses incurred on official business within the county in which the magistrate resides. (1977, c. 945, s. 5; 1979, c. 838, s. 84; c. 991; 1979, 2nd Sess., c. 1137, s. 11; 1981, c. 914, s. 1; c. 1127, s. 11; 1983, c. 761, s. 199; c. 923, s. 217; 1983 (Reg. Sess., 1984), c. 1034, ss. 84, 211; 1985, c. 479, s. 210; c. 698, ss. 13(a), (b) (14); 791, s. 39.1; 1985 (Reg. Sess., 1986), c. 1014, ss. 36, 223(a); 1987, c. 564, s. 12; c. 738, ss. 22, 34; 1987 (Reg. Sess., 1988), c. 1086, s. 16; 1989, c. 752, s. 33; 1991, c. 742, s. 14(a); 1991 (Reg. Sess., 1992), c. 900, ss. 41, 43; c. 1044, s. 9.1; 1993, c. 321, s. 60; 1993 (Reg. Sess., 1994), c. 769, s. 7.13(b), (c); 1995, c. 507, s. 7.7(a), (b); 1996, 2nd Ex. Sess., c. 18, s. 28.6(a), (b); 1999-237, s. 28.6(a), (b); 2000-67, s. 26.6; 2001-424, s. 32.7; 2004-124, s. 31.7(b); 2005-276, s. 29.7(a), (b); 2006-66, s. 22.7(a), (b); 2007-323, ss. 28.7(a), (b); 2008-107, ss. 26.7(a), (b); 2012-142, s. 25.1A(g), (h); 2013-382, s. 9.1(c).)

Vision Books Order Form

Fax Orders: 1-704-921-9271

Phone Orders: 1-704-921-9271

E-mail Orders: www.visionbooks.org

Mail Orders: Vision Books
                P.O. Box 42406
                Charlotte, NC 28215

Shipp To:
Name_____
Address_____
City_____State_____Zip_____
Phone_____Fax_____
Email_____@_____

Bill To: We can bill a third party on your behalf.
Name_____
Address_____
City_____State_____Zip_____
Phone____(_____)_____Fax_____
Email_____@_____

Pamphlet Number ($15.00 Each)	Qty	Total Cost
_____	_____	_____
_____	_____	_____
_____	_____	_____
_____	_____	_____
_____	_____	_____
_____	_____	_____
_____	_____	_____
_____	_____	_____
Full Volume Set 1-92	**92 Pamphlets**	**1,380.00**

Free Shipping Shipping & Handling on Full Volume Orders
Add $1.00 Shipping & Handling per pamphlet $_____

Total Cost $_____

DID YOU ENJOY THIS BOOK?

Vision Books, LLC would like to hear from you! If you or someone you know has been fasely imprisoned, we would like to hear your story. If the 'North Carolina Criminal Law and Procedure' has had an effect in your life or if you have suggestions, we would like to hear from you. Send your letters to:

Vision Books, LLC
Attn: Staff Writers
P.O. Box 42406
Charlotte, NC 28215
Email: staff@visionbooks.org

Order Additional Copies:

Fax Orders:	1-704-921-9271
Phone Orders:	1-704-921-9271
E-mail Orders:	www.visionbooks.org
Mail Orders:	Vision Books P.O. Box 42406 Charlotte, NC 28215

www.ingramcontent.com/pod-product-compliance
Lightning Source LLC
Chambersburg PA
CBHW071410170526
45165CB00001B/229